REGARDING NATURE

SUNY Series in Radical Social and Political Theory
Roger S. Gottlieb, Editor

REGARDING NATURE

Industrialism and Deep Ecology

Andrew McLaughlin

State University of
New York Press

I wish to thank *Environmental Ethics* for permission to draw from my "Images and Ethics of Nature," *Environmental Ethics*, vol. 7, no. 4; and the Research Group on Socialism and Democracy for permission to draw from my "Ecology, Capitalism, and Socialism," *Socialism and Democracy*, issue 10 (Spring/Summer 1990). Copyright © The Research Group on Socialism and Democracy 1990.

For kindly granting permission to reprint from their publications, I wish to thank the following authors and publishers:

From *Deep Ecology* by Bill Devall and George Sessions (Salt Lake City: Gibbs Smith, 1985). Copyright © 1985 by Gibbs M. Smith, Inc. Used by permission of Gibbs M. Smith, Inc.

From *Ecology, Community and Lifestyle: Outline of an Ecosophy* by Arne Naess (New York: Cambridge University Press, 1989). Copyright © Cambridge University Press 1989. Used by permission of Cambridge University Press.

From "Reflections on the Evolution of Mind and Its Environment" by Ragnar Granit, in Richard Q. Elvee, ed., *Mind in Nature* (San Francisco: Harper & Row, 1982). Copyright © 1982 by Gustavus Adolphus College. Used by permission of HarperCollins Publishers.

From "Defining the Moment" by Richard J. Barnet, *The New Yorker*, July 16, 1990. Reprinted by permission; © 1990 Richard J. Barnet. Originally in *The New Yorker*.

Published by
State University of New York Press, Albany

Printed in the United States of America

For information, address the State University of New York Press,
State University Plaza, Albany, NY 12246

Production by Bernadine Dawes
Marketing by Terry Swierzowski

Library of Congress Cataloging-in-Publication Data

McLaughlin, Andrew, 1941–
Regarding nature : industrialism and deep ecology / Andrew McLaughlin.
p. cm. — (SUNY series in radical social and political theory)
Includes bibliographical references and index.
ISBN 0-7914-1383-7 (acid-ree) : $49.50. — ISBN 0-7914-1384-5 (pbk. : acid-free) : $16.95
1. Green movement. 2. Environmental policy. 3. Human ecology. 4. Consumption (Economics) 5. Radical economics. 6. Comparative economics. I. Title. II. Series.
JA75.8.M35 1992
322.4'4—dc20 92-14076
CIP

2 3 4 5 6 7 8 9 10

For

Richard and Dorothy

and Karuna, Mitra,

and Colin,

my closest relations

CONTENTS

PREFACE

This book argues that industrialism is a primary reason for our current ecological misfortune, and it seeks new options that would help both humans and the rest of nature flourish. I argue that we need to fundamentally change our understandings of both nature and humanity.

Presently, we make some fundamental mistakes in our conceptions of nature. Consider, for example, the ways economies are usually understood. As I write, the economy in the United States is bad because there is not enough economic growth. More growth, it is said, would lead to a recovery, and times would be better—even good—if growth soared. Economic hard times within industrial societies entail serious human suffering, and this suffering is distributed very unfairly. The only solution to this suffering, so it seems, involves expanding economic production, and politicians across the political spectrum agree that economic growth is desirable.

But suppose that we are actually within a serious ecological crisis. Since economic growth generally involves expanding industrial production, it requires accelerating the consumption of nature as resources. There are many indications that we have strained various ecological systems to the point where they might generate serious, rapid, and unwanted changes. Global climatic change and the depletion of the ozone layer are but two items on a lengthy list of such threatening changes. From an ecological perspective, further industrial growth may be toxic. Making times economically better may make them ecologically worse.

We thus seem confronted with a fateful dilemma. Either we pursue economic growth and ecological collapse, or we seek ecological sustainability and economic collapse. Neither horn of this dilemma seems comfortable. As with all dilemmas, one way out is to rethink the assumptions which lead into it. Industrial economies seem to require perpetual expansion. If so, then this requires the assumption that we can transform nature in whatever directions desired. Nature, we assume, poses problems, not limits. Perhaps this assumption should be reconsidered. An alternative is to understand humans as living *within* nature, not separate from it. This implies that any wise human economy must resonate harmoniously with the larger cycles of nature which encircle humans and their economies. Such an understanding dissolves the dilemma by incorporating ecological sustainability into the very criteria for assessing the goodness of any economy. This would imply that no ecologically bad course of action would be understood as economically good. Such a new understanding of human economies gives rise to the substantial task of creating new social forms embodying a revisioning of humanity and nature.

Today, those who seek social justice often do not pay attention to ecological troubles, while those who care about the environment often do not concern themselves with social injustice. In what follows, I hope to convince both of these camps that they need each other, and that they should expand their concerns to integrate social justice with a respect for the rest of nature. By working together, both camps can look toward a future in which all forms of life can flourish within a healing earth. This book suggests a few steps to take along this path.

A large number of people have helped me write this book. Many of my teachers stimulated me to rethink my assumptions; I can only regret that they do not know how important they have been to me. Others, with whom I have shared the excitement, joy, fear, and naïveté of attempting to change society, have helped me to keep alive a faith that social change is worth the effort. The contemporary surge of energy in the young, and the not so young, of the radical environmental movement renews this faith. I thank them for giving me enough hope to write about changing industrial society.

I owe particular thanks to Alan Drengson, Joel Kassiola, Richard Schmitt, and Luke Charde, who helped with their generous comments on earlier drafts of this book. Roger Gottlieb not only made many useful comments, he gave spirit and timely encouragement which were particularly important. David Orton, Robyn Eckersley, and Warwick Fox have each, through their exceptionally generous and astute help, fundamentally influenced the final shape of this work. I cannot thank them enough. My debt to my parents, Richard and Dorothy, is enormously great and late in being acknowledged. Finally, Karuna, Mitra, and Colin relentlessly, and sometimes patiently, teach me what life is really about each day. Without them this would not be.

1 *Regarding Nature: A conceptual introduction*

How should we regard nature? Until recently, this question was decisively answered by the practices of industrial society. Under the enchantment of the Enlightenment story of progress from darkness to light, from ignorance to knowledge, and from scarcity to abundance, we understood ourselves as steadily advancing toward a better future. A sign of this progress, as well as one of its causes, was the ever-increasing domination of nature through science and technology. Thus, it seemed, we could regard nature as just formless substance to be molded into whatever shape we desired. Recently, however, an uneasiness has entered into our understanding of our relations with nature and "progress" no longer seems assured.

How *should* we regard nature? The question poses two intimately connected issues—how we should *think* about nature and how we should *act* within nature. Both thought and action affect the kinds of environments we construct, which in turn influence who we are, how we think, and what we do. When nature is viewed from the perspective of a market economy, it appears to be a collection of "resources" having the potential to be transformed into commodities. Within capitalistic economies, nature can be privately owned, while socialistic economies see nature as being owned by the whole society. Viewed through the lens of science, nature appears as instances of general laws, a perspective which invites and enables the transformation of nature. These and other presumptions frame the ways we collectively understand and deal with nature. They need to be unearthed and opened to critical reflection and revision.

But what is nature? The question requires clarification because the concept of nature is not only rich and heterogeneous, but also pivotal to quite diverse topics. For example, nature can be contrasted to the supernatural or to the immoral, as in "unnatural acts." It can be opposed to the artificial or other products of human activity, as in "natural" foods or "natural" beauty. This list, far from exhaustive, suggests the diversity of the concept of nature and shows the need for a preliminary specification of its meaning.

For the purpose of examining the relations between humanity and nature, two central meanings of 'nature' need to be distinguished. One meaning of nature is "all that is," at least on earth. In this sense, the primary relation between humanity and nature is that of part to whole because humans clearly are a part of "all that is." Within this understanding of nature, we are not outside of, nor exempt from, the natural processes which result in solar systems, cities, and forests. All human actions, even thinking itself, are natural processes. Values and ideas, as well as canyons and sunsets, are parts of nature. This concept of nature makes all events natural. It is descriptive and inclusive. Nothing, save perhaps the supernatural, is outside of nature.

Another meaning of 'nature' rests on a distinction between humanity and the rest of nature. This concept takes humanity as existing at some distance from nature and presumes a dualism between humanity and nature. 'Nature' is distinguished from 'humanity' as an "other." This concept of nature is common within many environmental discussions. Some, for example, claim that "nature knows best," suggesting that human intervention in natural systems is likely to be destructive to those systems.[1] In a similar vein, criticism or endorsement of the attempt to "dominate" nature presumes some separation between humanity and nature. Thus, the assumption that humans are separate from nature gets built into many environmental discussions from the start.

Each of these concepts of nature have their difficulties. The inclusive meaning of nature suggests a disinterested and nonevaluative perspective on existence. Conceived this way, the concept of nature precludes contrast to the "unnatural" because all that exists is natural. Beauty, as well as its destruction, war as well as peace, hate and love, all become natural. This understanding of nature is implicit in many scientific approaches to the world and life, both human and nonhuman. These inquiries assume that the various particular realities investigated exemplify less apparent but unchanging regularities described by "natural laws." Applied to nonhuman nature, the resulting sciences and technologies have enabled an astounding capacity for the directed change of the course of events.

However, when this perspective is totalized to include human life, deep concerns arise. Is human life just a part of nature? Is it best understood as exemplifying "laws of nature"? If such laws do apply to *all* human activity, then they must also apply to those who search for the laws which govern human behavior. If so, the search for such laws would not really be a matter of judgment and rational inquiry; rather, it would be a nonrational process of obedience to the laws of behavior. The realization of this project in the human domain is the nightmare of an orderly and totally managed society.[7] The very concept of "good" as a normative ideal regulating human choices must then be seen as a delusion. Under this conception of nature, all experiences of weighing evidence, considering alternatives, posing questions of moral or rational choice, as well as the freedom to make such choices would be deceptions and have no effective connection to reality.

The totalization of this deterministic approach to humanity yields conclusions that cannot be adopted by rational humans simply because, within this view, there are no rational humans. In this account of humanity, all beliefs are causally determined, rather than reasonably, or unreasonably, adopted. Accepting this approach requires embracing the claim that the ordinary lived experiences of reflection, choice, evaluation, and decision are illusions. Yet these experiences are fundamental to life-as-lived and can only be reasonably rejected on the basis of very strongly grounded evidence. The absence of success in scientific projects to control human behavior indicates that there is not yet, at least, sufficient evidence to accept this radical revisioning of human experience. The only possibility of there being sufficient evidence is the actual construction of a totally controlled society, within which the very experience of freedom and choice might be eliminated.

These problems, arising from the self-reference implicit in the totalization of this approach, can only be avoided by denying that laws of behavior apply to all human life. If this is understood as implying a duality among humans, it is both intellectually indefensible and morally repugnant. There is no reason to suppose that all humans, except social scientists or "scientific managers," are subject to inexorable laws of human behavior. Any proposal from those who would unreasonably exempt themselves from such behavioral laws in order to design a society for the "others" seems both self-serving and morally noxious.

Acknowledging some sort of duality within human life seems necessary. Clearly, much of human life—such as digestion—is governed by processes aptly described by laws of nature. If we grant a categorical distinction between such processes and the experiences of reflection, choice, evaluation, and decision, and if we allow for the efficacy of these experiences in the course of human affairs, we can avoid these difficulties. But such an understanding lacks comprehensiveness because the duality within humans remains unexplained. Considerations such as these lead back to the dualistic concept of nature which presumes some fundamental distinction between humans and the rest of nature.[3]

The dualistic concept of nature has its own difficulties. Historically, humans could comfortably understand themselves as both within and outside of nature. The Judeo-Christian tradition provides a metaphysical framework wherein humanity stands at the apex of a hierarchy in nature. This hierarchy also extended beyond nature to the divine. Humans, having souls, could be understood as both the best of nature and as outside of nature, partaking of the divine. The Cartesian tradition also provides humanity with a dual self-understanding, granting human bodies the status of natural objects, while reserving a different dimension of existence for human minds. But these self-understandings can no longer claim general credibility. The ascendence of science over religion effectively undercuts most dualistic understandings of humanity. If science is taken as the correct mode of understanding, then it becomes obvious that humanity is part and product of natural processes. Of course humans are part of nature. Where and what else could we be?

Although any dualism between humanity and the rest of nature seems arbitrary, it cannot be easily relinquished. The inclusive concept of nature does not seem to give adequate grounding for an understanding of life as each person experiences it. We find ourselves, at least as adults, "at a distance" from all else—both other humans and other kinds of existence. We are fundamentally *interested* in our worlds, seeking food, and much else, on the basis of needs and desires. We are each the center of our own life. This interested orientation distances each of us from all else and precedes any descriptive orientation. Any descriptive orientation presumes interest and engagement and proceeds within that context.

This primary context of an interested and engaged orientation requires the dualistic sense of nature, where 'nature' is understood on the basis of a distinction between humanity and the rest of nature. This concept of nature provides the conceptual space to understand the experiences of appraisal and choice. Just as we are surely within nature, we are also, just as surely, a distinct sort of creature, not to be simply identified with "all that is." We act on nature and transform it, creating artifacts—manufactured things and whole environments. We often experience ourselves as separate and apart from nature, confronting it as alien, fearing and striving to "humanize" nature. This understanding of humanity as different from nature makes clear the interested and engaged relation between humanity and the rest of nature.

There is, then, something fundamental about the dualistic concept of nature. To deny it would seem to require a denial of an essential element of the experience of being human. But there is also something fundamental about the inclusive sense of nature as "all that is." It seems clear that we are of a piece with nature, not standing outside it. The story which science tells us about the origins of our universe and the evolution of life on earth provides the most compelling understanding we have of our place within nature. And that story clearly locates us *within* nature. Thus, my provisional conclusion is that both concepts of nature must be retained.[4] Each concept of nature resists simple reduction to the other. Both can claim a certain primacy, and neither can happily subsume the other. The value of having two perspectives is that they make possible binocular perception, allowing a depth of vision not possible with only one perspective. Henceforth, I shall keep these two senses of 'nature' distinct by qualifying the dualistic use through reference to "the rest of nature" or "nonhuman nature" when the context does not make clear which sense is intended.

One fundamental way in which we differ from much of the rest of nature is that we live within a cognitive world and act on the basis of our ideas.[5] Our sensory experience is a product of interactions between our sensory organs and the stimulations they undergo. These stimulations are encoded by the sensory organs and processed by our neural system. This processing is influenced by biological, linguistic, and cultural factors, as well as by personal idiosyncrasies.

What we view as the world is actually our representation in our experience of the world. For daily living, it is certainly functional that we are unaware of the chasm between our experience of the world and the world, since constant awareness of this gap would leave us plagued by confusion. Nevertheless, it is sometimes important to recognize that our understandings of the world are only mappings, and we can make mistakes in the way we understand nature, including ourselves. One of the convictions which underlies this book is that our current mappings of nature are leading us astray.

Thus, the question, "How should we regard nature?" in part asks, "How should we map nature?" What patterns of ideas should we use to understand ourselves and our relations with the rest of nature? The question involves the problematic assumption that we can choose how to think about nature. This strains the idea of choice. Typically, we make choices only *after* we have adopted some cognitive mapping. Usually we have already conceptualized our situation when we contemplate choices. For example, when I wonder what I shall choose to eat, I have already cast the world into the edible and the nonedible. The choice of cognitive patterns requires recognizing that our worlds *are* cognitive mappings and also envisioning alternatives, both of which can be difficult. We can only choose how we will regard nature after becoming aware of the usually unquestioned assumptions which undergird ordinary thought and normal social practice. The "choice" ultimately involves the construction of culture. The question, then, is what sort of culture should we try to create, for it is only within cultural forms that the rest of nature appears to us. The question, "How should we regard nature?" ultimately asks what cultural forms we should create to map nature and thus our place within it. As a practical matter, calling into question the "normal" ways of regarding nature can only be effective when the established patterns have led to difficulty. They have.

Ideologies of Nature

The metaphor of mapping for understanding humanity's relations with the rest of nature obscures the active aspect of our relations with the rest of nature. Different sorts of maps make possible different agendas for action, and various sorts of actions require different types of maps. A topographical map of fine detail tempts and indicates ways of walking to the top of a mountain or planning a canoe trip down an unknown river. A map of interstate highways invites a rapid motor trip to distant places, while a tax map assigns responsibility for tracts of land to people who can be summoned to financially support the state. Maps of nature thus suggest programs of action, and as we use those maps, we may change the territory. Therefore, the metaphor of maps of nature needs to be supplemented with an understanding of the agendas for action implicit in the various mappings. I shall use the phrase "ideology of nature" to include both the images or maps of nonhuman nature that we create and the agendas for action implicit within such mappings.

The term "ideology" is contested.[6] It was coined by Destutt de Tracy in 1796 with the intention of naming a new "science" of ideas. Adopted by Marx, the term came to have a pejorative meaning. Marx's central claim about the theories that he views as ideological is that they cause that which is historically contingent and changeable to appear as necessary and immutable conditions of human existence. Thus, an idea that correctly identifies some important aspect of alterable historical reality can become a source of mystification if it is seen as identifying some necessary fact about human existence. This sort of mystification inhibits efforts toward change, because it seems fruitless or worse to attempt to change that which is necessary.

"Human nature" is a concept particularly susceptible to ideological use. The extrapolation of "human nature" from the typical behaviors of people within a culture is apt to be deceiving because there is a tendency to confuse behaviors that are typical within a particular society with "human nature." What appears to be human nature, within a particular culture, reflects both human nature *and* the habitual behaviors induced by that culture. Separating the two types of regularities is difficult. Evidence that is easily available to people within industrial, capitalistic societies indicates that all humans are "naturally" self-centered, greedy, and only out for themselves. This is, after all, how our culture trains us to behave, and it does correctly state a widespread behavioral pattern within capitalistic societies. But the claim that this is actually "human nature" is ideological, because it mistakes what is historically contingent for some form of transcultural necessity.

Ideologies of nature are similar to ideological theses about human nature. Both typically mistake a conditioned reality for some transcultural "truth." Built upon this fundamental mistake, these ideas are then used to effect massive transformations of natural systems. Ironically, these transformations can then provide validation for the ideologies that guided them. "If it works, it must be true." Opening conceptual space for critical reflection on this interchange between humanity and nature is the intention underlying the concept of "ideologies of nature."

The pages that follow are an examination of various ideologies which frame our views of the rest of nature. Ideologies of nature are clusters of convictions about the structure of nonhuman nature, its significance, and its value. They are composed of two essential elements—images or mappings of nature and agendas for action. Images of nature are cognitive frameworks within which nonhuman nature makes its appearance. They are explicit or implicit claims about what nonhuman nature is and how it is composed. Thus, an image of nature involves, for example, beliefs, perhaps unconscious, about nature—whether it is sacred or profane, infused with purpose or devoid of meaning, composed of discrete parts or organically interrelated, as well as a host of other assumptions. Agendas for action are intimately connected to images of nature, as images permit, invite, oblige, and prohibit various actions regarding nature. Conversely, agendas for action require various kinds of mappings, and actions change territories, confirming old images or requiring new ones.

Ideologies of nature are often only implicit in various social practices. Experimentation on animals or the paving of a meadow for parking places may not be done with any clearly developed theory about animals or natural habitats. Nevertheless, such practices tacitly presuppose answers to questions about the value of animals or ecosystems, and such values involve understandings of what animals and ecosystems are.

It can be difficult to unearth the ideologies of nature implicit in social practices for several reasons. Since interactions with the rest of nature are often based on habits of thought and action formed in the socialization process—rather than being based on careful reflection—the relations between those habits and their underlying ideologies may be rather loose. Thus, several differing ideologies may provide a conceptual basis for a single social practice. Some social practices are, in this sense, "overdetermined." In such a situation, revealing the inadequacy of one ideology may not create change but simply lead to the invocation of another ideology.

A related difficulty is that reflection on ideologies of nature often involves making precise what is only implicit. Much of our thinking and acting regarding nature is ambivalent and inconsistent. This is not surprising given the unconscious dimensions of most ideologies of nature. Trying to make precise that which is merely implied and indeterminate runs the hazard that the result—a more precisely formulated ideology—is not one which the participants in such a practice would, upon reflection, accept. This can make it difficult to confirm that the imputed ideology is indeed operative. Nevertheless, even unacceptable ideologies concerning nature can bring to the fore the necessity for justifying our current ways of treating nature.

In this way, trying to make implied ideologies precise may stimulate reflection on how we *should* regard nature. When the underlying rationales for social practices are brought to light, those rationales may not withstand scrutiny, creating a cognitive dissonance which stimulates change. Of course, such dissonance may only lead to another justificatory ideology rather than changes in practice, but then the process of reflection can start again. While this, in turn, might kindle changes in the way we treat the rest of nature, there is no certainty that reflection has the power to transform practice.

Ideologies of nature are intimately connected to ideologies of society. Relations taken as normal in one domain easily become operative metaphors in the other. If nature is cast in Darwinian language as "red in tooth and claw," then it may seem "natural" to think that society should be an arena in which the strong dominate the weak. If a relationship of domination between man and woman is deemed "natural," then so too is the attempt by men to master nature. The interaction between social ideologies and nature ideologies also has a material basis. Any society involves patterns of interaction with the rest of nature and thus presumes some ideology of nature. These patterns of interaction, if moderately successful in guiding the production of material life, provide people with what they desire. This in turn supports the social and political ideologies that legitimate the existing social order. Social domination and the domination of the rest of nature are intimate companions.

If ideologies can provide both implicit and explicit answers to a set of related questions, then the more general category of "traditions" refers to the clusters of associated questions themselves. Within the tradition of political philosophy, there are a number of competing ideologies. The various conceptions of the "good state"—for example, democratic capitalistic, democratic-socialistic, fascistic, anarchistic—give rise to specific ideologies. But the very set of questions itself constitutes an intellectual tradition. The tradition of social and political philosophy consists of various answers to questions about the legitimacy and proper role of political power, the best ways to select leaders, the nature of human freedom, and other issues concerning how human society should be organized. Few explicit ideologies of nature exist within the social and political tradition, although the social practices endorsed by the various ideologies constitute implicit ideologies of nature. Indeed, as I shall argue, the way we constitute our social and economic systems is one of the most fundamental determinants of how we interact with the rest of nature.

The nature tradition, as I shall refer to it, is another set of questions centering around the issue of how humans should interact with the rest of nature. Around 10,000 years ago, with the rise of agriculture and the domestication of animals, nature became a focus for alteration instead of adaptation. It was only with this new attitude toward nature that the concept of wilderness, denoting that which is not under human dominion, could arise. As Roderick Nash points out, civilization creates wilderness. Nash relates a conversation with a contemporary Malaysian hunter-gatherer who simply could not understand Nash's questions about "wilderness." Finally, Nash asked him how he would say, "I am lost in the jungle." The hunter's puzzled response was that he did not get lost in the jungle. The question was as nonsensical to him as the expression, "I am lost in my apartment," would be to a city dweller.[7] Hunting and gathering societies have no need for a concept of wilderness.

The advent of agriculture radically transformed the relation of humanity to the rest of nature. As Max Oelschlaeger notes, "The agriculturalist necessarily defines 'fields' (areas cleared of natural vegetation), 'weeds' (undesirable plants intruding upon fields), and 'crops' (desirable plants suited to human purposes). In contrast, the hunter-gatherer lives on what is conceptually the 'fruit of the earth' . . . fields, weeds, and crops simply do not exist."[8] With agriculture, nature becomes something to be fenced and planted, altered in accord with desire, rather than dwelt within.

A few hundred years ago, with the collapse of the medieval world and the rise of industrialism, the rest of nature became an object of domination instead of mere alteration. The ever-increasing intensity of human domination eventually gave rise to countermovements aimed at the conservation or preservation of aspects of nonhuman nature. Recently, the project of dominating nature has generated a vigorous environmental movement which has questioned many dimensions of our relations with nonhuman nature. There has now been a sufficient history of concern for nature to warrant distinguishing a nature tradition within human thought. The nature tradition encompasses nineteenth-century thinkers such as Emerson and Thoreau, as well as twentieth-century thinkers like John Muir, Aldo Leopold, and Rachel Carson. It also includes the large numbers of contemporary environmentalists and social movements, such as deep ecology, ecological feminism, and social ecology. Within this nature tradition, a number of divergent ideologies of nature exist.

One of my intentions in this book is to build bridges between the social and the nature traditions. Historically, these two traditions have not communicated well with each other, ignoring or giving woefully weak answers to the central concerns of the other. While the social tradition has attended to the problem of human society and human liberation, it has often ignored or assumed the worst answers to the questions of central importance for the nature tradition. In fact, the social tradition has largely failed to recognize nonhuman nature as anything other than an arena for human domination.

The nature tradition has concentrated on the conservation, preservation, or liberation of nonhuman nature, ignoring questions of central concern to the social tradition, often appearing indifferent to the problems of poverty and other forms of human oppression. Consequently, it has often failed to connect its concerns with those who have an interest in changing the dominant social order. One thesis of this book is that these two traditions—or at least particular ideologies within each tradition—can be enriched through cross-fertilization.

One example of this cross-fertilization is the way some ideologies in the nature tradition could be enhanced by drawing upon one of the ideologies within the social tradition. Within Marxism, in order for any theory of human emancipation to be considered adequate, it must identify the agents who will carry out the necessary changes. This is one notable contribution of Marx and Engels in their critique of utopian socialism. The "requirement of agency," as I shall call it, directs attention to the need for any theory of emancipation to develop its analysis to the point of discerning the dynamics of the changes which can result in liberation.[9] Any nature ideology that is interested in effectively changing our current mode of relating to nature—and most are—could deepen its analysis and enhance its prospects for success by trying to identify the human agency that can bring about the desired changes. With an identification of such agents, practical efforts aimed at change could be more effectively determined and evaluated.

Ideologies within the nature tradition often have an inadequate understanding of the causes of destructive social relations with the rest of nature. Ideologies within this tradition often argue against the dominant ideology of nature and offer some alternative without discussing the social basis for that ideology. Consequently, proposals for changing the ways in which we relate to nature often amount to little more than utopian "oughts," paying no attention to the question of who, in a particular society, is likely to try to create a society that is harmoniously reconciled with the rest of nature. The nature tradition, so I shall argue, can be enriched by recognizing the problem of agency and striving to incorporate the requirement of agency into its analysis of the human situation.

The economic systems that we construct and live within are, I suggest, the primary immediate causes of the relations between society and the rest of nature. The compulsion to earn a living within organized societies compels most people to do what they do. Because economic systems are of central importance, the second and third chapters examine the ideologies of nature implicit within capitalism and socialism. These two socioeconomic systems are profoundly linked to the need for continually expanding material production. For somewhat different reasons, neither can easily choose to evolve toward an ecologically sustainable economy. The fourth chapter is an exposition of the ideology of "expansionary industrialism," which is the phrase I shall use to name the ideology of nature that undergirds both capitalism and socialism. Expansionary industrialism embodies a faith in technology and a technocratic organization of society, as well as an apparently insatiable consumerism. The fifth chapter is a consideration of the idea of control that is implicit in industrialism. I argue that industrialism and its project of dominating nature is problematic at its very foundation because the very possibility of control rests on a mistaken mapping of the human situation. It involves a sort of tunnel vision that is no longer tenable. The belief in the possibility of control, despite its impossibility, functions to legitimate bureaucratic managers and technocracy in general.

The sixth chapter is an analysis of the ideology of nature implicit in science. Science objectifies nature as a result of its methodological orientation toward purposive action. Although this orientation is essential for human action, it is typically totalized into an image of nature that makes all other ideologies seem absurd and unreasonable. It thus tacitly legitimizes the ideology of nature that is implicit in industrialism. It is the totalization of the scientific objectification of nature that requires critique.

In the seventh chapter, I discuss two environmental responses to industrialism that I call "reactive environmentalism" and "ecological environmentalism." Reactive environmentalism is a defensive reaction to the obvious excesses of industrialism, conceiving the environmental crisis as a series of "problems" to be corrected. Reactive environmentalism images nature in a piecemeal fashion and generates such concepts as assimilation capacity, which tries to determine the maximal amount of pollution that can be placed in an ecosystem without creating systemic collapse—and thus the "loss" of a natural "dump." Ecological environmentalism develops an ecological ideology of nature that provides reasons why economic expansion cannot continue indefinitely. Ecological environmentalism maps nature as a relatively tightly integrated system. Focusing on the connectedness of nature, it spawns slogans such as "everything must go somewhere," "and then what," and "nature knows best." This ideology shifts the burden of proof to those who advocate human intervention in natural systems. It provides an ecological basis for a critique of the status quo. One exponent of such an ideology, who leans toward the political right, is Garrett Hardin; an exponent on the political left is Barry Commoner.

In the eighth chapter, I begin to discuss the nature tradition and try to develop an ideology of nature which draws upon, but goes beyond, the science of ecology. This ideology of nature assumes that humans are part of nature and supports the idea of nonanthropocentric relations with the rest of nature. Some philosophers who are concerned with environmental ethics have developed strong critiques of any human-centered ethics, leading to the rejection of anthropocentrism—the idea that only humans have moral standing. The ninth chapter considers the difficulty of grounding any environmental ethic within contemporary ethical discourse and argues for the importance of social change. I argue that deep ecology offers an important foundation for an environmental perspective that accepts the project of social change. Deep ecology rejects anthropocentrism and proposes an eight-point platform that could be the basis for unity among all who seek to create a society that embodies respect for all of nature. Deep ecology seeks a transformation of people and society, advocating the joys of an expanded sense of identification with nature. In the tenth chapter, I consider the contributions that deep ecology can make to a radical environmental movement that understands industrialism as the root cause of ecological crisis. Despite significant differences, there is ground for a fundamental unity among radical environmentalists. Creating such unity may be a way for radical environmentalism to be effective in challenging and changing industrialism.

Since the focus of this book's analysis is on industrialism and its ideologies of nature, with the intention of fostering a greater unity among radical environmentalists, I shall pay relatively little attention to the problems of the Third World. There are several reasons for this. I think that the extent and depth of the ecological problems that all peoples of the world face have their roots in industrialism. Industrialism, I argue, is the core problem, and it is from within industrial societies that adequate solutions must arise. Further, industrial peoples cannot responsibly preach to less industrialized societies while continuing to consume the lion's share of global resources. Such a posture is morally dubious and likely to be of little effect.

Focusing on industrialism does not underestimate the severity of the problems of the Third World, which are intense and will almost certainly get worse before they improve. The projected growth of Third World populations, as well as current structures of debt and the power of international financial institutions and transnational corporations, guarantees desperate situations for the poor of our earth for some time to come. On the other hand, depending on how the ecological systems unravel, the relative independence of the poor from industrialism may work to their benefit. They are far less dependent than industrial societies on uninterrupted flows of energy and resources. It is hard to predict how the future might change.

Finding alternatives to industrialism within industrialism is likely to be the most important long-term project for the well-being of both industrial and Third World peoples. Much thinking about "development" and "underdevelopment" is dominated by an indefensible linear model which sees industrialism as an end point in a desirable process of change. Against this view, two points need to be made. First, it isn't happening. Most peoples of the Third World are falling behind those of the industrial world. The promise of development is not being kept, and the industrialized countries use the lesser industrialized countries as sources of cheap labor, cheap resources, and waste sites. Further, the promise cannot be kept. To bring all the people of the world up to the consumption levels of industrial peoples would require truly massive increases in energy use and manufacturing output. This would foreclose any chance, slim as it may already be, of coping well with problems such as global warming.[10]

What the Third World needs most right now is a clear understanding of why industrialism is the wrong path to follow and why, as an end point, industrialism is not the best kind of society. Showing this clearly is one of the tasks of radical environmentalism and success in this will facilitate the creation of better societies for people all over the world.

2 *Nature as Privately Owned: Capitalism*

Although the ecological problems of modern society have received wide notice and have been taken as cause for alarm, appraisals of the severity of humanity's ecological problems diverge widely. Some think that we are already in the midst of a crisis, and that we have already exceeded the global carrying capacity for human life. Others believe that the crisis will occur sometime in the intermediate future unless drastic changes in our modes of interacting with the rest of nature are undertaken now. Either analysis leads to a need for fundamental social change. On the other hand, some believe that environmental problems have been grossly exaggerated, which implies that no major social change is necessary.[1] Such divergence of opinion leads to little agreement on prescriptions for cure. In the midst of this uncertainty, it is not surprising that the solutions proposed by governments have been piecemeal and of small consequence. Reigning politicians rarely seek fundamental social change.

Philosophers, free from the fetters of political inertia, have raised fundamental questions about humanity's relations with the rest of nature. Their contributions to the analysis of ecological problems have been somewhat abstract, typically involving discussions of ethical questions concerning the foundations of an environmental ethic or the presence or absence of intrinsic value in nonhuman nature. So far, the role of economic systems in the generation of ecological problems has received relatively little attention by environmental philosophers.[2]

What value do such abstract questions have when humanity faces a wide array of serious environmental threats? What is the importance, for example, of discerning that anthropocentrism, which assumes that humanity is the central or only value, is a nearly universal presumption underlying most discussions of environmental issues? Certainly it is true that modern industrial peoples, in practice at least, presume that there are no moral issues involved in our treatment of animals and forests. Discussions of endangered species often simply assume that any justification for saving species or their habitats must involve finding some present or future benefit for humans. Nature, in any of its nonhuman forms, is typically granted value *only* to the extent that it is instrumental in achieving human ends.

Clearly the uncritical acceptance of anthropocentric assumptions about humanity's place in nature is a current cultural fact. But why is this important? If anthropocentrism were to become as discredited as leprechauns, would environmental problems be adequately resolved? Anthropocentrism may indeed be a central ideological factor in supporting current social practices, but it seems unlikely that its elimination would, *in itself*, lead to ecologically sustainable modes of interacting with the rest of nature. Such queries could equally be pressed for other issues focused on by environmental philosophers. If people did attribute intrinsic value to nonhuman nature, would that gracefully resolve our relations with all of it? If mechanistic conceptions of nonhuman nature were avoided, would that resolve ecological problems? If we arrived at a fully androgynous society, would that assure that relations with the rest of nature would be ecologically sound? In all these cases, it seems clear that the cultural changes urged by various environmental philosophers, necessary though they might be, would not in themselves be sufficient to arrive at ecologically adequate patterns of human interaction with the rest of nature.

Consider another problem. Did the abolition of chattel slavery and the resultant cultural agreement that no human could be owned by any other person resolve the problems of race in the United States? Clearly not. Certainly it helped, but just as certainly, more than a century after slavery's end, the United States has still not resolved the problems of relations between the races. While the roots of the problem of slavery did involve the ways in which some whites conceptualized their relations with blacks, changing those concepts alone has not been sufficient to resolve the problems of race relations. The roots of the problem extend into different soils as well. Understanding and ending racism requires understanding and changing the economic factors which push toward its continuance.

There is a lesson in the analogy to the Abolitionist movement. Although the critique of the ideological basis of chattel slavery has not been sufficient for the resolution of the problems of racism, showing the indefensibility of racist ideologies does have an important role in social change. Unless those ideas become discredited, they provide an important social "glue" which helps keep intact racist social practices. Racist ideologies legitimate practices whose primary causes are distinct from the ideology. Thus, the critique of anthropocentrism, social hierarchies, and patriarchy may have the same importance in delegitimating the domination of nonhuman nature.[3] But before this can be shown, consideration must be given to the value and limits of the analysis of the role of economic systems in generating environmental problems.

The lack of attention to economic systems in philosophical discussions of environmental problems is somewhat surprising. Agricultural monoculture, the clearcutting of old growth forests, the damming of free-flowing rivers, urban decay, and the suburbanization of farm lands cannot be adequately explained by seeing them as examples of cultural attitudes. The reasons given for the emission of over 2.4 billion pounds of toxic chemicals per year into the atmosphere by various companies within the United States do not require an appeal to profound cultural errors.[4] While presumptions such as anthropocentrism do underlie these practices, a less abstract and more grounded explanation is readily at hand. Disposing of unwanted by-products of production into the atmosphere in this society is less expensive than other alternatives for dealing with such substances.

Economies are the dominant factor in determining a society's interaction with all of nature. Attempts by businesses to make profits, and by governments to facilitate this process, are essential elements of any explanation, for example, of changing patterns of land use and the pollution of air and water. The compelling need to secure a living by earning wages propels most people to participate in activities that they might otherwise avoid. Without being compelled by material need and desire, most people simply would not do the labor they do. Many of the activities undertaken by people in the course of earning wages are destructive to ecosystems. If the economic system typically rewards ecologically destructive practices, then that system must be changed if a society is to find an ecologically sustainable pattern of living.

Economic structures are experienced by individuals as being compulsory and unchangeable. To the individual, they appear to be structures to which one must adapt. For all individuals, the economic system within which they exist offers a limited range of possibilities for gaining a livelihood. Economic rewards and deprivations are set independently of individual choices and constitute a powerful framework that structures individual choices.[5]

The intentional change of economic structures requires many people acting in consort. Political revolutions are examples of intentional social change, even though the results are often ironic. Any major change which is effective in intentionally transforming the ways in which societies interact with the rest of nature requires that large numbers of people join together and act collectively. That is, intentional social change requires organized social movements. One strength of the social tradition is its attention to the dynamics of social change, while inattention to these dynamics is a weakness of the nature tradition.

Capitalism

Given the importance of economic systems, the question of whether capitalism is capable of arriving at an ecologically sustainable form of interaction with nonhuman nature is of global importance. The collapse of centrally planned economies in Eastern Europe and what was the Soviet Union places the question of the ecological viability of capitalism at center stage. Understanding the importance of capitalism and examining its developmental potentials from an ecological perspective is the subject of this chapter.

Capitalism is the engine that has propelled a truly radical transformation of humanity's relations with the rest of nature. Only the agricultural revolution might be seen as having more profound an impact. The depth and breadth of current ecological problems are due to the changes that began with the explosion of European cultural and economic imperialism in the seventeenth and eighteenth centuries and which came to fruition with the industrial revolution. Although the process has continued from that point, it was the industrial revolution which laid the foundations of a global economy. This global economy is the context for transnational corporations and world-wide financial markets linked by nearly instantaneous communication.

Our present world economy allows ecologically unsustainable patterns of life not only to endure but to flourish, at least temporarily. In Raymond Dasmann's terms, in the last few centuries we have changed from being ecosystem people to being biosphere people.[6] Ecosystem people derive their livelihood from the ecosystems within which they exist. If they arrive at sustainable patterns of life, they do so by developing economic and cultural ways that enable patterns of interacting with the rest of nature and which do not destroy the ecosystems within which they exist. They are attuned to feedback from those systems that allows them to effectively coexist with them. This adjustment is not necessarily "rational" nor intentional. Rather, it may be effected through culturally enforced myths, stories, or patterns of religious belief that restrain them from ecologically destructive practices. Thus, Rappaport persuasively argues that the ritual activities of groups living in the interior of New Guinea help them maintain the biotic communities existing in their territory.[7] The feedback loops within which they exist are relatively short, and this facilitates social learning about mistakes. If ecosystem people fail to find such ways of coexisting with their ecosystems, they migrate or perish.

By contrast, biosphere people draw some portion of their livelihood from ecosystems that are far removed from the ones within which they exist. Rather than being limited to coexistence with only their local ecosystems, biosphere people can import resources from outside their local ecosystems and also export their wastes. By greatly enlarging feedback loops, they can easily fail to notice their ecological mistakes. Hence, they avoid the consequences of these mistakes for a long time and displace their errors onto other societies. Even worse, the flourishing of biosphere economies fosters the appearance that their modes of interaction with nonhuman nature are preferable to the "primitive" ways of ecosystem peoples. If this is an illusion, it has become an illusion of global consequence.

As dramatic as the impact of capitalism has been on the relations between humans and nonhuman nature, it is not at all easy to define its essence. The problem of defining capitalism arises from the difficulty of univocally naming a changing creature. Should one understand mercantile capitalism as being the same as industrial capitalism? Is a highly competitive market capitalism the same as an oligopolistic or monopolistic capitalism? Is a market system with extensive state regulation still capitalistic? Must competitive market capitalism, because of an internal developmental logic, evolve toward oligopoly? Or is oligopoly a preventable backsliding from the competitive marketplace capitalism? These conceptual problems need not be resolved here.[8]

I shall employ two ideal types to discern the dominant forms of economic relations with the rest of nature in industrial society. One mode of making decisions about how nature will be regarded is to rely on markets. This is an "ideal type," not in the sense of being good but in the sense that is has never existed. In every actual society, there are governmental processes that impact the functioning of markets. Nevertheless, markets determine one way in which decisions can be made. Such decisions are the indirect result of the many individual choices made by participants in the various markets comprising a market society. The other "ideal type" is an economy that determines its relations with nonhuman nature through direct collective social choice. This, again, is an idealization of tendencies that are never fully realized. Even the most highly administered society has some markets, even if they are covert. Many private choices are made, but they occur within the context of more encompassing social determination. Collective direct social choices about how the rest of nature will be regarded involve some form of administrative decision making procedures. Typically the procedures take the form of bureaucracies.

These two ideal types define a continuum along which industrial societies can be arrayed. In varying degrees, all extant industrial societies use both markets and administrative techniques to arrive at decisions about how nonhuman nature is used. The critical variable is whether the economy is the dominant mode of making social decisions or whether the economy is submerged within some larger social decision-making process. The continuum does not exhaust all possibilities. Other types of social decision making have been realized, for example, in hunter-gatherer societies, and still other forms of social choice can be imagined. But these two ideal types do, I believe, name the two extremes of the spectrum of actual modes of social choice within industrial societies.

Given the impact of industrial societies on the shape of the modern world, it seems important to focus on markets and bureaucratic administration as modes of social choice. In reality, all industrial nations utilize some mix of these two forms of choice, despite the political rhetoric about the differences between capitalism and socialism. For simplicity, I shall view capitalism as an economic system that relies on markets to make social choices and socialism as an economic system which relies on bureaucratic administration to make social choices.

The dominance of markets in determining how humans interact with the rest of nature is the fundamental determinant of the ideology of nature that is implicit in capitalism. Markets, of course, are not unique to capitalism. They are a common form of exchange among precapitalistic people and may be a significant feature of some forms of "market socialism." What is unique in capitalism is the centrality accorded to markets in the ordering of social life. In capitalistic regimes, markets move from the periphery of social life to the center, and fundamental social choices are made by markets. Traditions become nonrational and a myriad of individual choices within markets result in social decisions directly intended by no one. This reliance on markets is at the core of capitalistic ideologies of nature.

Nature as Privately Owned

The essence of capitalism's ideology of nature is that pieces of nonhuman nature can be privately owned. The idea of ownership presupposes that the objects in question belong in the category of things that *can* be owned.

Just what can be legitimately owned is not as obvious as it might seem at first glance. The struggle over human slavery was, in part, about what kinds of things can be owned. Could human beings be rightfully owned? The success of the struggle against slavery led to the belief that no person can own any other person. People, we now believe, are not the sorts of things that can be owned. But exactly what can be rightfully owned is not always so clear. Can wild animals be owned? Does a land owner own the deer that cross the meadow? Is it proper to allow living products of genetic engineering to be patented? Can forms of life be legitimately owned? Clearly the laws of nature cannot be owned, but can complex algorithms be rightfully patented? The United States Patent and Trademark Office has granted a number of patents for such mathematical equations, and a patent is a sort of temporary ownership. Is this proper? The answers, whatever they may be, are not obvious, at least within a capitalistic society.

Can parts of nonhuman nature be rightfully owned? The claim of ownership of them presupposes that they are the sorts of things which can be legitimately owned. Under capitalism, whose ideology of nature is that pieces of nature can be privately owned, most of nonhuman nature is regarded as "stuff" which can be owned and disposed of as a right of the owner. This ideology requires that nonhuman nature be drained of intrinsic meaning and value. If "Mother Nature" is sentient, loving, or vengeful, she could hardly be owned, although she could be tended and, perhaps, cultivated. Capitalism could not transform natural systems and their parts into commodities to be bought and sold until the wood sprites and leprechauns are banished. No culture could regard nature as both sensitive and alive and nevertheless strip mine the mountains. In short, nonhuman nature must be "disenchanted" before it can be viewed as "raw materials" and "natural resources" which can be owned.

The idea that pieces of nonhuman nature can be owned is so obvious within industrial cultures that it is hard to call into question, yet it has not been so apparent to many other peoples. The native Americans of New England, for example, had quite different conceptions of property than those of the colonists coming from England. The native Americans recognized the right to use a place at a specific time. What was "owned" was only the crops grown or the berries picked. Thus, "different groups of people could have different claims on the same tract of land depending on how they used it."[9] Such rights of use did not allow for the sale of property. These differences remain to this day. As Buffalo Tiger, a Miccosukee Seminole Indian stated recently:

> We Indian people . . . are not supposed to say, This land is mine. We only *use* it. It is the white man who buys land and puts a fence around it. Indians are not supposed to do that, because the land belongs to all Indians, it belongs to God, as you call it. The land is a part of our body, and we are a part of the land. . . . [W]e do not want to 'improve' our land, we just wish to keep it as it is. It's hard for us to come to terms with the white man because our philosophy is so different. We think the land

> is there for everyone to use, the way our hand is there, a part of our own body.

Jimmie Durham, a Cherokee, comments similarly:

> We cannot separate our place on earth from our lives on the earth nor from our vision nor our meaning as a people. We are taught from childhood that the animals and even the trees and plants that we share a place with are our brothers and sisters. So when we speak of land, we are not speaking of property, territory, or even a piece of ground upon which our houses sit and our crops are grown. We are speaking of something truly sacred.[10]

Even if nonhuman nature is regarded as the sort of thing which can be owned, how can it be owned privately? How can *one* person take claim to land or other parts of nature? By what right does one person exclude others from parts of the earth? If it was not created by those who claim to own it, how can such a claim be legitimate? Although private ownership of the earth is now a common dogma, it was not at the outset of the capitalistic regime. Then the conception of nature as privately owned required justification.

John Locke, in his *Second Treatise of Civil Government* published in 1690, provided a rationale for the private ownership of the earth. Locke saw that there was a problem in justifying how "that which God gave to mankind in common" could legitimately be privately owned.[11] To show how people could obtain the right to exclude others from parts of nature, Locke began with the theory that one has property in one's own person. Thus, one owns one's own labor. Therefore, "Whatsoever, then, he removes out of the state that nature hath provided and left it in, he hath mixed his labor with it, and joined to it something that is his own, and thereby makes it his property."[12]

The claim is that by putting labor into a part of nature a person incorporates that part into one's self. Indeed, Locke used the metaphor of eating to elaborate the idea of acquiring property by labor. But this claim is not as obvious as Locke thought because one might as easily argue that putting one's labor into some part of nature results in the loss of ownership of one's labor rather than occasioning the acquisition of property in nonhuman nature.[13] And why is removing some part not theft of the common heritage of all humanity? Further, suppose that a people invested their surroundings with symbolic importance, as it were, and mix their psychological life with their place. According to Warwick Fox, the Maori people of New Zealand and Australian aborigines do just this.[14] In such a case, the mixing of labor with what has been given symbolic importance might be worse than theft, more closely resembling a personal assault.

Locke recognized limits to this original right to property. First, one could not legitimately acquire more than could be used fruitfully. "As much as any one can make use of to any advantage of life before it spoils, so much he may by his labor fix a property in. Whatever is beyond this is more than his share, and belongs to others. Nothing was made by God for man to despoil or destroy."[15] As far as rights in land, Locke claimed that those who labor on the land have right to exclude others, for God commanded man "to subdue the earth," and those who, "in obedience to this command of God, subdued, tilled, and sowed any part of it, thereby annexed to it something that was his property, which another had no title to, nor could without injury take from him."[16] Importantly, Locke supposed that such annexation did no harm to others, since there was "still enough and as good [land] left."[17]

This, of course, is not sufficient justification for modern capitalistic forms of private property, which recognize no limits to the extent of private property. Limits to property based on the necessity for labor or on causing no harm to others would involve a radical redistribution of capitalistic property. Whatever the case in Locke's time, there clearly is not now "enough and as good" land left, so private ownership now does entail harm to others. Private ownership of land not only excludes individuals from particular places, but it excludes many from *any* place. Further, if one has a right to that with which one has mixed one's labor, then every worker has the right to take home the products that he or she made that day.

To justify capitalistic forms of private property, limits to private ownership must be disavowed. Locke abolishes all such bounds by a rather dubious theory of money. While, prior to money, it was "useless as well as dishonest to carve himself too much,"[18] the "invention of money gave them the opportunity to continue and enlarge" their possessions.[19] After the invention of money, "it is plain that the consent of men [to money] have agreed to a disproportionate and unequal possession of the earth."[20] And this inequality is prior to any social contract, being within the "state of nature." The unlimited right to private property is thus "natural," not due to any social convention, and based on the "consent" to the use of money.

It is hard to accept the claim that the use of money rests upon any relevant form of consent. To be sure, there is a consensual element in individual monetary exchanges, in that they may be voluntary as opposed to coerced. But within a monetary society, there is no significant sense in which the whole practice of monetary exchanges is voluntary. For this whole practice to be voluntary, there must be adequate alternatives present. Without such alternatives, the whole social practice is lacking in individual choice and consent. Within a monetary economy, if one wishes to engage in exchanges, then money is typically involved. And choosing not to engage in exchange is not generally possible. In any case, consent to monetary exchange is not an *informed* consent to the "unequal possession of the earth." The unequal possession of the earth is based on violence and fraud, not the use of money. Any doubts on this point can be resolved by even the most casual reading of the history of the relations between European settlers and American Indians. Even in the unlikely event that this inequality were, in fact, a consequence of the use of money, this consequence could not have been anticipated by those who first consented to monetary exchange. By no stretch of imagination is it a consequence consented to by those who use money now.

Although Locke's justification for unlimited property fails, it is nonetheless significant. At least Locke recognized the need for a justification for the private ownership of the earth. Modern attempts to answer such questions ignore the problem Locke tries to address and simply assume that the earth is the sort of thing which can be owned. The key question in modern debates is the foundation of property rights: Is property justified by the beneficent consequences of such an institution or is it justified by an appeal to some absolute or "natural" right? This debate has implications for the question of when, if ever, property rights can be justly overridden. If property rights are justified in terms of the good consequences of the institution of private property, then similar goods of society can justify their contraction or abolition. On the other hand, if property rights should be regarded as "absolute," then they can *never* be justly infringed or abolished. Significantly, this debate is not about whether nonhuman nature can be legitimately owned; it assumes that it can, and is a debate over the foundations of the assumed right.[21] Thus, the unargued assumption which underlies contemporary discussions is that the rest of nature is in pieces and that the pieces are, in fact, the type of things which can be legitimately owned.

Locke's concern with the question of the legitimacy of private property is understandable. He is trying to justify a nascent economic system which had not yet come to seem normal. The absence of concern with this question among contemporary theorists is equally understandable. They simply presume that which Locke tried to justify. Establishing capitalistic economies required force, enclosures of common lands, armies, missionaries, and justificatory ideologies. Over time, the character structure of the participants in an economy comes to embody the ideas required for the ordinary functioning of that economic order. The social order becomes crystallized in habitual and unreflective thought and action. Once the dominant economic order has become commonplace, the "right" to use and dispose of the pieces of nature that one "owns" is considered "natural."

Capitalism and Markets

Capitalism is an economic system in which the production and distribution of economic goods is typically effected through competitive markets. These markets are the arena within which social decisions are created. A capitalistic system, to simplify, is a collection of producers linked together by markets wherein exchange rates, (i.e., prices) are determined by unregulated auction. Some producers are only in a position to sell their labor while others own or can effectively dispose of the products that are produced by those who sell their labor.[22] Further distinctions could be introduced, but a finer analysis of the conditions of production is not necessary. The point is that people under capitalism typically confront various markets that regulate significant dimensions of their lives. This fact applies to laborer, bureaucrat, and corporate manager.

All participants in competitive market capitalism are confronted with conditions to which they must adapt. They encounter markets that set the prices of the elements of production which they must purchase in order to produce. They face another market that sets the price at which their products can be sold. Thus, workers do not control the costs of food and housing, and capitalistic producers typically do not control their costs for raw materials. Workers do not control the wages they are paid, and capitalists do not control the prices at which their products can be sold. The collection of such markets, it is said, leads to the best possible "mixture" of what is produced in society at the lowest possible cost. Thus, Adam Smith's famous "invisible hand"—a metaphor for the theory that when producers act only in their own interests, this leads to a socially optimal result—guides us all toward general prosperity without anyone explicitly intending such a result. Markets determine what otherwise might have to be decided by tradition or explicit decision.

The regulation of social life by market mechanisms has ramifications in all dimensions of human life, ranging from family life and schooling to the way people live out their lives as workers or owners. Markets tend to generate selfish behavior and discourage cooperative behavior. Typically, the participants in these markets act to enhance their welfare without regard to others. In short, they are self-regarding. That this is the ordinary pattern of behavior within capitalistic markets is not a reflection of human nature. Participants within a capitalistic market who do not attempt to enhance their economic position tend to suffer unpleasant consequences. For example, if those who manage centers of material production fail to maximize profit, they may be unable to attract investors. As a result, they may be unable to modernize their systems of production. This makes them less able to compete successfully with other producers. They then lose their position in their market.

To summarize, the social decisions about how nonhuman nature shall be treated are made within the context of an ideology which assumes that nature can be owned privately. The actual decisions made regarding the rest of nature are unintended byproducts of self-regarding choices made by a multitude of participants within an interconnected network of markets. Are decisions made this way apt to be ecologically adequate?

The Incompatibility of Capitalism and Ecology

There are three principal theoretical reasons for the inability of capitalism to cope with ecological problems. First, the reliance on markets to make decisions about the way society interacts with nonhuman nature implies that it can be adequately seen through the lens of a market economy. Second, capital must always be given a price, leading to a systematic disregard of the future which is incompatible with ecological sustainability. Third, capitalism requires growth, but growth cannot be indefinitely sustained within a finite world.

I stress here theoretical reasons for the ecological unsustainability of capitalism, because discussions of the particular ecological problems now prevalent within capitalistic societies often founder on the question of how likely it is that some future technological discovery will enable the resolution of present problems. If the question of the ecological adequacy of capitalism is restricted to the currently available evidence, the picture is indeed grim. The list of problems is long and distressing. It includes the possibility of significant and global climatic change and thinning of the ozone layer. These two possibilities portend major changes in patterns of human habitation, with massive migrations across national boundaries. The thinning of the ozone layer will disrupt the oceanic food chain with vast and unpredictable consequences for all life on this planet. Current agricultural practices involve major fossil energy inputs that cannot be obtained without ecological disruption and that will not last indefinitely. Air pollution and the acidification of rain affect the health of forests. Many species of fish, particularly those nearer the tops of food chains, now have such high concentrations of hazardous substances that consumption of them is dangerous to human health. Many dumps slowly leach dangerous materials into groundwater. This small sample of the range of ecological problems we now face indicates the severe threat to all forms of life which has been created by industrial capitalism.

Of course, the claim that future technologies will resolve environmental problems and provide means of surpassing apparent limits can never be decisively refuted. For example, is there some technological solution to nuclear wastes yet to be found? The fact that thirty years of intense effort has not yielded such a solution does not prove that one cannot be found. Some wastes must be contained for 10,000 years or more, a time span far exceeding the existence of any civilization, but this fact is not decisive for those with faith that technological solutions can always be found. Is there some technological solution to the problem of global warming? One recent proposal was to place a large opaque surface between the earth and the sun to diminish the amount of sunlight reaching the earth. One can marvel at or mock the hubris of such an idea, but it could not be decisively disproved, even if it were tried unsuccessfully several times. The faith in technology is as resilient as the faith of the religiously devout in the face of counterevidence. The pervasiveness of this faith in technology is why I stress the theoretical reasons for capitalism's ecological inadequacy.

Markets and Nature

Markets are not an ecologically adequate mode of interacting with the rest of nature. Within a market economy, social choices are a composite result of decisions made in the buying and selling of commodities. The decisions made in various markets indirectly regulate the daily activities of the members of society in accord with seemingly objective forces governed by the so-called laws of economics and consumer preferences. If people with money value some commodity sufficiently to purchase it, then that product will likely be produced. Finite resources will be devoted to the production of those things and not to others. Wage labor will be purchased to produce some commodities and not others. The result is a social decision to produce certain things and not others, to use parts of nonhuman nature in some ways and not others. No particular person will have made that decision. The social choice is, instead, the unintended effect of many other choices made by purchasers in various markets. The ecological consequences of this social choice likely will not have been considered at all. Capitalism, by leaving its fundamental social decisions to market forces, only accounts for the rest of nature insofar as it is measured by money and markets.

How does the rest of nature appear when seen through the lens of a market economy? Parts of ecosystems are plucked like fruits to be transformed into commodities, parts are used as sewers, and parts are invisible because they are not given value by the human participants in markets. The value placed on parts of nature is determined by prices that are in turn determined by markets. Thus, it may or may not be economically profitable to strip-mine a mountain—it depends on the market conditions—but it will destroy the mountain's ecosystems. Soil conservation may or may not be economically justifiable for a farmer, but erosion beyond the rate of soil replacement cannot lead to sustainable agriculture. It may or may not pay to "mine" rain forests for exotic hardwoods and use what remains for cattle pastures—it depends on market conditions—but it does destabilize global weather patterns, disrupt atmospheric chemistry, and destroy the habitats of primal peoples and myriad species of plants and animals. Nature as a network of biotic communities disappears when viewed from the perspective of a market economy, and becomes visible only as bits and pieces of it are brought to the marketplace for sale. It is seen as meaningless clay that can be molded through human intention realized by exchanges made in marketplaces.

In fact, human economies exist within the larger matrix of nature. To regulate human interaction with the rest of nature solely by markets inverts this relationship. The faith that this inversion will endure rests on the assumption that the dynamics of markets are harmonious with the dynamics of ecosystems. The only empirical support for this assumption is found in the past successes of market economies in transforming nature into resources to be marketed. The adequacy of this evidential support becomes suspect if the past successes have proceeded within a "slack" in natural systems which have so far been relatively tolerant of human exploitation.

The concept of slack names the degree of tolerance which may exist in an interconnected system because of a looseness of connection between the elements of that system. When there is a high degree of slack in connection between the elements, the consequences of changes in one part of the system are muted in their effects on the rest of the system. When there is less slack, consequences spread more robustly throughout the whole system. If nonhuman nature is understood as an interconnected network, then the presence of slack permits disruptions of parts of the system to be of mostly local consequence. When there is less slack, the same kinds of disruptions may have far reaching and unexpected consequence. If disruptions of a natural system tend to lessen the degree of slack, then the kinds of actions which once had little noticeable effect may, at a later time, have more wide-spread consequences.

The evidence against the belief that the dynamics of markets are harmonious with the dynamics of ecosystems is substantial and growing, as the range and depth of environmental problems within capitalistic societies expand. This mismatch of markets and ecosystems is not merely contingent. The market image of material flow in society is that nature, under the concept of "resources," is developed into commodities which are produced, brought to market, purchased, consumed, and discarded. It is assumed that materials flow through the system, disappearing from markets when placed in a landfill.

By contrast, the central concepts ecologists use in studying ecosystems are energy flows and material cycles. Within a relatively contained ecosystem, energy flows through an ecosystem affecting the various cycles of material—living and nonliving—within that ecosystem. Material does not disappear, it only changes form. The only thing *not* recycled in a closed ecosystem is energy.

Thus, from an economic perspective, material flows through society, whereas, from an ecological perspective, energy flows through ecosystems. Since economies are nested within ecosystems, market societies will have problems with their wastes. If their products cannot be decomposed by natural processes, which is typical in industrial processes of production, a garbage crisis *must* develop.[23] The dynamics of markets do not include the dynamics of ecosystems, and this omission is of fundamental importance. The mismatch between market processes and ecological processes is tolerable only when there is sufficient slack in the relevant ecosystems. In the long run, however, ecology is a more fundamental determinant of existence than economy. This becomes readily apparent when the slack disappears and, for example, the biotic systems of a lake collapse through an algae bloom.

Of course, capitalism does not exist on markets alone. Economies based on markets generate a reaction wherein political regulation of the extremes of the mistreatment of humans and the rest of nature develop.

Capitalistic societies differ significantly in the degree to which they politically moderate the working of the labor market on human beings. Some societies view certain human needs, such as medical care, housing, food, and clothing, as rights which must be met, irrespective of the workings of the market. Others do not. So too, some communities set more limits than others upon the "owners" of parts of nature. Thus, restrictions on pollution and waste disposal are common, but they vary widely in their stringency. Most societies recognize that the community has the right to control at least some aspects of the choices that individuals make with regard to their property.

The general logic for restrictions on individual choices about property within capitalism is that some decisions affect the value of property owned by others. Thus, zoning laws in the United States reflect the fact that property owners' decisions may have significant impact on the value of neighboring properties. The baseline of such restrictions is the idea that those who are recognized as the owners of a piece of nature have the right to do whatever they choose with it, unless their choices harm others in prohibited ways. The presumption is that the owners may do whatever they wish with the pieces of nature that they "own," as long as others are not harmed.

As noted above, there is controversy about the moral basis of property rights among proponents of capitalism. For them, the central issue is the moral foundation of "property rights." Should such rights be regarded as absolute? Or are they founded on the basis of their usefulness to society as a whole? The libertarian view is absolutist in regard to property rights. It denies the legitimacy of any political regulation of the rights of owners to use their property in any way that they choose, as long as no harm comes to other people or their property. Such an absolutist view of property rights has a strange consequence—industrial society is morally illegitimate! This is because pollution is an inevitable result of many industrial processes. Air pollution, for example, inevitably spreads beyond the property of the polluter. Factories, as well as automobiles, pollute the air breathed by others. It is difficult to imagine industrial processes that export *no* pollution. Such pollution erodes the property rights of those who are unwillingly subjected to it. One can suppose that compensation could be paid, but how much? Suppose some parties would accept no price? In such a case, when viewed from the perspective of a believer in the unconditional right to property, the pollution must be prohibited. "No one has the right to benefit from acts or practices that violate the rights of others."[24] Thus, such activity must be legally prohibited, thereby making industrial society immoral.

Libertarianism views the rest of nature in a manner consistent with competitive market capitalism—nonhuman nature is a collection of pieces that can be owned by individuals. If processes were developed that did not spread pollution beyond the property owners' boundaries, then there could be no restriction on what they did with what they owned. Mountains and forests could be used or abused with abandon and for profit. The only limits are the contingent ones of harm to neighbors. The assumption is that the rest of nature can be dissected into private parcels without regard to anything except property rights. This assumption is at sharp odds with the interconnectedness of nature discerned by ecology. In fact, it is precisely this pervasive connectedness that compels the consistent libertarian to morally condemn industrial society.

The alternative to the libertarian solution within the framework of market capitalism is to accept restrictions and political regulation of property rights and markets through a political process. Consider the problem of pollution from the perspective of the individual producer of paper, for example. Given that the costs of materials and labor are set by one market and that the price of the paper is set by a different market, the individual producer is strongly pushed by the system to pollute the adjacent stream as much as possible. Any efforts to voluntarily refrain from polluting the river with waste effluent will increase the cost of production. This raises the producer's costs, possibly beyond the price at which paper can be sold profitably. Thus, the producer can plausibly and, in a limited sense, truthfully argue that there is "no choice" but to pollute. If a locality prohibits such pollution, then it must face the possibility that the producer will relocate to a place where rivers can be used as free sewers. The solution to this problem requires a general regulation of pollution applying to all paper producers. This cannot be achieved within any market, but rather requires an effective political process which regulates *all* producers.

The problem of mitigating the mismatch of markets and ecology must, then, be dealt with through a political process. It cannot be done by markets alone. The system of a competitive market economy compels its participants to regard parts of nonhuman nature as resources to be obtained at the least cost and to use other parts of it, such as air and water, as dumps for wastes. The destruction of ecosystems is the necessary consequence.

The political regulation of the environment means setting politically determined goals and controlling productive activity through laws and bureaucratic rules. As such, it involves restrictions on the rights of owners to do as they please with their property.[25] The exclusive reliance on markets generates a political reaction because the workings of the marketplace have no inherent limit on the exploitation of people or nonhuman nature. Whether it is child labor, or rivers that catch on fire, the extremes of abuse evoke a response by the body politic.[26]

The need for political regulation of market relations with nature is inherent in capitalism's development into a system that uses machinery extensively in the productive process. Investment in elaborate and expensive forms of production requires assurance that raw materials will be available for purchase. In a prescient remark, made over forty years ago, Karl Polanyi noted:

> Machine production in a commercial society involves, in effect, no less a transformation than that of the natural and human substance of societies into commodities. The conclusion, though weird, is inevitable; nothing less will serve the purpose: obviously, the dislocation caused by such devices must disjoint man's relationships and threaten his natural habitat with annihilation.[27]

The crucial question thus becomes whether or not the political process and bureaucratic administrative structures can adequately regulate competitive markets in humanity's relations with the rest of nature.

Political restrictions on markets are created through a process that works from a baseline assumption that individuals own pieces of nature and can do whatever they want with them. All restrictions that are placed on this "right" must fight an uphill battle against the presumption of private property, and the hill is significantly steepened by the influence of accumulated wealth on the political process. The influence of concentrations of wealth on the political process is a large topic in its own right. Suffice it here to note that the crucial political decisions in United States national politics are made before the ballots are printed. The central decisions concern who will be put forward as the candidates for the two major parties. These decisions are strongly influenced by who bankrolls the candidates and by corporately owned news media.

The effects of the concentration of wealth do not end after elections. Corporate centers of power exercise considerable influence aimed at maintaining their social control. Such concentrations of power have been used to obstruct the use of less profitable technologies, ones which might be ecologically more benign. In the 1920s, General Motors, along with Standard Oil of California and Firestone Tire, gained control of and subsequently dismantled mass transit systems in forty-four urban areas.[28]

The political regulation of markets is inherently conflictual. The results are, at best, compromises between ecological imperatives and powerful economic interests. Further, the regulation is apt to come only after the problem in question becomes politically visible, and the public has become too alarmed for corporations to be allowed to do as they wish. This means that the process is always one of trying to catch up with damage already done. It is not clear that ecological problems can be adequately managed this way. If the behavior of an ecosystem is not linear, changes happen rapidly and reflect past, not present, actions. For example, the pollution of a pond with sewage can proceed without much obvious change for some time. When the slack in the system is gone, conditions ripen for a massive increase in algae. This consumes the available oxygen rapidly, killing the fish population all at once. One of the most ominous facts about the depletion of the ozone layer by chlorofluorocarbons is that these gasses can take up to one hundred years to rise high enough in the atmosphere to affect the ozone. This means that the thinning of the ozone now being noticed is the effect of actions taken decades ago. No matter what is done now, the effects of past actions will continue for many decades into the future. For ecological problems that are nonlinear and for ones that have long delays between the action and its result, political regulation will tend to be of little effectiveness.

In actual fact, no industrial society leaves social decision making up to markets alone. Since the depression of the 1930s, governments have regularly intervened in economies in order to moderate the effects of markets. The influence of the state permeates the economy in all capitalistic countries. At what point will the political regulation of economic decisions change the system from capitalism into some fundamentally different system?

There is a spectrum of possibilities for the regulation of society's interaction with the rest of nature. The key issue is the degree to which either the economy dominates politics or politics dominates the economy. The end of the spectrum, at which point politics regulates the economy, is some form of socialism, fascism, or technocracy. This involves eliminating markets as a mechanism of social choice. At the other end of the spectrum is a pure market capitalism in which the political regulation of private actions is absent. Neither of these exists in reality. In currently existing industrial societies, there is a range of differences in the degree to which the state regulates economies. There are, of course, major differences in the types of political processes which determine state decisions about economies. But underneath these differences there is the same problem of regulating the impact of industrial society on the rest of nature. To the extent that capitalism relies on markets, it is ecologically flawed. It now seems inescapable that ecological problems will require increasing political regulation of processes once left to markets. This raises the question of how adequately such decisions can be made through political processes and techniques of public administration. Can industrialism be effectively managed? This is the topic of the next chapter.

Discounting the Future

A second theoretical reason for the incompatibility of capitalism and ecology stems from the fact that capital must always cost something. The ecological significance of this may not be immediately apparent. Capital cannot be free, but must always be priced through interest rates. Interest rates are one of the frameworks within which the profitability of various options for investment are evaluated. A dollar now is worth more than a dollar in the future because it can be invested now, and it will increase at the prevailing rate of interest. Thus, economic "rationality" requires that a possible future profit must at least equal present value plus interest. If interest rates are 10 percent, $100,000 today is worth more than $250,000 ten years from now. The greater the time horizon, the more the future is discounted. $100,000 now is worth more than $670,000 twenty years in the future. Higher interest rates also increase the rate at which future profit is discounted.[29]

Another important factor in such decisions is represented by the probabilities attached to possible outcomes. Uncertainty increases as time horizons extend further into the future. This increase of uncertainty also tends to discount the future. Thus, consequences of actions that extend beyond a rather limited time frame—in practice, ten years—are usually steeply discounted. Economic "rationality" requires that the distant future be disregarded.

There are exceptions to this compulsion to discount the future. Resources can be reserved for future use by ignoring "rational" calculations of profit. This requires a degree of wealth sufficient to insulate decisions from the pressure of market conditions. For example, wealthy families have purchased and held real estate with low or even negative rates of return, expecting to wait an unpredictably long time until the real estate market in that area changes. They are prepared to stockpile some portion of capital in unprofitable real estate for their children or grandchildren, who may realize gains (possibly truly enormous ones) at some unknown point in the future. This happened on Manhattan's West Side, where a slum area eventually became the wealthy Lincoln Center area. A similar stockpiling of real estate may now be happening in the South Bronx.

A recent example is even more obviously related to environmental problems. Pacific Lumber, a relatively small timber company in northern California, held large tracts of old-growth redwood forests, slowly and selectively cutting timber from those forests. The timbering was managed with a concern for the long-term health of the forest and surrounding communities. They "irrationally" husbanded their timber resources, seeking a sustainable yield over generations. Unfortunately, their timber holdings constituted an asset which was used by another corporation to leverage a buy out of the smaller company. The new company, the Maxxam conglomerate, having used the timber assets to finance their takeover, no longer had the luxury of insulating their assets from market pressures. They were thus compelled to attempt an ecologically unsound program of the rapid cutting of timber to pay their debts. Thus, within capitalism, avoiding the pressure to discount the future requires sufficient wealth and a desire for a sustainable yield to enable an ignoring of economic "rationality."[30]

Market pressures to discount the future will probably intensify. It is reasonable to anticipate significant scarcity of resources in the future. This increasing scarcity of resources will result from depletion and manifest itself as the increasing cost of obtaining such resources. The first barrel of oil is far easier to get than the last. Increasing costs will tend to raise the prices of resources. Such increases will push the economic system towards inflation. Of course, increasing costs will also intensify the development of alternatives to those resources, by changing production processes or by creating functionally equivalent alternatives. Even though such substitutes may be available, it is likely that they will be more expensive. This inflationary bias, introduced by the increasing cost of resources, means that interest rates will tend to be pushed upward. Higher interest rates discount the future at a more rapid rate. Further, as ecological problems intensify and the call for effective political regulation becomes louder, uncertainty about the future will increase. The fear that political regulation may restrict profit will only intensify the "rationality" which discounts the future, and the tendency to take the money now will only intensify. As Charles Hall points out, at least one neoclassical economist, in discussing renewable natural resources, advocates managing fish stocks by harvesting them to exhaustion. The monetary gains could then be invested elsewhere. As Hall points out, this so-called logic results in a truly absurd and impossible world with "lots of money but nothing real left to invest in."[31]

The ecological significance of this is that the rhythms of ecosystems and the fluctuations of interest rates are not closely connected. In particular, the time frames necessary to achieve ecological rationality may extend across generations, while the time frames for economic decisions rarely stretch out past a decade or two. Thus, capitalistic economies will not likely be ecologically rational. Such rationality as they can achieve must arise from political regulation. This, as we shall see, is not much.

The Necessity for Growth

A third and especially significant dimension of capitalistic markets is the necessity for the continual growth of production, albeit with occasional contractions along the way. Capitalistic economies require growth of production because of the role of competition in the dynamics of capitalism. Producers are vitally interested in their profit. One way to increase profit is to sell products at a lower price than others sell the same or similar products. This can be done by lowering the costs of producing such products. Cheaper labor, perhaps to be found in a different location or by paying lower wages, is one way of lowering costs. Another historically effective way to reduce production costs is to devise ways to produce the product (or one similar to it) by a less costly process. Such innovations typically involve the use of more elaborate machinery to produce larger quantities of goods with less labor per unit. Thus, the successful producer finds a cheaper and faster mode of producing something, enabling that producer to come to the market with a cheaper product.

This confronts competitors with the problem of finding some innovation themselves or being driven from the market by cheaper goods. In this process, more is produced with less labor. If wages are the dominant form of income, the increase in the productivity of labor threatens to generate unemployment. But increased unemployment means fewer consumers able to purchase what is produced. There is, therefore, a systemic need to expand consumption of what is produced. The needed expansion is usually found in new consumers, increased per capita consumption, and governmental purchases. This cycle, in which an increased productivity on the part of labor requires increased consumption of the rest of nature, repeats itself again and again. It is called "economic growth" and is widely regarded as good.

The continued expansion of production bodes ill for nature, human and nonhuman. Growth accelerates the process in which more and more of nonhuman nature is converted firstly into "resources" and somewhat later into "waste." The necessity of selling what is produced in order to realize a profit, in later capitalism at least, tends to foster a consumer culture wherein people conceive of the "good life" as the maximum consumption of things. The inner psychic life of people becomes a focus of attention, with continual attempts made to convince people to appraise their worth in terms of how much they own. But this way of achieving a sense of self-worth becomes a source of dissatisfaction when affluence becomes widespread and therefore no longer serves as a socially recognized mark of being "better" than one's neighbors.[32] Thus, the treadmill toward increased material consumption does not lead to satisfaction, but rather an unending quest for more. This may in part explain the fact that Americans now have many more material possessions than they did three decades ago, yet they consistently report lower levels of happiness than they did in 1957.[33] The point is not that material consumption is irrelevant to human happiness. Clearly there are basic needs that must be met for a dignified human existence to be possible, and these basic needs are regularly unmet for the poor of the world. Nevertheless, material consumption, beyond a certain level, does not lead to increased human happiness.

This process of expanding production will not be endless because growth cannot continue forever within a finite medium. As this process is an integral part of the logic of capitalism, changing it involves a transition to another form of economy.

To appreciate better the necessity for the expansion of production under capitalism, consider the conditions under which the requirement of growth can be avoided. In particular sectors of the economy, producers may establish monopolies. By exerting conscious control over markets, they can avoid the dynamics of growth generated by competitive markets. Occasionally participants are successful in this, but monopolies tend to generate political regulation.[34] If the whole economy of a society became one monopoly, the imperative of growth could be avoided. But such a society would no longer be capitalistic. Replacing markets as the mode of social decision making involves eliminating them or submerging them into the context of social control. This amounts to a transition to some form of state capitalism, technocracy, or socialism, as long as the scale of industrial societies is maintained. A central question in morally assessing such a change is whether social decisions are made in the interests of maintaining existing inequalities or decreasing them.

The alternative to capitalism, which leaves existing relations of advantage and domination in place, involves retaining control through the manipulation of politics and seems to be a regulation of the economy in the "common interest," but it actually leaves the fundamental structures of domination in place. Such a publicly controlled monopolistic economy would amount to a mammoth bureaucratic state capitalism. The path to a publicly controlled capitalistic economy raises a host of problems with its associated legitimating belief systems.[35] It means the loss of the ideological justification for present inequalities. Those who suffer from relative deprivation in a capitalistic society must give up their hopes for rising in the economic order. The loss of competitive markets would end moral arguments offered for capitalism that claim that markets are the fundamental condition for human freedom. It is an open question as to how far people can be cajoled, bribed, and/or coerced into leaving control of the economy in the hands of those who profit from it. This is especially true in the absence of any compensating ideology promising that these same people will also be "free" to enter the market as owners and to "get ahead." I assume that there is some limit to the extent to which people will tolerate such a situation, although I do not know where it is.

A managed economy might find it difficult to survive the decline in living standards that may arise from ecological constraints. Such contractions and their associated suffering, within a publicly managed economy, appear to be the responsibility of politicians (presumed to represent the interests of all citizens), rather than the results of "blind" forces of the marketplace. Calls for the regulation of the economy in the interests of all members of society, not simply the few who happen to "own" the productive apparatus, would have increasing appeal:

> The division of gains which [poor people] accepted on the way up will not be the division of losses which they will want to accept on the way down. . . . Passing (say) $2,000 annual income per head on the way up, a society may be very unequal; passing the same figure on the way down it is likely to be more equal, or more bloodstained, or both. Even if growth

> merely slows or stops without actual losses, equality may suddenly seem more important.[36]

Quelling such demands for the social control of the means of production would likely involve suspending political democracy and/or fostering mass irrationality, wherein the citizens surrender their material interests and sacrifice them to some symbolic "higher" good, such as race, *volk*, or flag—plausibly the description of some form of fascism. Thus, while capitalism requires economic growth as a condition of its existence, ecological considerations indicate the impossibility of such growth continuing indefinitely. Avoiding the imperative of growth requires abolishing capitalism for some form of fascism if existing relations of inequality are maintained. To the extent that equality is fostered, the transition towards political regulation is socialistic.

There are, then, three fundamental reasons why capitalism cannot respect the rest of nature. In the first place, regulating human interaction with nonhuman nature exclusively through market processes rests on an unjustifiable faith that the dynamics of markets adequately account for the dynamics of the ecosystems within which human life exists. Further, the cost of capital leads to a discounting of the future. Finally, the requirement of growth makes capitalism unsustainable over time. The alternative to continued growth within capitalism is to freeze structures of privilege and domination through political fiat. Although I do not know that such a bureaucratic state capitalism is impossible, I do know that it is undesirable.

This discussion does not encompass every possibility. In particular, society could devolve into more decentralized organizations. Bioregions, for example, could become the basis for social and political organization. This will be discussed in my last chapter. This would require a fundamental reorientation of industrial social forms and their tendencies toward the integration of economies and the centralization of control. This alternative is also discussed in the last chapter. Before discussing such a major break, we must examine the socialistic alternative, to which we now turn.

3 *Nature as Owned by Everyone: Socialism*

To speak of socialism at this juncture in history may be irrelevant because almost all of the societies that proclaim themselves to be "socialist" are trying to adopt various forms of market economies. If socialism seems to be an endangered species, why consider it at all? This line of argument involves two questionable assumptions: first, that Eastern European and Soviet societies were, in fact, socialistic; and second that their mistakes are irrelevant to the future. Both of these assumptions are, I think, wrong.

The "socialist" societies that are now deconstructing themselves have not embodied the socialistic ideals of freedom and democracy. Rather, they have been dictatorially managed by political and technocratic elites in the interests defined by those elites. The twentieth-century development of the Soviet Union into a world power is remarkable and attests to the strength of a particular form of social organization in certain historical conditions. The Soviet Union shows that centrally administered economies can be effective in rapidly industrializing society. The presence of hostile enemies helped, as they contributed to internal social solidarity. Industrial development was also facilitated by quasi-imperial relations between the Soviet Union and Eastern European states.

The Soviet and Eastern European experiences, however, have little relevance in assessing the democratic-socialistic ideal of a free society in which the collectively produced social wealth is distributed in accord with plans devised through democratic processes. I do not know if such a society will ever come to pass, but it remains as yet an unrealized ideal, not one that is refuted by the collapse of these regimes.

This does not mean that the history of Soviet and Eastern European societies is irrelevant to the question of the how nonhuman nature fares under socialism. This history is relevant in assessing how effective bureaucracies can be in managing industrial society's relations with the rest of nature. In the previous chapter, I suggested that one could array social decision-making modes along a spectrum with markets at one end and bureaucratic management at the other. While markets are highly problematic, the Soviet and Eastern European experiences show that the bureaucratic end of the spectrum is also unpromising.

A photograph of a small town in Romania shows a shepherd walking down a dark grey street herding a flock of very black sheep.[1] The picture does not depict an unusually high incidence of black sheep. Rather, it reveals an almost unimaginable degree of carbon pollution, for the wool from these sheep is white underneath the soot and is washed before it is sold. The workers in the plant that produces this carbon pollution are pitch black at the end of each day. They drink large quantities of milk to coat their stomachs in the hope that they can protect themselves from ingesting the carbon. Outside of an administered society, it is hard to imagine citizens tolerating such a degree of pollution. This is only one of many examples of the failure of socialism to achieve ecological sanity that have surfaced with the opening of Eastern Europe to Western scrutiny. Some estimate that the economic costs of environmental degradation amount to about ten percent of the gross national products of Poland, Czechoslovakia, and the Soviet Union.[2] Costs of this magnitude indicate environmental mismanagement of striking proportion. What was the ideology of nature that led the Soviet Union into such a spectacular failure of ecological wisdom?

Some friends of industrial capitalism claim that environmental problems are overstated and unduly alarmist. They see the future as fundamentally continuous with the past, with technological innovation providing the solution to whatever problems might arise. Thus, Herman Kahn and Julian Simon, in their refutation of Gerald O. Barney's *Global 2000 Report to the President* report, proclaim:

> The nature of the physical world permits continued improvement in humankind's economic lot in the long run, indefinitely. Of course, there are always newly arising local problems . . . But the nature of the world's physical conditions and the resilience in a well-functioning economic and social system enables us to overcome such problems, and the solutions usually leave us better off . . . that is the great lesson to be learned from human history.[3]

Kahn and Simon are not alone in their confidence. Evgeni Federov, a politically influential scientist, claims:

> In fact, the entire history of humankind has proved . . . that [the] possibilities [for humankind's satisfying its requirements] have continuously been growing . . . natural characteristics or resources of our planet may create considerable problems from time to time. These problems can be overcome, even anticipated, in a society which will have at its disposal the entire complex of natural resources of our planet, and which will be able to make rational use of them. Such a society [can] . . . ensure the existence of approximately ten times the present population of the earth. . . . The present trends of development of science in general, and the earth science in particular, furnish enough proof that in the future, too, all ecological problems will be tackled. We will have sufficient scientific and technological capabilities to "design" and create the environment necessary for our development, to make the earth as "big" as we need it to be . . . human society will have truly unlimited possibilities for progress.[4]

Federov, like Kahn and Simon, envisions nuclear power as the key energy source by which limitations to the continued expansion of industrialism can be overcome.

Federov is a well-known Soviet scientist and a member of the Presidium of the Supreme Soviet of the USSR. The striking parallels between Federov's views and those of Kahn and Simon indicate a shared perspective on environmental issues within the governing circles of both the United States and the USSR. In particular, these writers all believe that material progress is possible for the indefinite future, as long as science and technological innovation are not restrained and that no significant ecologically based limits on future production exist. They also believe that technological innovation can make the earth vastly "larger" and that the central need is for the expansion of the human domination of nonhuman nature, not its restraint. Federov assumes that humanity is virtually unlimited in its ability to control the rest of nature, believing that we can ultimately control global climate.[5] The only important way in which he differs from his United States colleagues is that while Kahn and Simon believe that a well-functioning society rests upon unfettered capitalism, Federov considers socialism to be the only rational principle of human organization. From an ecological perspective, this may be a difference that makes no difference.

Socialism

The concept of socialism is contested. No simple definition of socialism can claim anything like universal assent. For example, those who claim to be socialists do not agree about whether the Soviet Union is a socialistic society, a flawed socialistic society, a statist system, or a version of state capitalism. Bobbio claims that "the only people to defend the socialism of the Soviet Union turn out to be . . . the ones who want to demonstrate by invoking the example of the Soviet Union that socialism is a bad option."[6] The astonishingly rapid transformations in Eastern Europe and the dissolution of the Soviet Union further confuse attempts to devise an abstract definition of socialism that has significant historical example. Happily, it is not necessary to discern the true definition of socialism. For my purposes, the important question is whether any variant of socialism, real or ideal, can adequately manage society's interaction with the rest of nature.

Socialism, as I shall use the term here, is any social system that consciously subordinates economic decisions to social plans in the interest of social justice and equality. By submerging the economy within society and by refusing to allow economic considerations to dictate social policies, the economy is subordinated to the social determination of the good.[7] Within socialism, social policies determine material life, which is a reversal of the capitalistic process of using markets to determine social life. Various forms of socialism can be distinguished by their mode of arriving at such social plans.

A variety of possible socialisms can be described by determining the degree to which they systematically incorporate all members of society into the process of devising, assessing, adopting, and implementing social decisions. Socialisms, then, can be arrayed on a spectrum ranging from democratic to autocratic. This implies that there are degrees of democracy. Although it is possible to define democracy as an "all or none" condition, a recognition that procedures for making social decisions can be "more or less" democratic is more fertile. Although representative democracy may be far less democratic than a fully participatory democracy, this does not imply that representative democracy is not democratic at all.[8] And democratic procedures for social choice can be implemented in few or many dimensions of social life. For example, a political democracy is more democratic than a political dictatorship, but a society which has some form of political democracy and a capitalistic economy is far less democratic than a society which embodies both political and economic democracy.

In whatever form it takes, socialism theoretically holds great promise for ecologically sound relations between humanity and the rest of nature. The ecological blindness of markets is unnecessary. And since there is no necessity for the future to be discounted, socialistic societies could preserve environments for future generations and adjust to the rhythms of ecological systems. Further, unlike capitalistic economies, socialistic economies have no inherent necessity for economic growth. A socialistic society could decide that growth is a mistake and adopt a steady-state economy.[9]

Further, profound changes in humanity's current relations with nonhuman nature could be adopted and socially implemented. There is no inherent necessity for a socialistic society to adopt an exclusively exploitative orientation toward the rest of nature. There is no inherent economic need for a socialistic society to treat nonhuman nature as merely a collection of resources to be developed. Large tracts of wilderness could be preserved without the need to appeal to merely utilitarian justifications. Social planning could fully incorporate ecological insight without compromise to private economic interests. It is possible for socialism to be ecologically sound.

Some of these possibilities were, in fact, realized in the early history of the Soviet Union. Shortly after the Bolsheviks took power, Lenin gave conservation an urgent priority, resting authority with the Education Commissariat instead of with the Agricultural Commissariat, precisely because the former was not involved in an economic orientation toward the land.[10] This attitude led to the creation, in 1920, of a *zapovednik* (nature reserve) in the southern Urals within which all hunting, fishing, and even egg collection was prohibited. Several other reserves were also created. As early as 1921, these reserves were criticized, but preservationists successfully resisted attempts to make them "pay" by modeling them after Yellowstone, with its admission fees, hotels, and guided tours. They successfully argued that the "exploitation [of the nature preserves], like that of some industrial enterprise, contradict[ed] their very essence."[11] There was to be no logging or even collecting of deadwood. The reserves had to remain free from human intervention to serve as baselines for the scientific study of the dynamics of ecosystems.

Significantly, a less human-centered attempt to preserve wilderness tracts met with less success. A minority movement among the preservationists based the prohibition of human activity within the reserves on an nonscientific moral obligation to nonhuman nature, challenging the anthropocentric presumption that humans are the only form of life having intrinsic moral worth. A prominent entomologist, Andrei Petrovich Semenov-tian-shanskii, argued that industrial society is a flaw, from which the rest of nature has to be protected.

> Nature not only nurtured us, she brought us up, educated us. She feeds us, educates us, and nurtures us yet. . . . [O]nly thanks to the various forces of nature . . . did man at the dawn of his existence 'become human.' . . . [We must realize the right] of all living things to their existence. [We have a] great moral obligation toward Nature [like] the son's duty to his mother. . . . The tasks of conservation . . . boil down to the immediate fencing off and protection of every spot that has still been spared from the devastating onslaught of mankind. [The conservation movement should] serve as a counterweight to the ever greater dispersal and accelerated growth of the human population and to the seizure by humans of a greater and greater percentage of the world's land.[12]

This minority movement ran counter to the rising status of science at the time and was condemned in 1927 as a "saccharine-sentimental" approach by those higher in the bureaucratic hierarchy. Its proponents prudently became silent.

The growth of nature preserves from 1925 to 1929 in the USSR was rapid. In 1925, there were about 4,000 square miles of state nature preserves, while there were more than 15,000 square miles only four years later. However, these preserves were managed by different agencies with divergent ends. Some nature preserves were simply game preserves where commercially valuable species could propagate. Others were viewed as scientific preserves (*etalon*) with the aim of studying ecology to bring the economic practices of society in line with the carrying capacity of ecosystems.

These scientific preserves were to be a "laboratory" for the ecological study of the dynamics of unaltered ecosystems. This approach meant that the scientific preserves should be totally free from human intervention so that the natural dynamics of ecosystems could be understood.[13] There was a latent tension in the concept, however, because of the conflict between the goal of the pure scientific study of the evolution of natural ecosystems and the preservation of endangered species, which was also a concern of the conservationists. The evolution of an ecosystem may lead to new conditions which might threaten existing species within that ecosystem. Such a development would bring to the fore the conflict between the goal of understanding the dynamics of ecosystems and that of preserving endangered species of flora and fauna. Should humans intervene in favor of preserving an endangered species? But doing so disrupts the dynamics of the ecosystem. Of course, the conflict could be abated by allowing sufficiently large areas to remain free from human interference, as this would allow the speciation process to continue. To date, no government has contemplated such vast expanses of wilderness. In any case, this tension within the conservation movement never surfaced because drastic threats to any form of conservation soon arose.

The Conservation Congress of 1929 decided that the preserves had to be justified in economic terms, conceding that pure science had to "pay off."[14] This concession occurred within a changing social context in which pure science no longer enjoyed the same degree of acceptance. At least part of this decline in the status of pure science was rooted in the middle-class origins of Soviet scientists, a fact that brought them under suspicion.[15]

The exaltation of applied science became a dominant part of Soviet ideology and practice. Natural science came to be seen as the tool which, under socialism, would solve all problems through "the great transformation of nature." Struggles over the use or nonuse of the nature preserves for animal breeding and "acclimatization" projects continued, with those favoring the "transformation of nature" in accord with "socialist planning" triumphing through political force.

The struggles against nature preserves and their defenders led to purges of some Soviet ecologists in 1934 and the arrest of V. V. Stanchinskii, a prominent ecologist of the time. His work on the nature of ecosystems was denounced as reactionary by I. I. Prezent because Stanchinskii had argued that there were "natural limits to humanity's capacity to transform nature."[16] Prezent and his student Lysenko also conducted a campaign against Mendelian geneticists. Both ecology and Mendelian genetics suggested that there are limits to the extent to which humans can remake the rest of nature in accordance with their desires. Mendelian genetics "imposed limits to the progress of plant breeding that were socially unacceptable to Soviet agriculture because of its needs. On the other hand, a model [Lysenkoism] in which the creation of hereditary variation proceeded at the same pace as its selection promised unlimited progress, once physiological knowledge was sufficiently sophisticated."[17] Ecology was also seen as reactionary because it cast doubt on the view that socialism could and should transform nature. Writing recently about the history of the development of energy production in the Soviet Union, Boris Komorov (pseudonym for a high-ranking member of a Soviet ministry) argues:

> All the grandiose plans to "harness nature," to divert river courses, to correct "millennial errors by nature" were advantageous for the ruling bureaucracy politically, and they became facts. The economic benefits were secondary, and ecology was not taken into account at all. On the contrary, the more such projects contradicted the laws of nature, the more highly they were regarded. . . . [T]he illusion of their success demonstrated the power and wisdom of the new leaders of the country.[18]

In accord with this logic, the nature preserves were redefined as being "models of what the creative will of man can do with nature under socialism" and were meant to serve as "prototypes of the nature of the future."[19] The results were not as hoped, with newly introduced species of plants and animals wreaking havoc on the ecology of the preserves. Economically prized species flourished at first as predators were removed, but then their populations collapsed. Massive epidemics arose and spread to surrounding livestock. Wild dogs moved into the ecological niches vacated by the exterminated wolves.[20] In short, the "creative will" provoked the collapse of numerous ecosystems.

The breakdown of the conservation movement in the Soviet Union continued unabated. By the early 1950s, two-thirds of the already degraded nature preserves were given over to farming and lumbering; the remaining ones were turned into agricultural experimental stations. Their total area went from 48,000 square miles to 5,700 square miles.[21] Oil prospecting, hunting (both by poachers and by high government officials hunting from helicopters), fishing, dams and canals, cattle grazing, haying, nut gathering, and tourism are all not uncommon now within the nature preserves.[22]

Other intelligent attempts to deal with ecological problems followed this pattern of unrealized intention. In 1935 there was an ecologically sound plan for limiting the size of Moscow to five million residents and surrounding it with a "greenbelt." This limit was to be achieved by restricting migration into the city.[23] Despite the plan and efforts to implement it, the population of Moscow grew to 6 million in 1960 and to 8.3 million in 1983, with at least 3 million more living in the greenbelt and satellite cities.

The history of the Soviet Union suggests the following lessons. First, insofar as ecological concerns are given priority, a centrally administered economy, such as the Soviet Union, can achieve remarkable goals. The Soviet Union established the first preserve in the world exclusively devoted to the ecological study of nature and aimed at restricting urbanization by placing limits on migration.

But this strength is also a weakness. Programs instituted by central governments can also be dissolved or left unenforced by administrative fiat. The paramount goal of the USSR was industrial production, not the development of sustainable and ecologically sound relations between humanity and the rest of nature. When conflicts between these goals arose, nonhuman nature lost. The rest of nature was viewed as a resource to be exploited for human welfare. Decision makers in the Soviet Union assumed that nonhuman nature can be transformed through science and technology and that it should be changed solely for human ends.

The managed society became a corrupt dictatorship, with its secret police, gulags, psychiatric institutions for dissenters, and restricted press. Only such a depoliticized and autocratic regime could carry out the ecological devastation exemplified by the blackened sheep of Romania. This degree of devastation would not have been tolerated in a society where its citizens could know of and respond to such environmental destruction. Censorship denied citizens the information that might have led them to demand greater environmental sense from the state.[24] This restricted flow of information to the public, as well as the presence of the secret police, dampened the possibility of the formation of independent environmental groups and made less likely the environmental consciousness which might have stimulated significant social change.

Centralized Socialism

The rise and fall of ecologically based preservation in the Soviet Union is a story of competition within and between bureaucratic agencies, in the context of an administratively managed society. To discern the developmental possibilities for an ecologically rational society within such a context, one must look to the evolutionary possibilities of centrally administered societies. Within any centralized socialism, bureaucracies will be of fundamental consequence.

Centralized administrative structures, while necessary within capitalistic societies, are not overly pervasive and do not constitute the primary locus of social decisions. These structures arise out of the need for governmental regulation of markets. Under capitalism, each producer tries to externalize the costs of environmental degradation, imposing the costs of production on those outside the producing firm, while retaining the profits from such production. Thus, pollution is one of the businesses of capitalistic business. The response is political regulation aimed at internalizing the costs into the production process. Such a political process is uncertain in result and inherently compromising of environmental integrity. The result may even be worse because such regulation typically leads to the formation of bureaucratic agencies that fall under the control of those whom they supposedly regulate, while offering an unjustified symbolic reassurance to the public.[25]

One might expect that socialism could avoid the problem of externalization because theoretically the people own the producer and there is no inherent conflict of economic interest between producer and the public. No pressure for profit prevents the producer from internalizing all costs of production. But, in fact, this is not what happened in the Soviet Union. Production was carried out through the coordination of multiple ministries, agencies, and productive units. Each of these organizations had goals set for it from outside and incentives were attached to the achievement of these goals. These goals were assigned on the basis of some larger plan devised by a higher level of administration. Because production was a primary goal, ecological issues had great difficulty in gaining serious consideration. In terms of the Soviet experience, Komorov notes:

> The entire system of planning and managing the economy is built on narrow industrial alignments established long ago (ferrous and nonferrous metallurgy, chemicals, petroleum processing, petroleum extraction, a multitude of branches in machine building, etc.). By their very nature ecological problems cut across many branches at once, and their resolution usually cannot help but alter the existing mode of operation of any of these branches. In other words, these problems must be resolved higher up, in the USSR Council of Ministers. . . . [T]he departments concerned with nature conservation [could] take such problems to sessions of the Council of Ministers only after the approval by all the parties involved.[26]

To be effective in addressing ecological problems, the bureaucratic structure would have to be radically redesigned so that the priority of production was not built into the administrative organization of society.

The goal of increasing industrial production is difficult to give up for both administrators and those who are administrated. Clearly, a decent human life requires that people have a certain level of material production. Production beyond this level makes for more obedient citizens. Expanding production also makes existing patterns of inequality more tolerable. Thus, Soviet leaders found the ideal of economic growth to be justified both in terms of human welfare and also as a means of maintaining political control and their own material advantages. Failure to achieve growth in the consumer sector, as we have recently seen, led to extreme political crisis and the dissolution of the Soviet Union.

Since industrial production was a primary objective for the Soviet Union, rewards and penalties for the various agencies and ministries were set up to encourage this end. Thus, a factory manager's situation within the Soviet economy paralleled that of a manager within a capitalistic economy. Each productive unit had an interest in externalizing production costs as much as possible, a tendency directly related to the imperative for growth assigned from above. Regulations to prevent this externalization led to concealment, not compliance. Generally, the parties involved in the upward flow of information through the bureaucracies had an interest, given the incentives involved, in understating the ecological costs of various activities. As a result, there was a bias within the Soviet system toward understating the environmental costs in the interest of expanding production. Hence, ecological problems were displaced to the domains of other agencies, or they were denied, kept quiet, and left unsolved. Some mitigation of these problems is possible within a centralized socialistic system.[27] Public organizations could be allowed and encouraged to review the performance of industries and the responsibility for ecological oversight could be severed from the ministries involved in production, much as Lenin placed the function of conservation within the educational sector, which had no ties to the economic exploitation of land.

The significant difference between capitalism's and socialism's relation to economic growth is that the push toward growth within capitalism is absolutely fundamental to the capitalistic economic system. By contrast, the imperative for economic growth within socialism lies in the desire of industrial societies for material consumption and the political need for social control. This implies that a socialistic society could change from a growth-oriented industrialism far more easily than could a capitalistic society. People living under a socialistic regime could come to desire a "steady-state" economy. Effectively realizing this could even become a source of political power within socialism, *if* the populace adopted such an economy as a desired end.

The logic of the problem for centralized socialism is that of bureaucratic ministries and agencies competing with each other, coupled with an industrial mode of production. Formal ownership of the means of production and the rest of nature by "the people" does not by itself resolve the ecological problems of industrial society.

The urgent movement towards market economies in Eastern Europe and Russia threatens the loss of even a semblance of environmental regulation. Markets, as argued in the previous chapter, cannot achieve ecological sanity. It will probably take many years to develop effective counterforces to markets in Eastern Europe, once the market economies become dominant. In the short term, the development of a market-based consumerism will probably be largely free from political regulation. Several environmental journalists from Eastern Europe report that with the opening of their societies to the West, there has been a decline in interest in environmentalism and a rise in interest in consumer goods. Iris Stoff, speaking of East Germans, says that it has gotten harder to gain people's interest in environmental issues. They are now "much too interested in consumer goods to want to hear anything about abstinence and moderation. So, the environmental impact of cars, for example, is of no interest." Ivo Bartik of Czechoslovakia says, "now we are free to write whatever we want—but, unfortunately, nobody is interested. . . . We [Czechs] want consumer goods, vacations in the Canary Islands, and fast cars. . . . [T]he general mood of the public is that we cannot afford environmental protection, that it's a luxury of Western countries."[28] It seems reasonable to expect nothing less than a severe intensification of the threat to local and global ecosystems in Eastern Europe and Russia.

Theoretical Socialism

Two kinds of issues must be considered in comparing the ecological reasonableness of capitalism and socialism. One concerns what has actually happened, and the other concerns the developmental possibilities of each of these systems. A consideration of only current practices in capitalistic and socialistic societies does not show the developmental possibilities for change inherent within each system. The "logics" of socialism and capitalism contain divergent developmental potentialities. As argued above, there seems to be no way that capitalism can arrive at an ecologically sustainable economy. The extension of political regulation into the domain of private property, a likely requirement for ecological sustainability, entails the abolition of social decision making based on markets. In contrast, under socialism people could choose to develop ecologically sustainable economies, even though they did not do so in Eastern Europe and what was the Soviet Union.

Several developmental possibilities within socialistic societies need consideration. The most obvious is the institution of a market system. If the evolution of market socialism leads to the determination of social policy through markets, then those societies are capitalistic and present problems characteristic of any capitalistic society. If such markets can somehow remain submerged within a larger social fabric, then such societies will remain under the sway of social planning. Then the critical question will become how such a plan is devised and implemented. Procedures for arriving at social plans may be more or less autocratic or democratic. In either case, they will require an extensive bureaucracy.

It is the expanse of society which leads to the need for an extensive bureaucratic apparatus. Modern nation states simply preclude any form of face-to-face governance and require extensive administrative organization. Nation states are not necessarily the only form modern society can assume. It is no longer hard to imagine a devolution of state power along historical, ethnic, religious, or, perhaps, bioregional lines. The possibilities and problems opened up by such a devolution are enormous and will be discussed in my last chapter. Now I want to focus on the potentialities of only those centralized systems on a scale of the nation state.

Centralization entails administration. Such an administration may be more or less democratic or authoritarian. At first glance, it is not clear that the difference between democratic and authoritarian systems is of fundamental importance from the perspective of achieving ecological sustainability. To be sure, the differences between authoritarian and democratically administered systems is of extreme importance in daily life. No one who has experienced the power of the state when turned against its citizens can doubt this. But it is not clear whether democratic or authoritarian systems have any ecological advantage. In fact, *prima facie*, one might conclude that administered systems have an advantage in being able to make tough decisions rapidly and effectively. On the other hand, such systems are thin on loyalty which makes the enforcement of decisions costly or impossible. To the extent that democratic systems are populated by consumers, the choices made by the society favor production over ecological constraint. But perhaps consumerism arises in part because people are not in control of their social life. If this is true, then a democratic socialism would provide a basis for developing a nonconsumerist way of life. My main point here is that the difference between authoritarian and democratic systems is not obviously central to achieving ecological sustainability. The problem of consumerism will be considered more fully in the next chapter.

Any centralized socialism on the scale of the nation state, whether democratic or authoritarian, must utilize the procedures of bureaucratic rationality to carry out the necessary administrative tasks of managing society. Political leaders quickly learn, if they did not know already, that bureaucracies cannot readily be controlled. As Max Weber notes:

> The question is always who controls the existing bureaucratic machinery. And such control is possible only in a very limited degree to persons who are not technical specialists. Generally speaking, the trained permanent official is more likely to get his way in the long run than his nominal superior . . . who is not a specialist.[29]

Thus, appraising the ecological value of centralized socialism becomes a matter of determining whether bureaucratic rationality is able to achieve an ecologically adequate society.

The administrative process of a complex society involves determining social goals, identifying problems, devising ways of solving them, dividing complex problems into their component parts, allocating tasks to various agencies, and monitoring the process of implementation to evaluate the whole process.

There are a number of reasons to doubt that a bureaucratically centralized mass socialism can achieve ecological rationality.[30] First, bureaucracies of even moderate complexity have great troubles in actually implementing any consistent policy. Orders from above are routinely translated into policies that are desired by those who are being commanded. In any moderately complex bureaucracy, this process of retranslation may occur several times. The process is difficult to detect or change because the information about results, which moves upward in the bureaucracy, is controlled by those who have already translated the policies into terms that are pleasing to them. Thus, the policy actually implemented is often only a distant cousin to the one directed by the upper ranks. The actual policies are far more "localized" as a result of this process. If this process of localization arose because of sensitivity to the local environment, this facet of bureaucracies might be welcomed from an ecological perspective. Unfortunately, this localization process is a function of adaptation by bureaucrats to higher level administrators, not to the local natural environment.

Even if the structures exist to effectively implement whatever policies are adopted, the process of goal formation is troublesome. Conflict among priorities will make all but the primary goal extremely difficult to realize. If the primary administratively set goal is material production and incentives are arranged to encourage this goal, then there will be significant troubles in achieving any additional goals, particularly ones which conflict with increasing material production. Ecological goals are apt to be precisely the sort which conflict with increasing material output.

If the problem of effectively implementating policy were solved, the next major difficulty that any bureaucratic socialism faces is that of correctly discerning problems in need of resolution. Accurate information as to what is actually happening in society is hard to obtain through bureaucratic structures. The information that is generated will reflect the bureaucratic organization that exists to receive and process the information. Since information is often a source of power within organizations, interagency rivalries will impede its flow. "National security" considerations, for example, often lead to the concealment of vital information.[31]

If adequate goals can be set and problems correctly discerned, then the next concern is dividing the problem into tasks to be carried out by various agencies. Ecological problems are often difficult to break into separate elements. Population is connected to agriculture, which is in turn connected to land use, chemical production, climate, technology, water supplies, energy, and so on. There is little reason to think that task assignment will work well for ecological problems that cut across the lines of bureaucratic structures that have been set up to foster industrial production.

Even if adequate knowledge of the actual state of affairs could be obtained, and even if administrative structures capable of operating effectively across traditional bureaucratic lines could be devised, would the people working within such structures know what should be done? This is perhaps the most doubtful of a series of doubtful assumptions. We have now accumulated a significant track record of intervening in ecological systems only to find that the so-called solutions have led to more complicated problems.

Not only do we not now know enough to manage the environment, but perhaps we never will. In the past, humans have altered their ecosystems without untoward results. Industrial society has effected the most massive alterations to ecosystems in human history. We can now begin to discern that our past practices have been carried out within a set of ecosystems that have exhibited a strong tendency toward resilience. This "slack" seems to be disappearing and there are ominous signs that the stress we place on our ecosystems may lead to irreversible and unfortunate changes. It is within this context of increasingly brittle ecosystems that the commitment of centralized socialism to managing its environment becomes dubious and dangerous.

Some of the reasons for the failure of socialism to develop in an ecologically sound direction are cultural. First, the continued development of industrial production coheres with socialistic ideology. Marx praises capitalism for developing the means of production which, under socialism, will make possible a reduction in the amount of labor required of all humans. He also envisions a general material abundance as the substratum of communism. Marxism, as well as capitalism, is under the spell of the idea that material production is the key to human social development. Labor falls within the realm of necessity. Marxism promises the maximum possible emancipation from this realm, a freedom which is based on the development of the means of production and on a rationally administered social organization. For Marxism, there is simply no basis for recognizing any interest in liberating the rest of nature from human domination.[32]

Advanced capitalism requires a culture which identifies the good life with consumerism. Equating the good life with material possessions is one of the few compensations left once mass society becomes the dominant way of life. With such a mass society, each person's lot is to labor at the direction of others for purposes set by others, and the only return for that labor is money, which is useful only to buy things and services. People in industrial societies have become helpless and mostly passive victims of systems that they neither understand nor control. There seems to be a developmental logic wherein industrialization leads to a mass society, which leads to passive and helpless humans.[33] Lacking any form of transcendent meaning, or a sense of being effective in public life, or meaningful participation in community life, all that is left are the satisfactions available in material consumption. Industrial people literally surround themselves with concrete, which both causes and reflects a psychic and sensual numbing. The environment of daily life within which industrial people live, itself being a technological product, cannot but make nonsensical the claim that nonhuman nature itself should be respected.

The primary conclusion which follows from this examination of capitalism and socialism is that neither system holds much promise for effectively coping with ecological problems. Socialism would have the potential for far greater competence in this area if the priority of industrial production were rejected in favor of the goal of ecological sustainability. This would involve enormous changes both in the desires of people and in the social structures that are orientated toward industrial production. No societies now extant give hints at trying to do this. It is now only a theoretical prospect. One fundamental impediment to solving ecological problems is the scale of industrial societies. Mass society itself, with its tendency toward consumerism, whether capitalistic or socialistic, may be an essential part of the ecological problem. It is to this question which we now turn.

4 *Nature as Resource: Industrialism*

Capitalism, with its reliance on blind market processes, cannot achieve an ecologically sustainable society. Socialism, by managing the relations between society and the rest of nature, through political choice, offers the potential for sustainability, even though the reality of existing socialist societies has been disastrous. A truly democratic socialism might create humane and just forms of society which could dramatically expand our vision of how good the good society can be. One might imagine a society in which substantial equality of life prospects has been achieved for all groups, where racial, ethnic, and sexual differences no longer disadvantage anyone. In this vision, some form of vital democracy may be realized. Human relations involving racial or sexual domination disappear entirely. Public discourse involves all citizens of society, and the outcome of such discourse effectively determines the direction of public life. Social plans represent the developed views of the citizens, and democracy is finally realized. We can at least still imagine the realization of such a just and democratic socialism.

Would such a just and democratic society also attain ecologically sustainable relations with the rest of nature? Would such a society realize that it is part of nature, not on top of it? Would it regard nonhuman nature with respect? Or would the citizens of such a society chose to follow the consumerist path within industrialism? If they did, then the prospects for ecological sustainability would be slim indeed because more people consuming more and more goods would substantially increase the strains on local and global ecosystems, however reasonable and humane their society might be. Unfortunately, there is no compelling reason to believe that a society that evolved beyond human relations involving domination would also automatically reject domination over the rest of nature. The prospect of a consumerist democratic socialism is not unlikely for at least two reasons. First, most socialists walk in the shadow of Marx, who was at best ambiguous about humanity's proper relations with the rest of nature.

Second, the logic of industrialization seems to lead toward a consumerist ethos.

Marx understood progress in social development as essentially connected to the increasing domination of the rest of nature in the interest of minimizing the labor required for the flourishing of human life. Capitalism, Marx perceived, is uniquely effective in developing methods of production that minimize labor. Particularly in the later stages of capitalism, one way to increase profit is to reduce the amount of labor required for each unit of production. Hence, there is a constant pressure to develop technological innovations that decrease the amount of labor time needed in production.[1] This process, under the pressure of competition, leads to a continual revolutionizing of the ways in which social livelihood is produced. Socialism, according to Marx, would both take over and build upon the means of production, developed with ruthless effectiveness under capitalism. This technological base, further developed in socialism, would eventually make possible a reduction in both the amount of labor required to produce what is needed, and also a general material abundance for all.

Marx thought that material abundance within a socialistic society would undercut the basis of the social conflicts that are rooted in scarcity. Thus, the profound conflict between the concept of equality, implicit in human rights, and the actual inequalities among humans could be resolved in a "higher phase" of communism when "all the springs of cooperative wealth flow more abundantly." Then the slogan, "From each according to his ability, to each according to his needs," could finally be realized.[2] However much existing socialisms deviate from Marx, they remained at one with his hope for a general material abundance and its promise for a resolution of social problems. Surely one of the reasons for their dissolution has been their failure to make good on the promise of abundance.

The process of reducing necessary labor, through the development of an industrial mode of production, gives rise to utopian possibilities. The reduction of socially necessary labor time, within a rationally organized society, offers the prospect of a life of free creative activity or what might be called "play."[3] In the third volume of *Capital*, Marx recognized this possibility in an ambiguous way.

> Just as the savage must wrestle with nature to satisfy his wants, to maintain and reproduce life, so must civilized man, and he must do so in all social formations and under all possible modes of production. *With his development this realm of physical necessity expands as a result of his wants; but, at the same time, the forces of production which satisfy these wants also increase.*[4]

Only beyond the realm of necessity can the "true realm of freedom" exist.

There is a fateful ambiguity in this perspective. Marx understands want as being dependent upon historical circumstance—that is, that wants are at least partially socially determined. He also believes that developments in the productivity of labor go hand in hand with the expansion of the realm of necessity due to an increase of want. Can want expand indefinitely, keeping up with developments in productivity, so that the realm of necessity is never diminished? It is at least theoretically possible that people can democratically decide on a social plan that involves working as much as before, but that produces more and more for their efforts. Are human wants subject to expansion and then satiation, or would we choose not to regulate and control them? Are our desires infinite? Perhaps consumerism is a "natural" development, even within a truly democratic socialism. This ambiguity within Marx's perspective about the nature of human wants becomes truly fateful as consumer-oriented ways of life threaten global ecosystems.

The process of industrialization has long-term cultural consequences that may be independent of the ownership or control of the process. Industrial societies have given rise to cultures that place high value on material consumption. If the process of industrialization tends toward consumerist cultural forms that are ecologically unsustainable, then industrialism itself becomes an important category for any social analysis based on ecological concerns. The categories of capitalism and socialism, arising in the context of the nineteenth-century, may no longer be adequate for understanding modern society.

Industrial Production

The industrial revolution constitutes a decisive change in humanity's relations with nonhuman nature, yet it is difficult to define or determine exactly when a society has become industrialized. No single technological change is sufficient to mark the onset of the industrial revolution. For example, to point to the steam engine as the keystone of the industrial revolution obscures those developments that preceded it and that made the steam engine so important.[5] Any sharp conceptual line of demarcation through what is actually a historical process, and not an isolated event, must be arbitrary to some extent. Nevertheless, it is clear that the gradual global dominance of industrial modes of production has fundamentally altered the ways in which people live and labor, with concurrent changes in social organization and human subjectivity. Its effects upon the rest of nature have been equally profound.

Industrial modes of production are not simply the concentration of laborers in one place nor the use of energy to power machines. Prior to the nineteenth century, there was a certain degree of concentration of laborers in the manufacture of textiles and other goods. Factories using energy sources, especially water, existed in mining, ship building, and other industries as early as the sixteenth century.[6] By the nineteenth century, material production with machinery powered by outside energy sources became the dominant form of production. Such machinery is expensive and requires a significant outlay of capital. Braudel argues that "the industrial revolution was above all a transformation of *fixed* capital: from now on, it would be more costly but more durable: its quality would be improved and it would radically alter rates of productivity."[7]

Several social conditions had to be met before large investments in fixed capital could dominate the production process. Relatively stable social and political organizations had to exist for such endeavors to be of tolerable risk, and there had to be opportunities for profit that compensated the risk. Perhaps the most important point for understanding industrialism's impact upon all of nature is that capital investment in machinery and other conditions of industrial production requires an assurance that human labor and raw materials will be available in sufficient quantity.

> Since elaborate machines are expensive . . . [t]hey can be worked without a loss only if the vent of the goods is reasonably assured and if production need not be interrupted for want of the primary goods necessary to feed the machines. . . . Unless this condition is fulfilled, produc-

> tion with the help of specialized machines is too risky to be undertaken both from the point of view of the merchant who stakes his money and of the community as a whole which comes to depend upon continuous production for incomes, employment, and provisions.[8]

The need for large and consistently available quantities of nature as resources and humans as labor is as necessary within industrial socialism as it is within capitalism. These imperatives of industrial production press hard whether capital investment decisions are made publicly or privately.

As industrial production increases in complexity and expense, the need for social planning increases. Modern industrial production requires the subdivision of any task into its component parts so that organized intelligence can be utilized. As the span of time between the inception and completion of the task increases, there are corresponding expansions in the amount of capital "fixed" to the performance of particular tasks. The need for specialized manpower and the need for forms of organization to coordinate these specialists also expands. This requires a high degree of planning.[9] From the nineteenth to the twentieth century, there has been a steady expansion in the need for planning. This need has grown from the provision of resources and labor into other dimensions of social life, including the state, the work place, all levels of education, scientific and technological research, mass communication, and entertainment.[10]

Industrialism's Ideology of Nature

Within industrialism, nonhuman nature is not seen as what it is but as what it might become. It is regarded as a conglomerate of resources. Forests are thought of as so many board feet of lumber; lakes, rivers and oceans are viewed as fisheries or sources of water or dumps, in which case they are analyzed in terms of their "assimilation capacities" to absorb pollution. Farms come to be seen as potential subdivisions, a self-fulfilling perception because farm land is taxed according to its "potential," making agriculture difficult to sustain when pressures for suburbanization arise. Heidegger, in his critique of technology, notes, "Everything everywhere is ordered to stand by, to be immediately at hand . . . the real everywhere, more or less distinctly, becomes standing-reserve."[11] Under industrial regimes, nonhuman nature becomes something to be restructured in accord with human intention, a collection of resources to be "developed" for human use.

Industrial production crowds out all other forms of production. The cost of industrially produced commodities is so much less than handcrafted goods that the industrial system of production spread relentlessly. Marx and Engels saw this clearly a century ago.

> The cheap prices of its commodities are the heavy artillery with which it batters down all Chinese walls, with which it forces the barbarians' intensely obstinate hatred of foreigners to capitulate. It compels all nations, on pain of extinction, to adopt the bourgeois mode of production; it compels them to introduce what it calls civilization into their midst, *i.e.* to become bourgeois themselves. In one word, it creates a world after its own image.[12]

If craftsmanship remains, it is valued against the background of mass production and becomes an expensive "luxury" product.

The last century has seen a remarkable integration of the global economy.

> Increasingly, global resource systems are being managed by multinational corporations. . . . Viewed from space, the Global Factory suggests a human organism. The brain is housed in steel-and-glass slabs located in or near a few crowded cities . . . The blood is capital, and it is pumped through the system by global banks assisted by a few governments. The financial centers . . . function as the heart. The hands are steadily moving to the outer rim of civilization. More and more goods are now made in the poor countries of the southern periphery under the direction from the headquarters on the North and most are destined to be consumed in the industrial heartland with the new postindustrial look.[13]

National economies which engage in export and import are tied into global markets. The greater such international trade, the greater the impact of such markets on the life of such nations. Transnational corporations and international financial markets corrode the reality of autonomous nation states through the mechanism of international markets.

In my second chapter, I discussed the difficulty that people in a particular area have in controlling a local polluter. The necessity for a political solution involving the regulation of all producers was noted. The globalization of markets recreates this problem at a larger and more intractable level. Global markets and transnational corporations tend to diminish the power of nation states to regulate production processes in order to temper their impact on people and ecosystems.

> The fundamental challenges posed by the age of globalization are how to make economic actors accountable to political communities and how to modernize government so that it can protect the public interest in the territory that it is expected to govern. Despite the cry for democracy now heard round the world, the great global enterprises that make the key decisions—about what people eat and drink, what they read and hear, what sort of air they breathe and water they drink, and, ultimately, which societies will flourish and which city blocks will decay—are becoming less and less accountable to the people whose lives they change. Global corporations, whatever flag they fly, have outgrown national laws and national cultures, and the world has not begun to address the problem.[14]

Thus, entering this global marketplace is a fateful decision for existing socialistic societies. It sets severe limits to the ways socialism can structure its social life and strongly influences the internal possibilities of socialistic economies. Social plans dealing with job security, medical care, housing for the aged, child care, energy prices, housing, and others, will come under pressure as the need to be competitive in global markets intensifies.

The internationalization of national economies leaves decisions about global ecology to markets and transnational corporations, with the attendant problems of any market economy. If the effective political regulation of national markets is difficult, and it is, then the problem of global regulation is vastly greater. One can already see that political movements toward "free trade," by setting up more regional economies, involve a settling downward of environmental regulation.[15]

The particular ways in which industrial processes use nonhuman nature have profound and widely noticed ecological implications. Many modern industrial processes generate products and wastes that are outside the ecological cycles of production and decay that have developed over millions of years.[16] These problems could certainly be abated. Sufficient political determination could enforce production methods that are more aligned with organic processes, even though market processes alone cannot achieve such a change. Recycling and waste reduction are clearly possible, having been successfully implemented in limited areas. Valuable as such measures are, they do not bring into question industrialism and its ideology of nature. Indeed, the belief that ecological problems can be solved solely by revising industrial production processes may reinforce the idea that industrial societies can successfully manage society's relations with the rest of nature.[17]

Industrial Culture

Most industrial people live lives that are fairly similar in structure, despite surface differences. Industrial peoples generally live within technologically constructed urban environments. This "technosphere" is so overwhelmingly present that it is hard to become aware of the profound effect that such a mode of life has upon our sense of reality.

Within modern societies, urban life is the locus for the formation of cultural attitudes. One can view human history as a steady rise in the dominance of urban centers over their surroundings. Roszak might be right to see the "empire of cities" as the oldest imperial interest "incessantly forcing itself upon the traditional, the rural, the wilderness at large."[18] Whether or not cities have had such a profound effect upon all of history, the rapid rise of urbanization in the last century makes a compelling case for the enormous influence of cities in the present. Indeed, cities have been flooded with migration from the countryside, in part due to the industrialization of agriculture. Suburban sprawl should be understood as a mutating form of urban life, as it is fueled by urban centers of economic activity. Many United States cities are now undergoing a process in which economic centers disperse into the suburban rings formed around the cities, leaving a wake of central city decay and fostering another larger ring of suburbanization. Although the most striking demographic change of our times has been the sheer increase in human population, the second most important change has been urbanization. From 1950 to 1986, the number of people living in cities increased from six hundred million to two billion. Cities will be the dominant habitats for humans by the early part of the next century.[19]

Life in cities might appear to be a liberation from nature. Daily life is insulated from the changes of weather and the seasons. Central heat and electricity level out the seasons and turn back the darkness of night. Within urban life, connectedness to organic nature is traded for convenience. No longer must one venture out regularly into the night and thus experience the changes of the night sky through the seasons. We no longer depend upon the phases of the moon, nor do we notice the seasonal patterns of changing constellations with the advent of electricity and indoor plumbing. The rhythms of the universe are collectively forgotten.

At the sensory level, urban life is relentlessly distracting. The hum of machines and vehicles and the sounds of radios and televisions surrounds city life. Silence is lost. People live by clocks and by schedules set by work and amusement. Daily life is a celebration of material consumption, as people are surrounded by things to be purchased and exotic foods to be consumed.

Our experience of the rest of nature has been transformed. The earth itself is sold in plastic bags, "sterilized" for potting houseplants. For many people, the closest contact with unmediated nature allowed by urban life is that contained in parks, where ironically the sense of danger resides in encounters with one's fellow citizens, not with the elements nor other species. The so-called reality of urban life is confirmed by the its contrast with lesser "realities" such as Disneyland and the like. Jean Baudrillard claims that these imaginary worlds "make us believe that the rest is real, when in fact all of Los Angeles and the America surrounding it are no longer real." Such theme parks are not false representations of reality, rather they conceal "the fact that the real is no longer real."[20]

Nonhuman nature appears to be infinitely malleable and worthy of any transformation which promises greater "ease and comfort." This attitude gives rise to the idea that there is no limit to the collective ability of humans to impose their will on the rest of nature. This apparent liberation from the rest of nature, however, conceals a deeper dependency on a vast and fragile network of human and natural systems. I remember returning to a city apartment after living in a rural area in a small cabin heated by a wood-burning stove. One morning I awoke to a cold apartment and no hot water. In my cabin, I had been able to deal with such a situation by cutting wood and lighting the stove, but in an urban apartment I was totally powerless to get heat in the absence of oil. The convenience of urban life involves a little noticed loss of autonomy. The individual feels correctly that he or she is relatively powerless, dependent upon systems over which the individual can exert little control.

Urban centers cannot do without vast imports of water, food, and fuel, and they cannot avoid vast exports of wastes. This process of meeting needs by relying on distant resources heightens dependence and risk, the avoidance of which requires that increasingly complex systems function without flaw. When there is a failure in such systems, blame is characteristically assigned to one particular element of the system. The whole pattern of centralization which creates such catastrophic risks is rarely identified as a source of trouble.

Within industrial societies, politics becomes that of mass society. People are "informed" by experts and become "knowledgeable" through mass media. Information becomes reduced to what is purveyed by corporately owned media. Face-to-face meetings of citizens having effective decision making power are exceedingly rare, and politics becomes a spectator sport.

Work

In the last few hundred years, the texture of human labor has also been transformed by industrialism. The preindustrial system of merchants "putting out" raw materials for country laborers to process left those laborers at home with a significant degree of autonomy. They were not dependent for survival on the income they got from the merchants because they were able to support themselves on their own labor in their own locality. Later, when labor became concentrated into urban centers, people lost the autonomy which derived from having other options. People could now only survive by laboring within the mode of industrial production. They now had to earn their livelihood outside of their household.

Work has also been severed from the local community, although to a lesser degree. People no longer expect to live out their lives where they were born. It has become normal for people to move away for education and employment. Friendship and ties to family and place have lessened.

Some corporations regularly transfer their higher-level employees to ensure that their primary loyalties are to the company, rather than to the place they live.

Industrial modes of production also seem to require the suppression of spontaneity and autonomy within the work place.

> Supposing a social revolution dethroned the capitalists. . . . Will authority have disappeared or will it only have changed its form? . . . [T]he will of the single individual will always have to subordinate itself, which means that questions are settled in an authoritarian way. The automatic machinery of a big factory is much more despotic than the small capitalists who employ workers ever have been. . . . If man, by dint of his knowledge and inventive genius, has subdued the forces of nature, the latter avenge themselves upon him by subjecting him, in so far as he employs them, to a veritable despotism independent of all social organization. Wanting to abolish authority in large-scale industry is tantamount to wanting to abolish industry itself, to destroy the power loom in order to return to the spinning wheel.[21]

Even labor that is not directly regulated by the rhythms of machines still exists within hierarchical organizations where relations of dominance and submission are routine.

In sum, industrialism involves regarding nonhuman nature as a potentiality, a mere resource. This attitude is fostered by an urban culture where organic nature ceases to be a part of daily life and individuals become atoms within a mass society. Convenience trumps connectedness. Work becomes degraded and degrading, an occasion for the loss of autonomy. If labor and community life are not sources of satisfaction, then it is not surprising to see one's life as divided between labor and leisure. Life's satisfaction is sought in leisure and consumption becomes the "good life." More appears as better.

Consumerism

The industrial mode of production has been notably successful in providing consumer goods. The enormous increase in material production made possible by industrial modes of production has led to an astonishing level of material abundance for most members of such societies. This "success" is most fully developed in capitalistic societies and has become a model that evokes envy in lesser industrialized societies. The average home in capitalistic industrial societies has hot and cold running water, flush toilets, televisions, telephones, refrigerators, and central heating. Even during the rather short period of the last few decades, the rise in the level of material abundance in the United States is notable. Now homes often have air conditioning, clothes washers and dryers, dishwashers, videocassette players, and microwave ovens. The average car is now provided with air conditioning and high-quality musical equipment. Even though this takes place within the context of homelessness for some, the spread of material abundance is a notable feature of industrial production. Thus, it seems to be a success. Yet it does not yield contentment.

The development of consumerism involves a change from satisfying needs to the attempt to satisfy desires, and the mistaking of desires for needs. Locke thought that it was the rise of money which led people to desire the expansion of possessions beyond what was necessary for immediate use.[22] Locke's thesis is surely incomplete, as money without markets for exchange is useless. But it is surely correct to note that money and markets are essential underpinnings for consumerism, although not sufficient in themselves. Traditional forms of status, such as those into which one is simply born, must also be dissolved. Such a dissolution allows material things to become emblems of prestige, and the striving for prestige through material accumulation is the essence of consumerism. It now becomes possible to purchase moments of prestige by acquiring material goods.

Although one might have expected such a development to lead to widespread satisfaction, the opposite has been true. Ironically, with this abundance has come a chronic experience of scarcity. People have always experienced periodic scarcities, but we now see scarcity as a general and chronic condition.[23] That this system is a source of continual dissatisfaction has often been noted. Veblen put it well.

> But as fast as a person makes new acquisitions, and becomes accustomed to the resulting new standard of wealth, the new standard forthwith

ceases to afford appreciably greater satisfaction than the earlier standard did.[24]

The process of stimulating and managing consumer demand becomes more essential as industrialism develops. When goods offered for sale involve the satisfaction of basic needs, people require little persuasion that they need them. On the other hand, when what is offered for sale are things that one could easily do without (i.e., "luxuries"), the management of demand becomes essential. No one needs to be persuaded to buy food, but an electric toothbrush may require subtle persuasion. This process of managing demand by stimulating it, Galbraith remarks, may require an illusion of freedom to work well. "It is possible that people need to believe that they are unmanaged if they are to be managed effectively."[25] Thus, the development of industrial production involves an extension of planning processes, from labor and nonhuman nature in the nineteenth century to the management of politics and desire in the twentieth century.

It is too facile to claim that this feast on material stuff is solely due to a kind of hypnosis that is induced by a corporately controlled media. Certainly it is true that powerful images, both explicit and implicit, are used to induce people to spend their money on specific products. Beyond the merchandizing of specific products, mass media implicitly sells the faith that happiness comes from material consumption. Certainly such an attitude is essential for the continued existence of late capitalism, but this creed is voluntarily, indeed enthusiastically, endorsed by industrial peoples. People are not forced to spend their money on the trinkets offered; they do so willingly. Consumers willingly graze the malls and labor for the money to spend on goods that are far beyond the range of human needs.

In this context, one must ask why no industrial society has chosen to reduce labor time, why all resolutely retain the idea that economic growth is a good to be pursued at all cost. Although it is not correct to say that industrial society simply reflects the desires of its members, it does seem clear that industrial peoples *want* to participate fully in the consumer society, exhibiting a rather aggressive desire for the material fruits of industrial production.

Industrialism is both a process of material production and the development of a consumer culture. Without consumerism, industrialism's increase in the productivity of labor would lead to either vast unemployment or a shortening of the working day. Thus, the central problem is that industrialism is a social totality, encompassing both the external development of the methods of producing things and services *and* the subjective desire to constantly acquire more.

It is the close interlocking of industrial production with the development of consumerism that, I think, necessitates that industrialism be viewed as a central category of an ecologically based social analysis. Tradition and older forms of satisfaction, such as those based in community and in labor, are dissolved as societies industrialize. Real human needs are effectively met and desires become mistaken for needs. The distinction between need and desire is lost and people come to feel deprived, no matter how extensive their material possessions.

It seems hard to imagine that human societies will shift from industrialism toward some other social formation by choice. Recent events in Eastern Europe show that people, when they can grasp a chance for material abundance, will do so. Industrialism, urbanism, alienation from the earth, the division of one's life into work and leisure, the perception of nature as a mere resource, and the resultant consumerist orientation toward life seem to hang together as a social formation that most modern societies strive to realize.

There are, however, some signs of transformation. The spell cast by the prospects of yet another round of material abundance does not catch everyone, and the spell itself may have become less enchanting. Many people, out of concern for their fellow humans, for other animals, or for the environment, sense the trap of consumerism and willingly adopt less ecologically destructive ways of living.[26] Increasingly, people identify themselves as environmentalists, and this concern is being felt in the political systems of industrial countries.

The fact that consumerism is not deeply satisfying is itself hopeful. This implies that moving beyond consumerism might not be so painful. Increased material consumption simply fails to provide corresponding increases in happiness. Within a given society, the rich express more satisfaction than do the poor, but between societies one cannot find higher levels of expressed satisfaction. Beyond some point long ago passed in capitalistic industrial societies, the absolute level of material consumption is irrelevant to satisfaction. Instead, the degree of satisfaction experienced seems to depend on one's economic position relative to others in one's society, rather than on what one actually has.[27]

Even more significantly, Americans consistently express *less* satisfaction with their lives than they did four decades ago, despite a clear increase in material consumption and real income.[28] Indeed, there is a pervasive feeling of deprivation that permeates the psychology of consumers, despite the fact that they "enjoy" an incredible level of affluence (that they may not actually enjoy at all).[29] This decline in satisfaction opens the door to the possibility of change.

Understanding this decline in satisfaction is important for grasping its potential for social transformation. Several explanations for the decline in satisfaction expressed by members of consumer societies are possible. Hirsch distinguishes two fundamentally different types of limits to growth.[30] On the one hand, there are ecological limits to growth that Hirsch thinks are distant and uncertain. More immediately, there are social limits to growth. These contain inherent limits on the level of satisfaction that consumption can yield. According to Hirsch, there are goods which are valued precisely because they are rare, such as high fashion designs. These goods derive their value simply from their relative scarcity and the prestige they confer upon those who possess these rare things. Clearly these goods cannot be widely available if they are to fulfill their function of conferring high status. Another kind of "goods"—such as that represented by a cottage at the seashore—has a value that rests on its intrinsic characteristics. This kind of "goods," when widely available, changes in quality simply by virtue of its widespread use. Thus, the road to the cottage becomes clogged and its isolation is lost by its being surrounded by similar cottages.

There are then, according to Hirsch, two economies in advanced industrial societies—a material economy involving the satisfaction of material needs and a positional economy involving goods which are inherently socially scarce. Growth in the material economy cannot slake the thirst arising from the positional economy. Not understanding this, society relentlessly pursues economic growth, while dissatisfaction increases. This phenomenon is what Hirsch calls the paradox of affluence: "Why has economic growth become and remained so compelling a goal for all of us as individuals, even though it yields disappointing fruits when most, if not all of us, achieve it?"[31] Thus, growth in the material economy beyond a certain point is necessarily a frustrating attempt to solve problems which can only be resolved collectively. But however insightful, this explanation is incomplete. It leaves untouched the question of why people would regulate their lives by the external indicators of material consumption. Why does the pursuit of status permeate industrial culture?

A more complete analysis is put forward by Paul Wachtel, a psychologist.[32] Why, he wonders, do we persist in the pursuit of economic growth, even though we do not experience increased satisfaction, and even though we recognize—and at once deny—that industrial society is poisoning us. Wachtel locates the problem historically in the breakdown of a sense of community and belonging attendant upon the industrial revolution. This breakdown contributes to and is accelerated by social and geographical mobility, giving rise to the need to create for ourselves a place in the social order. Our social place is no longer simply given to us. This is coupled with a rapid rate of change in traditions and mores, leaving us all threatened by feelings of being "outsiders." Thus, we are fundamentally insecure. Consumerism is a quest to relieve this insecurity and vulnerability by providing a feeling of strength through our possessions. But the system of production which makes this increase in consumption possible also accelerates the loss of any sense of social locus other than that of the accumulation of possessions. Thus, a vicious and self-reinforcing cycle is established. Home, school, and community come to be viewed as "launching pads," rather than as integral elements of our identity, placing more emphasis on competition, self-interest, and the stimulation of demand. This pattern permeates society.

> There is something compulsive, irrational, and self-defeating in the way we pursue goods. Our overriding stress on productivity and growth and the toll it takes on our health and well-being are part of a tragically unnecessary treadmill on which we run, ever more desperately, with ever

> more strain, committing more and more of our lives to the hopeless chase to keep up.[33]

This historical change from a society in which status was assigned at birth to one in which social identity must be achieved has been celebrated as a great social advance by many theorists. Thus, the French and American Revolutions are routinely noted as watersheds in the movement from tradition-based inequalities to democratic freedoms. But this advance has a shadow which we have not yet appreciated. The overthrow of tradition leaves open the process by which our sense of personal identity is formed. Consumerism is one result of this freedom from tradition, once the basic problems of material production have been solved. A consumerist society is, then, a psychologically frustrating and ecologically lethal mode of forming personal identity.

This implies that solutions to consumerism involve changing the process of identity formation. Within advanced industrial societies, the formation of desire is left to socializing institutions and mass media. The domination of these institutions by corporate interests assures that they continue to encourage frivolous behavior and implicitly conveys the ethos of consumerism. How can a society become free from this sort of influence? Can humans be satisfied with a certain level of social production? Or are they inherently driven to compare themselves with others and to strive to have more than their neighbors?

From an anthropological perspective, the answer is obvious—many societies are free from the striving for material abundance. They have found ways of existing in harmony with their environment, and at least some observers have portrayed the lives of these societies' members as being more pleasant than the average industrial life. Life in such societies involves less labor, less stress, more pleasant social interactions, as well as freedom from the insecurities that plague most industrial peoples' lives. As Marshall Sahlins puts it, "there are two possible courses to affluence. Wants may be easily satisfied either by producing much or by desiring little."[34] It is, of course, implausible to think that industrial peoples can become hunter-gatherers, and I am not suggesting that we can or should. The question is whether we can move forward toward a society that chooses a course of affluence by desiring less or whether we are compelled to continue the fruitless search for satisfaction through the relentless pursuit of industrial products. The latter course is ecologically unsustainable.

This question is of considerable importance for any Green politics. A wide spectrum of meanings for the term "Green politics" is possible. Here I only intend to name those political movements which give a high priority to the interconnectedness of all human life within the larger interconnected community of all life on Earth. As Jonathon Porritt puts it: "To 'see green' is to see all nations and all people, however divided or different they may appear to be, as members of one interdependent human family, linked by their responsibility to each other and to the care and maintenance of our planet."[35] If one assumes that there is no way of transcending industrialism, then some accommodation must be made. But such an accommodation assumes that the level of material consumption presently "enjoyed" by industrial peoples can be maintained. This seems to write off the Third World, since the present levels of material consumption in the industrial world cannot be generalized and achieved by *all* peoples of the world. We need only consider one factor, the output of carbon dioxide:

> If past trends continue, developing countries will be emitting 16.6 billion tonnes of carbon annually by 2025—over four times as much as developed countries today. Assuming industrialized nations manage to stabilize their emissions per person at current levels, the total output per year would be 21 billion tonnes—*three times the present level.*[36]

Numbers of such magnitude indicate a profound problem in relations between industrialized countries and developing countries. Industrialized nations have already mined and deforested vast tracts of the developing countries, organized their internal economies toward production for export, and used them as dumping grounds, first for wastes and now for industrial production processes that are "too dirty" for industrial societies. Green political analysts must confront the problem that the planet cannot bear the burden of a consumerist life-style for over ten billion humans.

Within the German Green movement, there is one faction which wishes to accommodate industrialism. Saral Sakar quotes German Green Party member Joseph Hubner as claiming that "there are alternatives in industrial society, but not to it." This accommodation is due, Sakar argues, to the formation of the Green Party and its interest in parliamentary power, as well as to the influence of leftists in the movement. Their belief is that technological progress, material affluence, and high productivity are necessary for socialism and that the working class is the agent of social change. Accommodating industrialism, as realistic as this may appear to be in terms of political change, seems to implicitly advocate either continued domination of the Third World by the industrial nations or a totally unrealistic image of an ecologically unlimited biosphere. Going more deeply, Sakar recognizes the importance of the definition of need—is it subjective and hence infinite, or is it objective and based on ecological limits? He concludes that "we should be seeking freedom in work, not freedom from work; and self-realization and emancipation within and not outside of everyday life."[37]

Alternatives to industrialism and its consumerism must be envisioned and given emphasis in the Green analysis and program. Fortunately, less developed countries are not locked into industrialism. For example, suburban society is committed to its needs for petroleum and automobiles. Societies that have not yet traveled very far down the industrial path have more options and are less dependent on an uninterrupted flow of resources. It is possible that they can create ways of leapfrogging over industrialism, if they recognize it as a dead end.

If the process of establishing a sense of identity lies at the root of consumerism and if consumerism lies at the root of the continuing expansion of industrialism, then serious concern with the process of personal identity formation is essential for any ecologically based social philosophy. This is an important focus of Deep Ecology, which is discussed in Chapter 9.

To sum up, both capitalism and socialism have a systemic need for economic expansion, although their needs for growth stem from different foundations. Capitalism requires growth economically, while socialism requires it politically. The political requirement is based on the need for legitimation and the production of consumer goods. The similarity is that both systems are based on industrial modes of production and both require growth. They are both forms of expansionary industrialism. An ultimately frustrating consumerism develops directly from the logic of industrialism, with its destruction of traditional social forms and modes of creating a personal identity. Thus, economic efficiency and the expansion of industrial production become an objective of all industrial societies.

Industrialism requires a strong commitment to managing society's relations with the rest of nature in order to satisfy desire. The expansion of industrialism intensifies this commitment. Underlying this project is the assumption that nature can be controlled, a question to which we must now turn.

5 *The Ideology of Control*

Industrialism regards all of nature, human and nonhuman, as a reservoir of resources to be used in the production of a variety of goods. As a project, industrialism assumes that nature can be controlled, and its need for control expands along with the swelling of industrialism. The need for control within industrialism expands in two directions—inwardly into human subjectivity and outwardly into external nature.[1]

Efforts to control subjectivity and the rest of nature are interconnected in that failure in one dimension makes success in the other more urgent. For example, "we" simply cannot control our own numbers. One aspect of that failure is the subjective desire to have more children than a simple replacement birth rate requires.[2] Being unable to control our collective desire for children, hope for dealing with population becomes indirect. On the one hand, changing social conditions—such as improving the status of women and access to education, health, and family planning—seem to slow the increase of population. But even if these measures were widely introduced, we still face a doubling of the world's population in the next century, and this occurs within an already stressed set of ecosystems. Thus we become compelled to try to increase the human carrying capacity of the earth. This requires increased efforts at managing nonhuman nature to support the increasing human population.

Technology, another fundamental determinant of the shape of the modern world, is also out of control. How do we collectively decide what sort of technologies we will develop and which we shall neglect? Such decisions are, after all, absolutely crucial in shaping the texture of the world that we and our children will inhabit. Within market economies, technological change is determined by the search for profit, and the direction of the development of technology is left to the blind forces of the marketplace. Effective political control of technology is virtually nonexistent. We are under the spell of what Langdon Winner has aptly called "technological somnambulism," sleepwalking into a technologically restructured world without political discussion about the kind of world we are constructing.[3] For some, even questioning technology seems hopelessly utopian.[4] As we cannot control our numbers, our desires, or our technological creations, we seek to extend our control over external nature.

The assumption that nature can, in fact, be controlled may not be true. I want to suggest that the aim of controlling nature may actually be unrealizable—that control is an illusion. This claim may seem incredible on its face, given the obvious manifestations of control over some parts of nature, but I believe the appearance of control involves a sort of tunnel vision. When we pay attention to the whole context of industrialism, control might, in fact, be seen as beyond our reach.

Clearly, questioning the possibility of controlling nature is difficult because the appearance of control is deeply embedded in our social life. Everyday we experience situations where all participants share the belief that someone is "in control." Social organizations typically take a hierarchical form, with boards of directors, various levels of management and workers, and a "top" that supposedly controls a "bottom." People commonly expect, even desire, that others will exercise leadership in political life. We believe that parents should control their children, and that we should control ourselves. Our relations with the rest of nature also reflect the appearance of control. We heat our houses, drive our cars, construct bridges and plastic toys, manage farms to produce food, and shop in "climate-controlled" malls. This experience of control is so pervasive that it seems beyond question.

Several assumptions are embedded within the idea of control. First, control presumes a duality between the controller and the controlled, with the controller commanding some other "it" to act in a particular way. This involves the assumption that the controller is separate from what is controlled—I call this the "separation assumption." Second, control assumes that the controller has sufficient knowledge of the structure of "it" to cause it to conform to the intentions of the controller—this is the "knowledge assumption." It is doubtful whether either of these assumptions apply to humanity's relations with nonhuman nature.

Consider a simplified case of control involving a puppeteer and a marionette.[5] The puppeteer seems to be in absolute control of the marionette, which moves along the floor and dances when the puppeteer pulls its strings. A jiggle of a finger and a slight twist of the wrist results in the puppet taking a step. Anyone who has tried it, knows that this appearance of control is misleading. A novice trying to make a marionette walk along the floor or fall down realistically learns that the relationship between puppeteer and marionette is complex; the novice's jiggling finger does not have the desired result. The "control" manifested by the experienced puppeteer is actually a learned skill, wherein the puppeteer has learned to calibrate his or her movements with that of the marionette.

The adept puppeteer actually has an extensive learned relationship with puppets and this context of knowledge is necessary to achieve the appearance of effortless control. Learning to work with the marionette results in an expanded puppeteer/marionette system, with the puppeteer in a complex feedback relationship to the marionette. To think that the puppeteer simply controls the marionette is to neglect the complex interrelationships of the puppeteer/marionette system.

One might object with a claim that the experienced puppeteer is, in fact, in control of the puppets. Simple maneuvers have been learned, building up from simple walks across the stage to a complex sequence of walking, falling, and a leaping recovery. However, this appearance can be dissolved by enlarging the context. What leads the puppeteer to learn these maneuvers? The sense of these maneuvers cannot be understood outside the context of why such motions are of interest. In fact, the puppeteer is trying to create a performance, and the parts make sense only within this even larger context. The puppeteer/marionette system is part of a larger system that includes an audience, perhaps imagined, and its anticipated responses. It is the performance context that gives sense to the practicing novice, as well as to the skillful puppeteer.

When a simple act of technological control is considered in context, it too becomes vastly more complex. When we use tools and wood to construct a set of stairs, we can separate ourselves from the tools and the materials, thinking we are in control of them. If we expand the context, we see that we actually have had to calibrate our motor responses to the saw and the hammer and the wood. And if we trace the genesis of the project back to the desire for these stairs or to the very idea of stairs made of wood with nails, we find ourselves enmeshed within much larger systems of which we may be only vaguely aware.

Consider a furnace connected to a thermostat. Which element is in control? One is apt to say that the thermostat controls the furnace. But is the thermostat in control if there is no fuel to burn in the furnace? What if the electricity powering it fails? Is the thermostat in control of its own temperature setting?

Consider another example. I drive down the road thinking I am in control of my automobile. I imagine myself as being separate from the car. This illusion can be corrected by brake failure or by an empty fuel tank. Further, when a deer darts across the road or another driver swerves toward me, even larger systems indicate their presence. At such moments, I have the potential to realize that the car/driver system is part of still larger systems over which I do not exercise control.

Consider the model of control when it is applied by an individual to him or her self. It seems apparent that I can raise my arm if I choose. But if I enlarge the context, certain puzzles arise. Perhaps I raised my arm because I wanted to. From whence came this desire to raise my arm? Did I control the origin of this desire? How can an individual control, for example, a desire? If one is going to control one's desires, *who* is controlling the desire?

The idea of controlling any aspect of one's self suggests an image of a small but very smart homunculus residing inside the body controlling various parts of the person. This might seem intelligible enough if we impute the desire to raise an arm to the homunculus, which then does whatever it must to make muscles and nerves raise an arm. But this duality invites the question, Who or what controls the homunculus? Is it some other yet smaller creature within the homunculus? And so on. This hierarchical model of the homunculus to explain self-control implies an infinite regress to increasingly smaller homunculi and cannot adequately describe a person exercising "self-control." Am I the homunculus, or am I the arm?—or both, or neither?

If we reject the homunculus theory, then perhaps an individual is better imaged as a system akin to the thermostat and furnace, embodying a complex set of feedback loops. There is no single locus of control in such a system. The thermostat is controlled by relations between the temperature of the room and the temperature setting on the thermostat. The temperature of the room is controlled by outside temperature, by the rate of heat loss through the walls, by the rate of air infiltration, and by the amount of heat delivered from the furnace to the room. The furnace is controlled by the signals from the thermostat, by the proper operation of its components, by a continuing fuel supply, and so on. Control is diffused throughout the whole system, which means, of course, no control at all.

It is only when there is some specific purpose in mind—for example, to make the room warmer I can turn up the thermostat—that a part of the system might be fruitfully regarded as "in control." For certain purposes, this perspective on control may be useful, but it is a misunderstanding of the system to view a part of it as actually being in control. The larger context gets noticed when I ask where my desire for a warmer room comes from. The reality is more like a set of interconnected systems, each of which may be necessary for the functioning of the larger system.

Most of these examples are simplified, as they have not dealt with situations where the object of control has some degree of autonomy. Autonomous systems respond to outside influences in more unpredictable ways, making the intention of control even harder to realize. Thus, training a dog is more complicated than learning to use a marionette, because dogs respond more autonomously and less predictably than do marionettes.

A striking example of this complication is found in the effort of the Jains—a 2,500-year-old religious sect still vital in India—to reduce the suffering of nonhuman nature to an absolute minimum. The Jains embody a profound reverence for all life and consistently strive to avoid injury to any living thing. They structure their economic lives and their diet around the idea of not harming living creatures. They obviously, then, do not hunt, but they also do not farm. Tilling the land would kill worms and other small creatures. They eat only the fruits of plants, not the plants themselves. They believe that eating a plant whose harvesting kills that plant, such as a carrot, is a killing to be avoided. But for all their care, they have ironically generated, in contemporary India, the practice of trapping wild birds. Outside Jain temples, vendors sit with caged birds for sale. Because the Jains will purchase the birds in order to set them free, others trap them, place them in cages, and sell them to the Jains for release. However much the Jains control their own behavior, others within the larger context react to these efforts at nonviolence by creating violence. Although the Jains are exemplary in their efforts at control, within the broader context that surrounds them, they indirectly create a violence which, without their actions, would not exist. Thus, believing in control involves forgetting about context. Control can often be seen as being only an appearance by widening the context.

So also with the project of controlling the rest of nature. We can think of ourselves as controlling nature when we imagine ourselves as separate from nature. But this is simply not true—we are enmeshed within nature. When we expand our understanding of our situation to include this embeddedness, then the concept of control misleads. If this larger context is noticed, it becomes clear that we are not in control. Rather, we exist within a web of a complexly interrelated nature. We are parts of the web.

The Control of Nature as Progress

The thought that we cannot actually control nonhuman nature is unsettling to the adherents of the ideology of industrialism. As the slogan goes, the victors write history, and within industrialism progress is construed as the expansion of human domination over nature. This is supposed to lead to social progress. Viewing control as progress, industrialism's story is that of a progressive development of increasingly powerful technologies. Progress appears as those technical and cultural achievements that yield an increased level of control over the vagaries of the external world. In fact, this concept of progress is a cornerstone in the justification of industrialism.

Viewing progress as domination over the rest of nature masks the social dominance of humans. If we look for the origin of technology, I think we find its most decisive moment to be what Lewis Mumford calls the development of the "megamachine." The megamachine is composed of human beings hierarchically organized "under the rule of an absolute monarch whose commands, supported by a coalition of the priesthood, the armed nobility, and the bureaucracy, secured a corpselike obedience from all the components of the machine."[6] The megamachine allows the collective labor of many to be focused on mammoth projects such as flood control or the building of roads, elaborate cities, tombs for rulers, and the like.

The social consequences of the megamachine for daily life are immense. It organizes daily life into a mechanical pattern wherein work done at the direction of others, for ends set by others, becomes the lot of many humans for most of their lives. Work becomes a lifelong task imposed by a social order, instead of a series of sporadic events dictated by natural necessity. The state comes into being, developing institutions of socialization and control. "Terror has changed into fear and fear into caution."[7] Bureaucracies, priesthoods, and armies became organs of the megamachine, which had to be supported by the labor of the many.

When progress is understood as a progressive domination over nonhuman nature, such a development seems like a great step forward. Through social organization, humanity becomes able to literally change the face of the earth. The pyramids seem to be a great "wonder" of human achievement, and their social context is forgotten. Technology is at first an artifact of this process of increased repression of spontaneous human activity. Later it becomes instrumental in maintaining and intensifying centralized control of human activity.

A critique of this image of progress requires a different concept of the human good. Such an alternative might invite a view of humans as being, fundamentally, creators of meaningful symbolic systems. If humans are essentially generators of meaning, then progress is that which increases the richness of human cultural experience. This criterion, while more difficult to apply to concrete cases, takes as its context the texture of human life *as lived* and uses this context as the crucial variable in assessing historical progress.

If we understand ourselves primarily as producers of meaning and culture, our history no longer appears as a linear progressive development. If progress is the degree of cultural richness present in daily life, then the megamachine, with its increasing centralization of power and the loss of personal autonomy, is a human calamity. History, when seen as the movement from tribal life to the modern state, appears to be ambiguous, with profound losses accompanying the technologies and hierarchical social organizations that grant an increase in the control of pieces of nature. This increase in control has afforded some security from the vagaries of untamed nature, but the cost of this security is substantial. We have lost the face-to-face societies of "primitive" peoples, which often involve proto-democracies, flexible sex roles, and a linkage of authority and competence to the tasks immediately at hand. Stanley Diamond captures at least part of this process when he notes, "Civilization originates in conquest abroad and repression at home."[8]

Typical reactions to such considerations are that "we can't all become primitives" or songs of praise for the material fruits of the megamachine. These reactions indicate the power of an image of progress that is based on the domination of nonhuman nature. The point here is not to suggest the impossible—that we should all go "back"—but to raise a critical framework within which we can reconsider the question of what human progress really means, and thus consider deeply the kind of future we should create.

Progress, I suggest, should be understood as an expansion of personal development, a flourishing of human individuals and other forms of life, rather than either as an increase in our domination over the rest of nature or an expansion of the megamachine. The questions to be asked about our history are whether or not we have become more competent, happier, more capable of love and compassion, more developed in spirit, and more autonomous in our personal lives. Asking these questions opens the door to a closer look at the evidence about "primitive" cultures. Such evidence seems to suggest their lives *are* generally less constrained by the need for daily labor, with more time for music and dance, and with greater equality and freedom.[9] This can help us effectively question the idea that progress demands increasingly powerful technologies, an idea that is rooted in the view of progress as control over nonhuman nature. Rather than simply remaining entranced with technology and the illusion of power that it brings, we can assess new technologies within the context of life and culture.

Critique of the Control of Nature

A powerful objection to the argument in this chapter needs consideration. So far, I have suggested that control is an illusion which involves forgetting about context. I have also argued that progress should not be understood as an increase of control over nonhuman nature. These two claims might seem contradictory because one implies that there can be no control and the other warns against an unreflective increase of the control embodied in the development of technology. But this assumes that control is possible. Is control an illusion or is it a danger? It cannot be both.

This apparent contradiction can be resolved by distinguishing between wholes and parts. Earlier in this chapter, I argue that a part cannot control the whole of which it is a part. The idea of control assumes that the controller and the controlled are separate. But perhaps parts of wholes can control, at least to some degree, other parts. Thus, I have also suggested, in this chapter, an alternative concept of progress to counter industrialism's image of progress—that of increasing control over *parts* of nature. This raises the critical question of whether humanity can be appropriately understood as apart from other parts of nature. Deciding this requires knowing whether nature is a single whole or whether it is composed of relatively independent pieces. Pursuing this latter question would involve a long excursion into complex questions about wholes, parts, and the fundamental structure of reality. This would be an extensive diversion from the problems at hand.

Fortunately, the venerable history of philosophical speculation about the issue of holism versus individualism need not to be reviewed here. Our actions have changed our situation—we have changed the degrees of relative autonomy of the parts of nature in the last century. Whether or not the ultimate nature of reality is one or many, as a practical matter the rest of nature has become more and more tightly integrated. Even if the world were aptly understood as many independent pieces, it is now becoming increasingly integrated into a whole, at least on this planet. We have not yet incorporated this fundamental fact into our thinking about humanity's relations with the rest of nature.

The technological approach to nonhuman nature assumes that the world within which we exist is separable into at least relatively independent pieces. This piecemeal approach seems amply verified by the technological marvels of the modern world. We proceed on the assumption that we can remake aspects of nature in accord with our purposes, and we seem wildly successful at it. But this purposive approach may introduce an epistemic bias into our understanding of reality. Gregory Bateson argues:

> Consciousness . . . is a short-circuit device to enable you to get quickly at what you want; not to act with maximum wisdom in order to live, but to follow the shortest logical or causal path to get what you next want . . . Purposive consciousness pulls out . . . sequences which do not have the loop structure which is characteristic of the whole systemic structure. If you follow the "common sense" dictates of consciousness you become, effectively, greedy and unwise.[10]

The epistemic bias of purposive consciousness is that reality appears as being separable into disconnected parts. Although past success based on purposive action confirms that humans can control parts of the rest of nature, the increasingly interrelated set of ecological crises cast doubt on this assumption.

What image of reality could reconcile the past successes with the present problems? Imagine some creatures existing within a world in which all parts are actually interconnected, a web of existence. They approach their world in terms of purposive action, and their basic mode of activity is to seek what they want. To do this, they pull on the strings of the web to bring what they desire within reach. Their success confirms their image of their world as a collection of many independent strands.

For a time, things go along quite well. They are intelligent and learn to pull on strands using power mined from the network itself, thus satisfying an increasing range of desires more efficiently. This success leads to more and more creatures pulling on more and more strands. They would, quite reasonably, believe that they can control their world by strand pulling. What they fail to notice is that pulling strands has effects beyond the mere satisfaction of desire. The intensity of such effects would depend upon how much overall slack exists in the network within which they exist.

What evidence would appear to them if their world were actually an interconnected network, not many independent strands? Evidence might come from an increased frequency of negative "side effects" resulting from strand pulling. They might realize that they cannot do just one thing and that actions always have multiple consequences. This would create the need for experts to assess likely consequences. Unfortunately, these experts, if they are trained to examine reality in a piecemeal approach, would likely proceed under the assumption that efforts at control will be successful with more detailed studies by more experts.

If they persisted in their old theory about the efficacy of strand pulling, they would continue to stress their network. As the slack in the network is used up, further strand pulling will have wider and more intense consequences for the whole net. Unexpected events might arise that threaten the creature's way of living. The tragedy would begin in earnest when the creatures realize that the network within which they live has undergone fundamental change, and therefore they redouble their effort. As they generate even more intractable problems, such measures might lead to another round of intensifying the patterns of thought and action that had created the problems.

It is possible that they could focus their attention on the increasing tempo of the side effects and conclude that their world is really *one* network, not *many* strands. Since our current experience is that we find massive untoward consequences of our actions threatening our ecosystems, it seems warranted to reexamine the assumption that our world is many separate pieces. If the world is characterized by an increasingly tight interrelatedness, then knowing the parts in isolation from each other is inadequate. Rather, the object of our knowledge must be broadened from that of the pieces of systems to that of the systems themselves. If we understand our world as being fundamentally interconnected, and if we insist on being in control, then we must expand our domain of control to include the whole system. Is such a form of control possible?

The project of controlling the whole system is dubious. What, after all, is our "whole" system. Human society is nested within a complex set of ecosystems, each one of which presently defies total comprehension. Even the relatively simple system of a pond escapes anything approaching full knowledge. The set of human societies within those ecosystems is of such complexity that it eludes understanding and control. Even subsystems of a particular society are beyond our full knowledge, much less our control. Who can claim to understand fully the educational or political or economic subsystems of an industrial society, much less the interactions between these subsystems?

Consider the problem of assessing whether or not some proposed change constitutes an improvement in a given system. How, for example, does one assess a proposed change in the educational system? To assess it, one needs to know if implementing the change will be better than doing nothing and if it will be better than other possible changes. One must, therefore, determine what other changes are possible, which involves knowing the paths of potential change in the educational system. Moreover, the present state of the subsystem is a product of the larger systems within which it is nested. It might be that the best possible change is to change the larger society. Changes in the family, for example, have fundamental impacts upon educational possibilities. Perhaps more resources (or fewer) should be devoted to education by the larger society. One would then have to know the effects of a transfer of resources on other subsystems. Is it better to devote more resources to the educational system and fewer to the health (or defense or welfare) subsystems?

In fact, we are nowhere near the point of being able to determine the optimal allocation of resources within the educational system, much less the optimal allocation among *all* the subsystems of any society. To know the best action in one part of any system, one must know the entire system at the present moment and all its developmental possibilities.[11] Clearly, such knowledge is simply not available for even the simplest of actual situations. The idea of controlling society or nonhuman nature, depending as it does upon knowing the status and dynamics of many subsystems, is simply impossible to realize.

One response to this thesis is to reject the attempt to find the "best" or optimal change. Some decision theorists, recognizing the impossibility of finding the best decisions, seek a more realistic approach to decision making. Herbert Simon, for example, proposes a theory of "bounded rationality," that recognizes that the human capacity for problem solving is small in comparison to the complexity required for "objectively" rational maximizing behavior. Simon rejects maximization as unrealistic and reformulates the goal of individual and organizational decision making in terms of "satisficing." He believes that people seek courses of actions which are "good enough," rather than the "best possible." Instead of examining every possible course of action and assessing all relevant probabilities associated with each, actions are sequentially examined until one that is "good enough" is found. What is good enough depends upon levels of aspiration, that are related to past successes and failures.[12] Surely Simon is correct to notice that decision making in the real world does not proceed by maximization.

Accepting a "satisficing" approach assumes a tolerance in nature which allows us to continue "getting by" without knowing the whole system within which we exist. Increasingly extensive side effects are an indication of a decrease in the tolerance. Just how little we know is emphasized when we remember what our "whole system" is.

> The bottom line message of the global models is quite simple: The world is a complex, interconnected, finite, ecological-social-psychological-economic system. We treat it as if it were not, as if it were divisible, separable, simple, and infinite. Our persistent, intractable, global problems arise directly from this mismatch.[13]

We presently have not the slightest capability of controlling any actual "complex, interconnected, finite, ecological-social-psychological-economic system," much less one that is becoming global in scope.

The idea of managing the complex of natural and human systems becomes increasingly urgent as the slack in the relations between society and the rest of nature lessens. This declining slack in ecosystems means that past ways of making decisions might not project well into the future. Our ability to "satisfice," to just get by, becomes more and more constrained by the increasing brittleness of the context within which we act.

The impossibility of control, given the vast unknowns, makes the idea of management suspect. There may be, in fact, an ideological dimension to the illusion of control, for such an illusion makes managers seem necessary. Alasdair MacIntyre argues that the idea of management is a fiction that solidifies the control of society by a few people. He argues that the requisite social-scientific knowledge to justify claims to be "managing" society is simply not available now, nor is it likely to be available in the future.

> The concept of managerial effectiveness is after all one more contemporary moral fiction and perhaps the most important one of them all. The dominance of the manipulative mode in our culture is not and cannot be accompanied by very much actual success in manipulation. I do not mean that the activities of purported experts do not have effects and that we do not suffer from those effects and suffer gravely. But the notion of social control embodied in the notion of expertise is indeed a masquerade. Our social order is in a very literal sense out of our, and indeed anyone's, control. No one is or could be in charge.[14]

The idea of control is a masquerade used to justify the status of the "managers," not to describe what they actually do. MacIntyre's claim, if plausible for the "social order," is even more credible when extended to the fiction of the control of the rest of nature.

The illusion of control is powerful. Someone always seems to be in control. Even if the ideological dimension of this illusion is realized, the power of the illusion needs yet further explanation. The crux of this illusion is a certain sort of blindness, a lack of peripheral vision. The illusion of control depends upon abstracting from the system of humanity/nature and attending to only selected aspects of that system. Control involves focusing on one small part of the visible, as if one were looking through a tunnel or a telescope. If we focus narrowly, then control appears to be possible. Indeed, it is possible, if the context is ignored.

For example, it turns out that we can make automobiles in a vast variety of shapes, with a wide range of characteristics. We clearly can "control" the pieces of nature necessary to result in automobiles. But this control is quite limited, which can be seen by expanding the context. We have not, nor could we have, controlled the consequences of introducing automobiles into our world. The effects of the automobile upon the rest of nature are vast and not fully known. We have hints of some of them in acid rain and the greenhouse effect, in the unquenchable thirst for oil, in the vast areas of pavement, and so on. In truth the effects of the automobile on the rest of nature are great, unknown, unknowable, and uncontrolled. The social consequences of the automobile are also unknown and unknowable, affecting patterns of recreation, habitation, adolescent sexuality, family life, and on and on. The point is that any significant intervention into a complexly nested set of natural and social systems has implications that stretch far beyond what can be known, much less controlled.

To extend the metaphor of tunnel vision, the illusion of control can be dispelled by shortening the length of the tunnel through which one looks. As the tunnel gets shorter, the larger context in which changes are introduced becomes visible. "Side effects" are a consequence of tunnel vision. Side effects are real but unintended effects. Every action has many effects and to label some as "side effects" is merely to notice that they were not wanted. As the tunnel is shortened and vision is expanded to include these unintended effects, the certainty of control becomes less sure.

If one were to leave the tunnel entirely, the idea of control would be obviously an illusion. Then the richness of the present moment would appear as such, in all its detailed particularity. The idea of seeking to discover the causal antecedents of *all* elements of this moment is patently absurd. When our vision expands to encompass the larger systems of which humanity is a part, then it becomes as absurd to say "we are in charge" as it is to think that a thermostat is in charge. The metaphor of control does not serve in a global context.

There is a danger of overstatement here. As parts of nature, we cannot but try to control some other parts of nature. We are bound by our very existence to act instrumentally in the world. My argument is that expansionary industrialism leads to an increasing need for control over a greater and greater domain. If the control of the "whole system" is truly impossible, then increasing the need for control is dangerous. Industrialism is the most radical extension of this need in human history.

The practical upshot of this critique of control is to seek ways to lessen the need for control. Technologies, for example, can be assessed by the degree to which they increase or diminish the need for control. The practice of monocropping increases the need to control pests, for they can wipe out an entire field, while mixed fields lessen the risks of any particular pest. Nuclear technologies vastly increase the need for control, while decentralized solar power decreases it. The Russian scientist Federov, noting predicted changes in global climate, believes that we must learn "to regulate the climate." He advocates taking control on an ever expanding scale.

> The steadily growing impact of anthropogenic activity on the environment calls for consciously directed restructuring of the existing ecological system, first locally, then over a larger area and, finally, on a global scale. It is only by way of such a deliberate, precalculated change that we can, with a fair degree of certainty, avoid adverse effects on the natural environment in the future.[15]

My argument is that this is precisely the wrong response to our situation.

The difficulties we face, in their scope and depth, are critically connected to industrialism and its invasive technologies. But the problem is likely deeper because it is not only industrial civilizations that have wreaked havoc on their environments. Ancient civilizations, such as Mesopotamia, Crete, Greece, and Rome all deforested their surroundings.[16] This reflection points to the importance of understanding that the roots of our problems extend to the megamachine and its consequences for social life. The cure, ultimately, must go to the roots if it is to truly reconcile humanity and the rest of nature.

What does the recognition that control is an illusion imply for social organization? Both capitalism and socialism require planning on an increasing scale and depth. A tightening ecological web means less "space" for just making do. Social structures that are sensitive to negative feedback from the environment are needed. This suggests that more local forms of social organization should be sought. I shall return to this in Chapter 10.

In sum, the control of a system is the ability to bring the system to a desired state. Our ability to control *parts* of nature supports the illusion of control. The existence of hierarchical societies also fosters the illusion of control and the need for "managers." The illusion of control can be seen by expanding the context of understanding. Thomas Birch argues that one of the important functions of wilderness areas is keeping open the possibility of seeing beyond the illusion of control fostered by the "imperial story of Western civilization."[17] He points to the importance of looking beyond the earth to the stars as an antidote to the illusion of control. Who, when gazing into the starred night, sensing its vast vastness, can believe that *we* are in control?

6 *Nature as Matter: Science*

The contemporary disenchantment of nonhuman nature is overdetermined. The industrialism that underlies both capitalism and socialism takes the rest of nature, obeying only the logic of force. The only justification for this enterprise is its success. Science, on the other hand, has created an image of nature that makes the project of its domination appear to be a reasonable response to a meaningless reality. When science depicts "reality" as tiny particles or waves constantly changing their combinations under the influence of external forces, all nature becomes, ultimately, lifeless, colorless, and without intrinsic meaning. Given such a picture, what grounds are there to object to the transformation of nonhuman nature? By undercutting any ontological basis for objection, science tacitly legitimates the domination of the rest of nature.

One could, of course, still argue that the domination of nonhuman nature is imprudent. Because we make mistakes and because the level of risk is increasing, one could argue that prudence requires much more caution in our dealing with the rest of nature.[1] Such an argument remains within an anthropocentric framework which recognizes only the validity of human interests. One could extend concern beyond human interests to include some other living creatures, basing such an extension on their similarity to some aspect of human life.[2] Extending concern to the rest of nature meets a fundamental barrier in the scientific image of reality as lifeless matter undergoing meaningless change.

Lynn White, in his famous essay on the historical origins of the ecological crisis, claims that the rise of Christianity over paganism was "the greatest psychic revolution of our culture." Although this may be an overstatement, he is surely correct to note that Christianity's banishment of pagan animism allowed the exploitation of nonhuman nature to occur "in a mood of indifference to the feelings of natural objects."[3] This conquest of animism does not in itself license an exclusively exploitative relation to the rest of nature. There is, for example, the possibility within the Christian tradition for an ethic of stewardship. If nature is God's creation, then it could be claimed that humanity is constrained in its relations with the rest of nature by the need to answer to God.[4] In this case, we are only tenants in God's domain.

While an ethic of stewardship could justify nonanthropocentric relations with the rest of nature, the dominance of Christianity is no longer secure and unquestioned. It has become a sect within a world only sporadically swayed by religious convictions. Christianity's victory over paganism has been secured, but its constraint on humanity in the West has been lost. It no longer fosters any general cultural orientation toward the rest of nature.

Science now stands in religion's stead, functioning as the equivalent of the medieval Christian church. The stature of the scientist in our society rivals that of the priest in theocratic societies. Proceeding in ways not understood by those outside their fold, scientists are regarded as the font of knowledge about reality. Science legitimates domination over nonhuman nature by depicting reality as a "discovery" rather than as a particular conception of nature based on a distinctive attitude. Science "discovers" a nature that is ultimately composed of particles combining and decaying in senseless, although intelligible, ways. These particles are inert, subject to motion through forces external to themselves. These ultimate bits of reality are exactly the opposite of life—inert, not self-moving; objects, not subjects.

Science did not arrive at this picture of reality *because* of industrialism, but its image of nonhuman nature fits in well with the needs of industrial society. Several writers have noticed this congruence with the needs of capitalism. Carolyn Merchant, for instance, argues:

> The removal of animistic, organic assumptions about the cosmos constituted the death of nature—the most far-reaching effect of the Scientific Revolution. Because nature was now viewed as a system of dead, inert particles moved by external, rather than internal forces, the mechanical framework itself could legitimate the manipulation of nature. Moreover, as a conceptual framework, the mechanical order had associated with it a framework of values based on power, fully compatible with the directions taken by commercial capitalism.[5]

And Robert Heilbroner maintains:

> Science thus becomes an ideology . . . [and] fills a social requirement indistinguishable from religion. Science is not ideological in the sense of an avowal of social values, or an overt partisanship for social interests. Its ideological aspect lies rather in the function played by its deepest conception—an indifferent and inert matter as the ultimate stuff of reality.[6]

Socialism finds science equally fulfilling in depicting nonhuman nature as being indifferent and inert. By undercutting any basis in the nature of reality for a protest against the domination of nonhuman reality, science provides a fundamental legitimation for all forms of industrialism.

One serious objection to this kind of critique of science is that science simply discovers the truth. If all of nature really *is* as science portrays it, then science can hardly be faulted, even if it does happen to legitimate the domination of nonhuman nature. If science really discovers the ultimate nature of reality, then the congruence of science and industrialism only shows that industrialism too is grounded on a proper conception of nature. Science is, on this account, just telling us "like it is," and faulting science is as foolish as killing the messenger. An adequate response to this objection requires considering three issues. First, what is science? Second, is science aptly understood as the "discovery" of reality? If not, is science nevertheless the most rational approach toward nonhuman nature? These questions are the subject of this chapter.

What is Science?

A minimal specification of science and its method involves emphasis on the intention to base belief on evidence, rather than simply whatever one wishes. Charles S. Peirce, a founder of American pragmatism, praised science as the best way to "fix" belief through the use of the scientific method. It was this method that would guarantee that "the ultimate conclusion of every man shall be the same, or would be the same if inquiry were sufficiently persisted in."[7] This perspective led Peirce to his famous dictum: "The opinion which is fated to be ultimately agreed to by all who investigate is what we mean by the truth, and the object represented in this opinion is the real."[8] This minimal specification of science seems unobjectionable in defining science as the aspiration to ground belief on the basis of reality rather than desire.

Peirce's view is also commendable because it *almost* avoids the highly problematic notion of 'truth'. A fundamental problem with the notion of truth is that the claim that any statement is true can itself never be known to be true. If truth is thought of as some sort of correspondence with reality, then knowing the truth of a statement requires that the statement be matched up with some piece of reality, compared to it, and determined to be in correspondence with that piece of reality. But what could it mean to determine that a statement corresponds with a bit of reality? Possibly we could construct a picture language that had some sort of isomorphism with bits of reality, as photographs can be said to resemble their subject matter. But such a language would not be our language, and its usefulness as a language is dubious. Could we ever begin to say what we wanted to say to each other by exchanging photographs?

As a matter of fact, our languages are far more complex than can ever be understood through the idea of language as a picture of reality. This is clearest when we acknowledge that particular beliefs are enmeshed *within* languages, which comprise whole structures of beliefs. Peirce avoids this problem by defining truth as that which will ultimately be agreed to by the community of inquirers. For Peirce, at the end of inquiry those conclusions ultimately fated to be "believed" will be true and will represent reality. Pragmatically, we need not now worry about the fruitless problem of truth. We can move on to an attempt to see which beliefs are best supported by evidence, recognizing that any of our present beliefs might be wrong.[9]

Peirce's minimal characterization of science as an attempt to go beyond the world of our particular hopes and fears is important. Each of us is trapped within our own particular perspective, and we have no direct access to anything but our own mental model of reality. To the extent that we never venture forth into discussion with others, we have no way of distinguishing our personal biases and fantasies from what is more generally perceived. It is, then, only through discussion with others that we can distinguish between our unique hopes and desires and those views which have wider assent. Inquiry requires a community of inquirers; it is inherently public. In science, that community intends to reach intersubjective agreements based on public and repeatable evidence. The agreements reached are ideally subject to no other coercion than that exerted by the available evidence. The methodological precepts of inquiry that are upheld and enacted by the community of scientific inquirers presuppose norms of a free discussion by humans using language.[10]

While individual bias is checked by the interplay of ideas that are regulated by a norm of free discussion within the community of scientists, there is a problem of more widely shared bias. There is no guarantee that the community will notice its own biases as such when they are shared by all members of the community. Thus, it is particularly important when the scientific community is challenged on a widely shared feature, such as for gender bias.[11] Such challenges not only bring to the fore the possibility of a systemic bias within the community of inquirers, but they offer the possibility of overcoming such biases.

The elimination of all such biases—be they based on social structure, economic class, ethnicity, or gender—would not mean that we could now arrive at the "truth." Our experiences are always enmeshed within the world that is made possible by our specific physiological and neurological structures. However ingeniously we try to become aware of the structure of our own physiology, such awareness remains *always* within that bound.

This embeddedness within our own bodies is the bias of our species. In itself, it is not a problem unless we follow the Peircean notion that, ultimately our beliefs will represent reality. If we surrender the notion that beliefs are representations, then the particular bias of being human need not cause trouble. Being human is a limit which we can strive to become aware of, but it need not constitute a fundamental threat to knowing as long as we reject the idea that science discovers "the reality" of nature. Science is simply one particular way of approaching nature. Fruitful as this approach may be, it does not in itself legitimate domination.

It should also be noticed that the Peircean idea of science as that which is agreed to by the community of inquirers implies that science will be about what is general. The *specific* experience of any particular moment, in being unrepeatable, falls through the grid of science. Ordinary experience becomes a surface appearance of some general reality. But as appearance, it retains standing as part of reality. This is only problematic if one presumes that science tells "the whole story" about reality.

Aside from its bias toward generality, the minimal specification of science as an attempt to found belief on intersubjective evidence agreed to within a community of inquirers does not, by itself, lead to the portrayal of nature as a meaningless and colorless collision of lifeless atoms falling through the void. The roots of this view of nature go back at least to the ancient Greek atomists, but the mechanistic view held by Bacon and Descartes in the seventeenth century, marks the start of its dominance in the modern mind.[12] Once the rest of nature is seen as "nothing but" a grand machine, it is a small step to the view that only considerations of efficiency apply and that there are no moral limits imposed upon science and technology by nonhuman nature. It is ultimately inert and can be regarded solely as an instrument to be used to satisfy human desire.

This process by which nonhuman nature comes to be seen as merely an instrument creates, in its synergistic interaction with technology, a world in which this seems to be true. Most of us are continually surrounded by environments molded by technology. The construction of this "humanized" nature within which we dwell—particularly when it becomes one's total experience—confirms experientially the scientific image of nature as being devoid of meaning and purpose. Nature comes to be seen as a plastic "stuff" capable of being molded into whatever shape happens to be desired.

What is forgotten is that this image is *constructed* by a methodological approach that, given its logic, can only yield an instrumental image of nature. This is due to the particular way in which science abstracts from experience the information upon which it bases its conclusions. The image, then, is an artifact of the method, not the "discovery" of reality.

The Construction of Experience

To understand the particular abstraction of experience that forms modern science, it is useful to notice that human experience in general is a construct, wherein the experiencer plays a crucial role in determining what is experienced. Human experience is dependent upon our biology (e.g., sensory organs, nervous system, and brain structure). It is also dependent on the cultural and linguistic frames within which we learn to perceive, the idiosyncratic expectations and beliefs we bring to a situation, as well as the stimuli that reach our sensory organs. I shall consider here only one aspect of the construction of experience.

A series of experiments developed by Adelbert Ames and others display clearly the interpretive element in experience.[13] The fundamental insight that underlies these experiments is that sensory experience is *always* underdetermined by the actual sensory input. The experimenters explain that

> in visual perception one is faced with the fact that any given visual stimulus-pattern can be produced by an infinity of different conditions . . . But we never see an infinity of configurations; we see just one. This means, of course, that perception cannot be "due to" the physiological stimulus pattern; some physiological stimulus probably is necessary, but it is not sufficient. There must be, in addition, some basis for the organism's "choosing" one from among the infinity of external conditions to which the pattern might be related.[14]

In one experiment, naïve subjects were asked to look through a peephole at an apparently normal room with two windows in the back wall. In fact, the subjects were viewing a very unusual room, with the rear wall receding sharply away from the observer. The apparatus had been constructed to provide the illusion of a normal rectangular room. When a face appeared, first at one window and then at the other window, the size of the head was *experienced* by the observer as changing drastically in size, shrinking or enlarging depending on the sequence of its appearance in the two windows. What had really changed substantially were the *relative sizes* of the head and the window. The rearward window was built much larger than the closer window in order to provide the perceptual illusion of equally sized windows. The subjects, based on what they experienced, made a preconscious assumption that the "real" size of windows is less mutable than the "real" size of heads. Given that assumption, then the heads "must" change size; this was the experience of almost all the subjects. The fact that almost all subjects experienced the same reaction indicates a general unconscious, cultural bias of sorts concerning the relative stability of window sizes and head sizes.

This phenomenon is highlighted by situations in which subjects differ in their preconscious assumptions. For example, one series of experiments showed that there can be a selective "distortion" based upon the emotional connection of the observer to the observed. This is called the "Honi phenomenon."[15] One subject, named Honi, experienced the expected changes in head size when she observed strangers through the different windows, but failed to experience such changes when she observed her husband through the windows. Discovered by chance, this led the experimenters to test for the importance of emotional connections in what is observed. In resolving the conflict between the apparent change in the size of a face and the apparent normalcy of the observed room, the emotional relationship of the observer to the person observed was found to be a determining factor in what was experienced.

One might object that such experiments are irrelevant to science since the procedures developed by science provide ways to eradicate or neutralize the subjective dimension of experience. Thus, it could be argued that the methods of science, through a critical and communal process, distinguish the reliable and intersubjective dimensions of experience, the "facts," from the idiosyncratic experiences of individual human beings.

While it certainly is the intent of scientific methods to achieve widely shared agreements, it is important to notice that some shared assumptions, conscious and unconscious, are not brought into question by the methods of science. To understand how the image of nature is constructed in modern science, it is essential to notice the role of certain widely shared assumptions in the constitution of science's reality.

The Construction of Facts in Science

The Latin root of "fact" is *factum*, which means "a thing done or made." Facts in science are not simply "out there" to be picked, as if they were ripe apples, but rather are constructed through scientific inquiry. Facts in science are formed by the application of method and theory to some part of reality. Accordingly, to understand what is involved in arriving at a fact in science, one must also understand the sculpture of facts by methods and theories.

A naïve image of science is that it proceeds by the accumulation of facts that are used to support more encompassing theories. The body of facts is viewed as being more epistemologically secure than the theories—a seeming necessity if facts are the grounds for theory. Considerable discussion within the philosophy of science over the last few decades has discredited this image of science.

The twentieth century has seen the ascendance and decline of positivism as an analysis of science. According to positivism, the empirical basis of science is a collection of facts that occupy a privileged epistemological position. In particular, facts are the neutral testing ground for all scientific theories. When attention turned to the history of science, this model came under severe attack as not accurately depicting the way science was, is, or should be carried out.[16] Philosophers of science came to recognize that facts are partially dependent upon theories and that theories are partially dependent upon paradigms or research programs, just as research programs and theories are partially dependent upon facts. If there is a fundamental shift in theory, then there is a fundamental shift in "the facts." This "theory laden" view of facts has received considerable attention and needs no further development here.[17]

One less examined aspect of the construction of facts in science is rooted in the method of science. Facts function in science to resolve disputes, and they are characterized by intersubjective agreement among scientific inquirers. Thus, facts in science hinge upon the process of arriving at intersubjective agreement. This is a social process, and underlying it are certain shared agreements that are *prior* to the establishment of facts. In particular, all science proceeds by way of definite procedures for conducting inquiry. An articulation of these procedures constitutes a methodological theory. Such a theory specifies rule-governed activities that are intended to describe reliable ways of establishing facts. Obviously, the reliability of the facts thus generated depends upon the reliability of the methods used.

The centrality of this shared agreement about method can be made clearer by noting what happens when particular methods become subject to controversy. Alleged facts can always be called into question by criticism of the method by which they were generated. What appears to those on one side of such a disagreement as a set of "facts" appears to those on the other side as not real facts, but rather "artifacts" of a particular method, for example, a particular experimental design.[18] Possible methodological disputes range from disagreements about experimental designs, to acceptable degrees of error and the required accuracy of instruments, to the appropriateness of using the method of experiment versus, for example, methods of simulation or statistical inference. These issues, crucial in deciding what to count as scientific fact, are not themselves settled by any straightforward appeal to "the facts." This methodological dimension to any alleged fact displays the embeddedness of scientific facts within a network of assumptions that may themselves become subject to dispute.

The Construction of Causality

Of particular importance in the construction of the scientific image of nature is the analysis of the world from a causal perspective. The world, when viewed from a causal perspective, is broken down into "relevant" variables. The connections between those variables are explored diachronically, looking for relations between changes in one variable and changes in others.

In the simplest of causal situations, two events are ordinarily viewed as being causally connected if they are constantly conjoined. (There are significant exceptions, but this need not concern us here.) The very idea of constant conjunction involves a series of abstractions that are so common as to escape notice. In particular, the condition of constant conjunction requires some notion of the repetition of the same event. However, the identification of two events as being the same itself involves a radical abstraction from experience. In its fullness, each event is idiosyncratic and never recurs. If this is not obvious, notice that a particular event happens at a specific time and in a specific place in history. For it to recur, it would have to do so at the *same* time and in the *same* place. It would then not be a different event, but rather the very same event.

What recurs is not the concrete moment, but rather some other moment that we identify as being "sufficiently similar" in relevant respects. Thus, two separate events can only be "the same" in certain respects. This abstraction at the very start of causal inquiry is based upon our interests, and it retains the mark of these interests. The identity on which the notion of causality depends is not given in any individual moment, but is constructed on the basis of a selective interest in certain aspects of experience. Thus, analyzing the world causally involves identifying certain aspects of concrete occurrences as being relevant and trying to determine whether or not one type of event leads to another type of event. In this way we construct a simplified world that we identify as "reality."

From this perspective, there was and is no necessity to arrive at a mechanical image of nonhuman nature. The key methodological step that leads toward such an image is a commitment to a reductive analysis of complex wholes into component parts, seeking some underlying "reality" of simple, unchanging parts out of which, it is supposed, one can reconstruct the wholes according to laws of motion and composition. This is, on the face of it, a reasonable procedure. Descartes proposed a version of it in *Discourse on Method* in the seventeenth century. His second rule was "to divide each of the difficulties which I encountered into as many parts as possible, and as might be required for an easier solution." The third rule was "to think in an orderly fashion, beginning with the things which were simplest and easiest to understand, and gradually and by degrees reaching toward more complex knowledge."[19] Such a procedure might be unobjectionable if one ever got back to the starting point. This, however, does not happen. We retain the image of the world disclosed through physics as discovered "reality," yet the "reality" of physics, complicated though it surely is, remains within the highly simplified world of the laboratory.

By taking physics as the paradigm of scientific knowledge, we reflect a narrowing of focus on all of nature that makes discovery easier, but not necessarily more adequate to reality. The simplified world of the laboratory is not the same as the more complex world within which we dwell. It is vastly easier to build a bridge across a river than it is to know the effects of doing so on the river or on the lives of the people living on each side of the river. In fact, we can build bridges, but we are quite incapable of predicting the environmental or social effects of doing so. The situations studied by physics are likewise distant from the real complexity of naturally occurring systems.

This restriction of focus on a simplified world accords well with the ideology of control, and it is likely one of the reasons our culture reveres physics as highly as it does. The narrowing of focus implicit in making physics paradigmatic of science leads to techniques that enable a limited form of control and that facilitate the illusion of control discussed in the previous chapter. Using physics as the paradigm of knowledge about reality is an example of the tunnel vision that underlies the illusion of control. The simplification implicit in the physics paradigm, useful though it may be, gives grounds for suspecting it as an adequate image of all of nature.[20]

Perhaps the most powerful form of abstraction comes from the application of mathematics to an analysis of the results of causally oriented reductive inquiry. Mathematics enables deductive elaboration of such results and tests them in, perhaps, quite different contexts. "Laws of nature" are developed using highly abstract concepts, like 'mass' and 'energy', to explain why things happen as they do. Success in doing so may lead us to reify these laws, taking them as describing some other reality that underlies our ordinary experience.

Nature, from this reductive frame, is radically simplified into a set of equations concerning masses and forces. The world becomes colorless microobjects colliding with one another. Anything that cannot be measured in the formulas and methods of science disappears from the resulting image. It becomes possible to create what could not even be imagined, and we appear to have an awesome ability to transform nonhuman nature in accord with our will. This encourages the belief that the world of physics and chemistry is the "real" world, and that the laws of science truly name a fundamental unchanging existence, one more real than the constantly changing world of ordinary experience.

This quest for an unchanging reality underlying the flux of experience is not unique to modern science. Its roots go back at least to Plato, who thought that only the unchanging could be the object of real knowledge.[21] But Plato's eternal realm included beauty and goodness, while the unchanging realities sought by modern science are represented by mathematical functions and describe a mechanism devoid of value and color. E. A. Burtt nicely summarizes the change effected by the Newtonian revolution:

> The world that people had thought themselves living in—a world rich in colour and sound, redolent with fragrance, filled with gladness, love and beauty, speaking everywhere of purposive harmony and creative ideals—was crowded now into minute corners in the brains of scattered organic beings. The really important world outside was a world hard, cold, colourless, silent, and dead; a world of mathematically computable motions in mechanical regularity.[22]

Of course, Newton has been supplanted by modern physics, but the contraction of the world of ordinary experience into "minute corners of the brains of scattered organic beings" remains the image of nature created by the reductive methods of modern science.

Why has this intrinsically less interesting image of nature gained such ascendancy? Clearly, it is because of the increased power it has yielded in our collective ability to transform parts of nature in accord with the interests that we happen to bring to it. Because the image of nature in science is nowhere to be seen or touched, only the fruits it bears tantalize us.

> Analysis by fragmentation has reached the summit in the natural sciences. The particles and waves of physicists, the single cell, its mitochondria, the isolated nerve impulse, the Boolean algebra, are all examples of this property of mind. Experience is fragmented until in the end the result is a world of symbols and causalities nonexistent to the world of the five senses. However, this is nevertheless a real world in its own right, because it stands for the language of applicability as spoken by our technology.[23]

But before we take the view of nature offered by science as being reality, we should remember that it is *our* construct, and that it is constructed from an "interested" point of view; in particular, the image depends upon our interest in successful instrumental action. This interest constitutes a fundamental orientation of modern science, and the validity of this image derives from the validity of our interest in instrumental action.[24] This point risks overstatement. Success or failure in instrumental action does give warrant to the scientific image, in that the activity is controlled by feedback. Science is, therefore, a learning process—not mere fantasy—and bears some relation to the world. But, however that relation is understood, the world portrayed by science is not nature itself. To take its resultant image as being *the* reality is a fundamental error.

The project of domination did not arise simply because nature is approached formally. Plato used mathematics to try to understand the rest of nature, yet he did not adopt the project of dominating it. His image of the world was that it was the expression of the creative power of the Demiurge, and, therefore, to understand the world was to approach the divine.[25] However, if the world is no longer seen as the expression of the divine, then a formal image of nature has no intrinsic interest, except for those few exceptional individuals, such as Einstein, who are motivated by a search for elegant abstract formulas. When an interest in the domination of nonhuman nature enlivens the mathematized image—as happens at the start of the modern age—then science and technology steadily rise in importance and gain epistemic dominance.

There are, then, two elements that need to be understood in order to explain the rise of science and its instrumentalized image of nature. One element involves the removal of divinity and animism from the rest of nature. What is lost is any sense of the sacred in nonhuman nature; human activity is no longer constrained by any understanding of nonhuman nature that limits human conduct. The most universal locus of value that makes sense, once the gods have left, is the human species.

The second element is tied into historical processes operating from the fifteenth century to the present. For a variety of reasons, the thirst for power over the rest of nature develops, albeit slowly at first, into a ravenous hunger when global markets and imperial cultures become established in the nineteenth century. The application of science and technology to the process of production is an essential element in the development of these imperial realms. It is at this point that modern science and modern technology enter decisively into the formation of the human image of the world.

Some of the confusion among contemporary discussions about environmental ethics stems from the incomplete dominance of the image of nature that is implicit in reductive science. Simply put, the world of science is not really the world in which we live our daily lives. It is still impossible for us to see a running stream as "nothing but" hydrogen and oxygen.

If the reductive scientific image were to achieve complete dominance, then nonanthropocentric ethical systems might become unthinkable. Although science may lead to diverse images of nature that do not reduce it to atoms falling through the void, the reductive approach makes questions about how we should treat nonhuman nature, outside of considerations of prudence, unintelligible. Accepting an image of nature that places value only inside the skulls of a few organic beings reduces questions of moral value concerning nonhuman nature to calculations of "costs" and "benefits." By implementing this image, we live ever more completely within a constructed environment. One might fear that future generations will never know the nonhuman nature that was. Could any environmental ethic be taught to a generation raised in a space colony? Their totally rebuilt world would be a realization of reductive science's image of nature.

It should be noted here that a nonanthropocentric understanding of all of nature is also implicit in science. George Sessions argues that the development of science has been a "two-edged sword," taking humans out of the central position they occupied in the Aristotelian/Christian cosmology.[26] Warwick Fox agrees, seeing science as a cosmology providing a basis for human identification with all of nature. Such an identification is based on the cosmological idea and a "deep seated realization of the fact that we and all other entities are aspects of a single unfolding reality."[27] The use of modern science to occasion a fundamental rethinking of reality is carried out most thoroughly by Freya Matthews, who uses Einstein's General Relativity theory to develop a metaphysics of the universal interconnectedness of all existence. Such a metaphysics leads Matthews to a fundamental justification for a nonanthropocentric attitude toward all of nature.[28] Since modern science is generally the most legitimate source of cosmological ideas in the modern world, the cosmological "use" of science may provide a counterforce to the rigorous anthropocentrism of reductive science. To the extent that science, as cosmology, tells a story capable of persuading humans that they are within, and a part of, a vast nature, it can increase people's sense of connectedness and be fundamental in reorienting humanity within the world.

But currently the major use of science, and at least one main reason for its prestige within industrial culture, is its efficacy in the project of transforming the rest of nature. It is impossible to deny the potency of reductive science and technology in its application to nonhuman nature. This potency involves a tunnel vision that reveals connections between parts of nature enabling their transformation in a variety of ways. The weakness of reductive science is that it ignores the larger context. Thus, what *can* be denied is the completeness of reductive science's image of nature. Fatefully, its potency now extends to all of nature on this planet.

Only if the reductive scientific image of nature is totalized into *the* truth does it justify the domination of the rest of nature. If any concrete situation is *only* a combination of invisible particles impelled by invisible forces to act in accord with timeless laws, then nothing in nature itself makes it worthy of respect. However, if reductive science is just one of several possible understandings of nature, then it does not follow that nonhuman nature can rightly be regarded as only an instrument for human use. As we shall see in Chapter 8, other understandings, grounded on nonreductive science, can legitimate a respect for the rest of nature.

There are two sorts of totalizations of the reductive scientific image of nature—the theoretical and the practical. We are, and have been for several hundred years, in the midst of a gradual practical totalization of the mechanistic image of nature. This project has been legitimated by science and required by industrialization. All along the way, there have been voices of protest. Some, such as Emerson and Thoreau and Leopold, continue to be heard. Increasingly, poets, scientists, environmental activists, and others are speaking out for nonhuman nature, against its colonization by industry. Remembering Thoreau's reveries about trout—"made beautiful, the Lord only knows why"—Bill McKibben laments the impending totalization of reductive science's image of nature:

> Through biotechnology we have already synthesized growth hormone for trout. Soon pulling them from the water will mean no more than pulling cars from an assembly line. We won't have to wonder why the

> Lord made them beautiful and put them there; we will have created them to increase protein supplies or fish-farm profits. If we want to make them pretty, we may. Soon Thoreau will make no sense. And when that happens, the end of nature—which began with our alteration of the atmosphere, and continued with the responses to our precarious situation of the "planetary managers" and the "genetic engineers"—will be final. The loss of memory will be the eternal loss of meaning.[29]

Such reflections motivate us to question the theoretical totalization that legitimates this "end."

Why totalize an instrumental image of nature developed under historically contingent circumstances? Surely some aspects of modern science are as they are because they developed within a particular culture. A science that developed within an animistic culture would be quite different from one that developed in the West after paganism had been banished. A science and technology which arose outside a Western milieu would likely have a different image of nature.[30]

One of the most fundamental contingencies that effect science's image of nature is the legacy of Plato. He bequeathed to us the ideal of philosophy as the contemplation of the eternal. The transitory quality of everyday experience is, for Plato, unsuitable for true knowledge. The "other" world is one beyond change, and this other world has remained the object of scientific inquiry—inquiry designed to discover the "true" reality. On this understanding of science, its laws are "discovered," not created. The ultimate particles of this other world would be exactly like each other, with no individual characteristics. They would not change through their combination into larger objects, and such combinations would happen in accord with timeless, historically unchanging processes named by scientific laws. True knowledge would be, in some way, a reflection of or a correspondence to this ideal world of true Being. Plato's legacy has enshrined this "other" world as the object of genuine knowledge.

There is something suspicious about the quest for an Unchanging Reality that is "above" or "underlies" the experiential world of constant flux. While the quest itself cannot be decisively refuted—neither can the quest for El Dorado—it can be doubted. John Dewey suggests that the roots of this Greek ideal are found in the class structure of Greek society. The elevation of the ideal of Unchanging Being bears some correlation with a slave society, wherein practical activity is devalued as being the labor of "lesser" humans, while the construction of theory is exalted, being the labor of citizens. Dewey also noticed a theological impetus behind the search for a realm of Unchanging Being. "Philosophy inherited the realm with which religion had been concerned. . . . The change from religion to philosophy was so great in form that their identity as to content is easily lost from view."[31]

If we were not so immersed within the tradition that readily accepts the idea of the "discovery" of laws, this construction of some other world with which we have no direct experience might seem simply fantastic. Is one to really believe that the laws of science exist independently of all human consciousness? Were these laws in existence before the earth? Before the Big Bang? If so, where are they?[32] What reason is there to believe that there is such a heaven of ideas? If faith in the world of Unchanging Reality were relinquished, then one's understanding of science would shift significantly. Science would not be understood as naming some other and better reality. Rather, as Dewey notes:

> a scientific object consisting of a set of measurements of relations between two qualitative objects, and itself accordingly non-qualitative, cannot possibly be taken, or even mis-taken, for a new kind of "real" object which is a rival to the "reality" of the ordinary object.[33]

Of course, this understanding of science as attending only to nonqualitative correlations between concrete qualitative objects reveals sharply the connection between science and the quest for control. "When these correlations are discovered, the possibility of control is in our hands."[34] Science, focusing on quantitative relations between events and ignoring their qualitative aspects, constructs an image of nature that enables control. Science and its reductive image of nature are *constructed* in the interest of control.

This understanding of science is important in unmasking its legitimating role in the domination over nonhuman nature. When science's image of nature is understood as a construction in the service of the project of domination, it can no longer be taken as legitimating this project. It is, rather, an expression of this orientation and cannot simultaneously justify it. Such legitimation as it has must then be found elsewhere.

Is Science the Only Rational Approach?

One important response to this line of argument involves conceding that science's image of nature is constructed, not discovered, and accepting the connection between an interest in control and science's construct. Nevertheless, one could maintain that this is, finally, the only *rational* relation humans can have to the rest of nature. Thus, it can be argued that the Enlightenment project of the eighteenth century was a genuine learning process from which there is no rational return. The Enlightenment thinkers saw Reason as the vehicle for human progress. Tradition was hampering the quest for Reason as well as happiness in dealing with the physical and the social worlds. Social enlightenment would lead to material comfort, spiritual happiness, and social progress. Thus, one could grant that the conditions that gave rise to the Enlightenment were contingent, but nevertheless maintain that the process of rationalization constitutes an emancipation from ignorance. Seen this way, the social learning of the Enlightenment cannot be undone through a "reenchantment" of nonhuman nature, which would be an irrational regression.

The twentieth century has generated grounds for doubt about the Enlightenment project. Human oppression has continued, reaching spasms of ferocity that rival any period in history. The horrors of fascism and techniques of social control make human progress seem elusive and uncertain. The fundamental threats posed by ecological problems suggest doubt about the application of reason to the rest of nature. The actual results of the Enlightenment project could, in fact, be used to suggest that the whole project is a mistake.[35]

Despite these horrors, the project could yet be defended by the claim that history as actually endured was a deformed version of what remains of the Enlightenment's emancipatory potential. With respect to the disenchantment of nonhuman nature, it could be claimed that objectification constitutes progress over any orientation that takes the rest of nature as alive and meaningful. Christianity's defeat of paganism, on this view, is a learning process which cannot be undone, and any "going back" would be unreasonable. Gregory Bateson, for example, remarked that "it would not be wise (even if possible) to return to the innocence of the Australian aborigines, the Eskimo, and the Bushman. Such a return would involve loss of the wisdom which prompted the return and would only start the whole process over."[36]

Marcuse and Habermas

The most able defense of the Enlightenment project along these lines has been developed by Jürgen Habermas, a theorist within the neo-Marxist tradition of critical theory. Habermas has been a vigorous critic of postmodern critiques of modernity and is one of the most important systematic thinkers in the social tradition.[37] Exploring Habermas's view will reveal the weakness, from the perspective of the nature tradition, of the social tradition's ability to respond to concerns about nonhuman nature.

Understanding Habermas's position requires a brief excursion into the Marxist notion of nonhuman nature. Marx envisioned humanity's relations with nature, historically developed through capitalism, as having an emancipatory potential that could only be realized through a transformation to socialism and then to communism. For Marx, the development of productive forces enabled the possibility of reducing the amount of labor necessary for human life to exist gracefully. He hoped for an eventual "resolution of the conflict between man and nature," but saw that this required a transition from capitalism to socialism and thence to communism. A later stage of communism would lead to a "consummated oneness in substance of man and nature—the true resurrection of nature—the naturalism of man and the humanism of nature both brought to fulfillment."[38]

Although there are subtle issues posed by Marx's understanding of nonhuman nature, it is clear that he understood it as something that could and should be transformed to reduce or eliminate the need for human labor. A transformed and remade—"humanized"—nonhuman nature was to be the foundation that could enable, given a rational society, the full development of human capacities.[39] Thus, the rest of nature within the Marxist tradition is viewed from an anthropocentric perspective. The development of the techniques to transform the rest of nature are potentially, but only potentially, the basis upon which a decent and humane society can be constructed. Science is an essential element in this project of rationally appropriating nonhuman nature for the use of humans. This instrumental orientation that lies at the heart of Marx's social philosophy has not generally been questioned by later Marxists.

Some Marxists have, however, sought a "new science" that would offer a fundamentally new mode of relating to nonhuman nature. Herbert Marcuse, for example, claimed that a new science involving qualitatively different relations between man and the rest of nature was possible. Such a science was not to be a reenchantment of nonhuman nature, but rather one that developed in an "essentially different experimental context (that of a pacified world); consequently, science would arrive at essentially different concepts of nature and establish essentially different facts."[40] This pacified world would, he claims, "open a universe of qualitatively different relations between man and man, and man and nature."[41]

These qualitatively different relations between man and nature would not be the end of the mastery over nonhuman nature. Rather, Marcuse distinguishes two forms of mastery, one repressive and one liberating. "Liberating mastery" involves the reduction of "misery, violence, and cruelty." According to Marcuse,

> all joy and all happiness derive from the ability to transcend Nature—a transcendence in which the mastery of Nature is itself subordinated to liberation and pacification of existence. . . . Civilization produces the means for freeing Nature from its own brutality, its own insufficiency, its own blindness, by virtue of the cognitive and transforming power of Reason. And Reason can fulfill this function only as post-technological rationality, in which technics is itself the instrumentality of pacification.[42]

Thus, Marcuse's "new science," with its qualitatively new relations with nature, involves the continuation of the project of the mastery of nonhuman nature. All joy and happiness come from the transcendence of nature. To be sure, the project would be radically transformed, because mastery would be subordinated to a pacified existence. But Marcuse's new science involves a vast reconstruction of the rest of nature, as he envisions eliminating or reducing its "brutality," ridding it of its "insufficiency," and ending its "blindness." Although Marcuse does not spell out just what these terms mean, it seems that wilderness and nonhuman carnivores would have no place in a "new nature" that has been rid of brutality, blindness, and insufficiency. Marcuse's new science, far from founding an ecologically harmonious mode of relating to the rest of nature, is a prescription for completing its domination. He remains firmly within Marx's project of "humanizing" nonhuman nature. Alford's criticism of Marcuse's "new science" seems accurate.

> The new science is rhetoric designed to soften Marcuse's otherwise terribly harsh . . . goal of the complete subordination of nature to human purposes. The new science is, in a sense, an ideology. It grants the aura of reconciliation with nature to what is actually projected to be humanity's final victory over it.[43]

Habermas, responding to Marcuse and others, denies that there is any possibility of a "new" science which is not a regression to some prerational perspective. "The resurrection of nature cannot be logically conceived within materialism" even if some, including Marcuse, have been attracted to "this heritage of mysticism."[44] Habermas understands the Enlightenment as a genuine learning process, which implies that we cannot return to the innocence of the past without the loss of wisdom. He distinguishes two categorically distinct types of rationalities that are, he maintains, irreducible to each other and rooted in the nature of the human species. One rationality is that of purposive action and the other is that of communicative interaction between human beings. The rationality of purposive action involves the efficiency of means toward pregiven goals and utilizes the sort of knowledge developed by natural science. Science provides the kind of information about the world that can be used in the project of changing nonhuman nature in accord with human goals. It generates a form of knowledge that is technologically exploitable. In sharp contrast is the kind of rationality that involves the interpretation of symbolic meanings. This is practical rationality, which is implicit in communicative interaction and has as its goal the achievement of uncoerced intersubjective agreement. Through communicative interaction, humans can, potentially, at least, arrive at uncoerced agreement about norms and collective goals. This process of reaching uncoerced agreement about norms would then become a normative basis for deciding the directions in which to change the rest of nature through science and technology.

One price to be paid for the learning made possible by the Enlightenment, according to Habermas, is that the only rational relations with nonhuman nature are instrumental relations. Habermas's totalization of reductive science's image of nature is expressly limited to the nonhuman world. He maintains a dualism between humanity and the rest of nature that is built into his analysis of the nature of reason. Indeed, one of his principal intentions is to preserve the dignity of humanity from the threat of a totally manipulated society. But this categorical dualism of reason compels Habermas to assert that nonhuman nature can *only* be understood through an objectifying science. No other possibilities exist without a lapse into "mysticism."

It needs to be stressed that, despite Habermas's complex analysis of reason and his restriction of the instrumental to the nonhuman world, his perspective still offers a vigorous legitimation of domination over the rest of nature. Indeed, one could argue that he offers a stronger legitimation than does a simple scientism, which renders itself dubious when totalized to include humans. Habermas's restriction of instrumental reason to the nonhuman world offers what appears to be a deeply grounded justification of a totally anthropocentric orientation toward all of the rest of nature, from apes to ecosystems to global ecology.

Some critics of Habermas have been concerned about the import of ecological crises for his analysis of our possible relations with nonhuman nature. Henning Ottman argues that control over the rest of nature can no longer be taken for granted, as we now see nature taking revenge. He notices a deep dilemma posed by "a will to control, whose legitimacy is based on our need to survive" which has become "itself a threat to our survival." In this revenge, nonhuman nature "reveals itself to be a *purpose-for-itself*."[45] Similarly, Joel Whitebook asks whether we can "deny all worth to nature," treating it as a "mere means" without destroying the ecological ground for the existence of humanity?[46] While Habermas recognizes the ecological problematic, he remains convinced that for external nature, "there is for *this* domain of reality only one *theoretically fruitful* attitude, namely the objectivating attitude of the natural-scientific, experimenting observer."[47] No other orientation toward nonhuman nature can further knowledge.

This does not mean that Habermas must forbid any foundation for a caring attitude toward the suffering of animals. Such attitudes and actions are founded on an ethical standpoint, rather than on an understanding of the essence of nonhuman nature. Unfortunately, the only basis for ethics that Habermas countenances is that of norms agreed to dialogically through communicative interaction. This hardly seems likely to occur between humans and nonhumans and seems certain not to occur between humans and nonsentient nature. It is possible, however, to imagine that an ethic founded on discourse between humans could extend moral consideration, on the basis of "compassionate solidarity," to the suffering of nonhuman creatures. They would not be included based on their participation in a ethical discourse, but rather because the participants in such a dialogue would extend ethical concern to the suffering of other creatures. This extension of concern would become possible by resolving the strife between humans. Given this social harmony, a communicative ethic could derive a good for nonhuman nature, based on its also being good for humans. This would allow the "preservation of the natural environment" without requiring any "qualitatively new relationship to the natural world."[48]

It is worth noticing that this way of posing the problem is abstract. To speak of the "preservation of the natural environment" says little about precisely what sort of environment should be preserved. If such a preservation is based solely upon human interests, are limits to the instrumental transformation of nonhuman nature based solely on human needs? Will any wilderness be left? Will this happen only because it is necessary for the preservation of humans and if so, how many? Will a communicatively founded ethic leave space for the survival of large nonhuman mammals? For their continuing speciation? What if this entails disinhabiting large areas? It seems to reflect a certain lack of vital concern about such issues to let them rest until the socially based disharmony of humans is resolved. These questions, of central concern to the nature tradition, have been only slightly discussed by thinkers in the social tradition.[49]

Habermas acknowledges that while the extension of moral concern to parts of nonhuman nature is not "absurd," it nevertheless remains problematic. The scope of any such concern is "blurry," extending at its farthest to plant life. Significantly, according to Habermas, the foundations for extending ethics beyond an anthropocentric framework remain in danger of regressing to "religious or metaphysical views" that have been overcome by the "learning attained in the modern understanding of the world."[50] While he is prepared to consider the possibility of extending ethical concern to include the suffering of other creatures, on the basis of that suffering, he is not sympathetic to the possibility of any theoretical grounding for such an extension. Science remains for him the only legitimate theoretical approach to the rest of nature.

At least one of the reasons for Habermas's view is that he only conceptualizes ethics from within the perspective of discourse, and discourse is necessarily reciprocal in intent. This limits the possibility of a "nonobjectivating" science to one which envisions "fraternal" discursive relations with nonhuman nature. Since this seems unlikely, so does any nonobjectivating new science. But the force of this conclusion is contained in the limitation that any ethic be grounded solely upon discourse. If one were not already convinced of this, it would not be necessary to categorize all nonobjectivating relations with the rest of nature as being akin to communicative interaction.[51]

Habermas's conceptual rigidity in regarding objectivating science as the only "theoretically fruitful" attitude toward nonhuman nature may not itself be theoretically fruitful. His conceptual schema freezes knowledge into one version of the prevalent orientation of science toward the rest of nature. As Alford notes, there is "a certain fixity or rigidity in Habermas' categories, which mitigates against speculation" and his system "downplays the creative freedom with which man constructs his philosophy and science."[52] Harking back to the discussion earlier about how science should be specified, the minimal definition of science as regulating belief on the basis of evidence gives no support to the thesis that science must yield an objectivating orientation toward the rest of nature. It is only a more specific characterization of science—as a reductive search for causal relations between parts of nonhuman nature within a mathematical language—that begins to derive an objectivated nature. It is this latter specification of science that need not be totalized. The fruitfulness of the objectivating perspective cannot be denied—but adopting it as the *only* valid cognitively grounded relation with the rest of nature is quite another claim.

There may be more room for alternatives than Habermas allows. Hans Jonas argues that the development of modern science and technology have given humans a vast power over the rest of nature. This power brings with it responsibility, suggesting that nonhuman nature has a moral claim upon us "in its own right." The scientific view of nonhuman nature

> emphatically denies us all conceptual means to think of Nature as something to be honored, having reduced it to the indifference of necessity and accident, and divested it of any dignity of ends. But still, a silent plea for sparing its integrity seems to issue from the threatened plenitude of the living world. Should we heed this plea . . . it would (if taken seriously in its theoretical implications) push the necessary rethinking beyond the doctrine of action, that is, ethics, into the doctrine of being, that is, metaphysics, in which all ethics must ultimately be grounded . . . we should keep ourselves open to the thought that natural science may not tell the whole story about Nature.[53]

It is precisely the metaphysical foundation for respecting the rest of nature that Habermas forecloses in his dualistic portrayal of reason. As a counterexample to Habermas's schema, it is worth seeing whether it is possible to construct an understanding of at least some form of science that does not legitimize domination over nonhuman nature.[54] Is it possible to construct an ideology of nature based on an ecological approach to all of nature? I explore this possibility in Chapter 8. This perspective does not entail a reductive orientation toward nonhuman nature, but rather it offers an alternative to regarding it as merely atoms falling through the void. Robyn Eckersley argues that such an "ecocentric science," guided by values that endorse the well-being of all life, could be a ground for the resistance to the domination over nonhuman nature.[55] Before the possibilities of such a new science can be appraised, it will be helpful to examine the ideologies of nature implicit in two prevalent types of environmentalism.

7 *Reactive versus Ecological Environmentalism*

The environment is widely recognized as a problem, but there is little consensus about solutions. Public concern is widespread, Earth Day is a major media event, and businesses seek shares of the market for "environmentally friendly" products. The Mobil Corporation claims that "where the environment is concerned, we all share the same basic goals."[1] Dupont, whose motto is "better things for better living," portrays cavorting dolphins in its commercials and sponsors radio reports to "encourage respect for the planet." Everyone is "for" the environment.

This proclaimed consensus rapidly evaporates when monetary interests are at stake. Mobil's goals, which they claim "we all share," include the exploration for oil in the Alaskan wilderness. Dupont wants only "responsible" regulation of greenhouse emissions. They lobbied for more research instead of governmental regulation of chlorofluorocarbons (CFCs), a major culprit in ozone depletion and global warming. In the late 1980s, they reclassified some CFCs as "soft" to avoid governmental regulation, and they continue to use them as aerosol propellants. Dupont produces between 15 and 25 percent of the CFCs used globally.[2] No business advises people to take the "greenest" action of all—stop buying.

When economic interest clashes with ecological interest, economic power usually wins. Consider, for example, the process of the environmental review of private and public projects. Environmental impact statements purport to assess the environmental consequences of a proposed action. Such impact statements generally require that alternatives to the proposed project be articulated and considered in terms of environmental consequence. Normally, one of the options that must be considered is "no action." This would seem to be a powerful way to effectively oppose any project that involves converting forests, meadows, or free-running rivers into shopping malls or housing developments. Letting nature be will almost invariably have less of an environmental impact than will any proposal to "develop" it. But this is not how such environmental impact regulations are structured. The New York *State Environmental Quality Review Act Handbook* is explicit about the relative value of profit over the preservation of nonhuman nature. "For many private sector actions, the no action alternative may be simply and adequately addressed by identifying the direct financial effects of not undertaking the action."[3] Thus, monetary loss is enough to rule out no action, and property rights trump meadows and forests.

In the last few decades environmentalism has become a political force, and the dominance of economic interests has been challenged by environmentalists. Today, environmentalism is an important political force in all industrial societies, contesting the transformation of nonhuman nature into commodities. Unfortunately, the environmental movement itself is not united in its analysis of the causes of environmental problems nor in the solutions to those problems.

One variant of environmentalism sees the problems as mistakes arising from ignorance, foolishness, or venality, and it understands solutions as increased governmental regulation and larger doses of expertise in the design and execution of industrial society. On this approach, no fundamental rethinking of our relations with the rest of nature are necessary, and no major social changes are necessary. We can, so it is believed, continue to regard nonhuman nature as a collection of resources that we can effectively control; we just need to be wiser in the particular ways we do so. Because this type of environmentalism shares industrialism's ideology of nature, it is simply "reactive" to the environmental problems generated by industrialism.

In contrast, another type of environmentalism sees a need for a new way of thinking about the rest of nature. Seeking an ideology of nature rooted in ecology, this "ecological environmentalism" conceives environmental problems as being interconnected. The roots of these problems are understood as extending to more fundamental mistakes in the structure of social decision making in modern society. This analysis leads to the judgment that major social changes are necessary to adequately resolve ecological problems.

These two types of environmentalism are "ideal types," rather than simple descriptions of environmentalists' views. There is significant ambivalence among many environmentalists as to what they should be doing. Some think that environmentalists should seek opportunistic alliances with a variety of politicians on issues as they arise. They lobby in the corridors of political power and pride themselves on being effective. Others think that they should form political alliances with other progressive movements, perhaps those within the Democratic party. Still others think that all such approaches entail excessive compromise and that they never deal with the real problems we face. They think that legislative victories are of little consequence because they mask a general failure to deal with the real scope of environmental problems lurking behind the facade of insignificant reform.

On the basis of international surveys in the early 1980s, Lester Milbraith reports that environmentalists are rather likely to think that some degree of basic social change is needed to solve environmental problems. Although most environmentalists in the United States, England, and Germany think that considerable basic social change is needed to deal with environmental problems, most do not think that a "completely new system" is needed.[4] Similarly, although most environmentalists tend to think that at least some of the rest of nature should be preserved for its own sake, about a third accepted the idea that nonhuman nature should be used as a resource to produce "the goods we use."[5] In fact, many environmentalists will identify with aspects of both reactive and ecological environmentalism. The merit of these ideal types is not descriptive. Rather, by bringing into clearer focus the implications of various ideologies of nature, they highlight the importance of how the rest of nature is understood in determining the type of environmentalism one adopts. Clarity on this issue is essential if environmentalists are to effectively confront industrialism.[6]

As capitalism called into being its opposition in the form of the labor movement, industrialism calls into being its opposition in the form of the environmental movement. Since its start, a division has existed in the labor movement between those who think workers should strive to make the best deal they can within capitalism and those who think that nothing short of some sort of social revolution can resolve the problems of capitalism. A similar split haunts the environmental movement. Reactive environmentalism is a defensive response to the obvious excesses of industrialism, while ecological environmentalism calls for a profound change in the ideology of nature implicit in industrialism. It may lead even further to a call for fundamental social change.

One or Many Problems?

One critical difference between reactive and ecological environmentalism has to do with the mode in which problems are conceptualized. Reactive environmentalism takes problems as they appear, assuming that each problem can be resolved with sufficient effort and expertise. This "one thing at a time" approach coheres perfectly with the belief that nonhuman nature is a relatively disconnected set of resources. Ecological environmentalism, on the other hand, looks for underlying patterns and the connections between seemingly separate environmental troubles. The belief in interconnections between problems coheres with an ecological image of nature as an interconnected set of processes.

For example, reactive environmentalism might view the problem of pesticides, such as DDT, as a technical mistake of introducing a long-lasting biocide into the environment. A reactive response to this problem is to seek more rapidly decomposable biocides, perhaps ones that act more precisely on the types of insects designated as "pests." The problem of plastics might be approached by seeking ways of recycling them. The problem of nuclear wastes might also be approached by seeking some mode of recycling, where feasible, and by isolating the rest for thousands of years.

An ecological environmentalist might go beyond these solutions to pesticides, plastics, and nuclear wastes by looking for connecting patterns between all three problems. Separable as these problems may be, they might also be, at a deeper level, symptoms of some profound mistake. Starting from the ecological insight that energy flows through systems but matter recycles, it follows that matter in a system must be recycled in some way. "Everything must go somewhere." If natural systems are to maintain their integrity as systems over long periods of time, they must recycle all matter introduced into the system. The introduction of wastes that cannot be decomposed *must* lead to problems of accumulation.

The difference between the two environmentalisms can also be seen in responses to the "garbage crisis." A reactive response is to consider building incinerators to burn the garbage. This alternative can be made more environmentally sound by using the heat from the incinerator to generate useable energy. The ecological environmentalist's response is to look for interconnections in assessing such a solution. "You can never do just one thing." What happens to the residue from incineration? Will it become even more dangerous "garbage"—as pollutants in the air and incinerator wastes of increased toxicity? Moving to social considerations, why not recycle to reduce the amount of garbage? Could changes in production processes create less material to be recycled? Will the high capital costs of an incinerator leave the community financially "addicted" to garbage in order to feed the incinerator?

Thus, one difference between the two environmentalisms is in the presumption as to whether or not environmental problems are interconnected. Reactive environmentalism assumes they are not, thinking that each problem can be solved in due course, whereas ecological environmentalism assumes that various problems are interconnected and reflect deeper problems.

Can Nature Be Managed?

Perhaps the most fundamental difference between reactive and ecological environmentalism is in the assumption that humanity's relations with the rest of nature can be managed. Reactive environmentalism accepts the premise of industrialism and its technocratic elites—that we can gain sufficient knowledge of nonhuman nature in order to effectively manage our relations with it. Reactive environmentalism simply urges changes in the details of the manager's agenda. It assumes effective management is possible.

This managerial assumption is implicit in concepts like "assimilation capacity." This concept tries to name the maximal amount of pollution which can be assimilated into an ecosystem without collapsing that ecosystem. It asks how much pollution an ecosystem can assimilate and at what rate. It is assumed that this can be known through studies of ecosystems. If known, then relations with ecosystems can be managed so that the assimilation capacity can be used without ecosystemic collapse. The ecosystem itself disappears behind the question of how much human abuse it can absorb.

Another managerial concept of reactive environmentalism is "maximal sustainable yield." When applied to ocean fisheries or forests, this concept introduces the difference between a maximum yield at a particular moment and a yield which is maximal over an extended period of time. The reactive environmentalist assumes that sufficient knowledge can be obtained to determine these maximum levels.

The Burden of Proof

Locating the burden of proof is critical in making decisions about the rest of nature. Does the burden of proof lie on those who would change natural systems for human use? Can we presume to change nonhuman nature as we wish, unless it can be shown that such changes are harmful? Or should we assume that any changes we make are likely to be damaging and require those who propose changes in natural systems to prove that those changes will not be harmful?

The language in which we discuss this issue is important. Typically, environmental projects are cast in the language of "risks" or cost-benefit analysis. This discourse subtly shifts the burden of proof to the critics of industrialism. Langdon Winner has analyzed the dangers of "risk assessment" language in discussions of environmental policy.[7] To speak of risks instead of hazards already slants the issue in favor of industrialism. As Winner points out, people know quite clearly what to do about hazards. You avoid them and stop people who place hazards in the way of others. Risks, however, are another matter. To conceptualize a danger as a risk implies some anticipated advantage. And taking risks has the aura of bravery. To know whether risks are "worth it," one must know a great deal about probable consequences. What is likely to happen if we do or don't do something? Further, one has to discern the relative costs of action or inaction, as well as the benefits. And we will have to discern some fair way of distributing the benefits and burdens. Such knowledge typically requires "experts." Thus, for example, if the issues of health and safety on the job are cast as risks, their resolution is far from clear. On the other hand, if the issue of health and safety on the job is conceived in terms of hazards and social justice, then the question is whether one person should endure hazards for the profit of another. Seen in this way, there is little need for experts to assess obscure probabilities. As Winner puts it, the language and techniques of risk assessment

> will delay, complicate, and befuddle issues in a way that will sustain an industrial status quo relatively free of socially enforced limits. . . . Because industrial practices acceptable in the past have become yardsticks for thinking about what will be acceptable now and in the future, attempts to achieve a cleaner, healthier environment face an uphill battle. The burden of proof rests upon those who seek to change long-existing patterns.[8]

Assessing actions in terms of economic costs and benefits means that whatever value is attributed to the forests and rivers is on the same scale as the profits and losses of a corporate balance sheet. The cost–benefit framework carries with it the assumption that the environment is only of value within the perspective of human monetary economies. "In couching arguments in these terms, environmentalists are implicitly accepting that environmental values can be traded off against other human wants . . . Environmental values become commodity values."[9] Once the environment is reduced to commodities, then the burden of proof rests on those who would deny the exploitation of the environment, or on those who urge expensive changes in current modes of exploiting the environment.

Where *should* the burden of proof lie? Differing ideologies of nature locate the onus of proof differently. If the rest of nature is a collection of relatively discrete piles of resources, then it is reasonable to think that expertise can be effective in resolving whatever difficulties arise in our dealings with it. After all, we have been very effective in the past at solving isolated problems, such as building bridges and flying in the skies. In this case, it may seem reasonable to place the burden of proof on those who would restrain industrialism from consuming resources.

On the other hand, if the rest of nature is a relatively integrated web of life, then all actions will have multiple effects, reverberating throughout the web in ways difficult to anticipate. All of nature, seen from an ecological perspective, is a product of a long evolutionary history. Human actions are apt to have many and various effects on the natural systems that have developed over thousands, millions, or even billions of years of natural selection. In this case, the burden of proof should lie on those who would alter natural systems. I shall return to this central issue shortly.

The Social Context

In the final analysis, reactive environmentalism tends to ignore the social context within which environmental problems arise. Environmental problems are taken as technical problems to be solved by the continued application of scientific and technological expertise. Such a perspective takes for granted and reinforces social systems that place technical elites as well paid consultants to the economic and political elites who make policy decisions.

In such a position of power, technical elites conceptualize problems as resolvable through technological innovations and/or an increase in legal regulation. This approach seeks policies within existing social hierarchies that can be legally or technically implemented. At its worst, reactive environmentalism insulates society from environmentally based critique by giving the appearance of reasonable attempts to balance environmental considerations with the needs of people and corporations. The average citizen is lulled into a sense of security that "they" are taking care of things.

Thus, reactive environmentalism remains within the sociopolitical framework of industrialism which generates ecological crises. It assumes that management of the problems is possible, which leads to calls for technological innovation, more research, and more legislation and regulation by the state. At its best, it is an approach which can make somewhat better a badly damaged planet. By treating the symptoms, it ignores the fundamental problems of industrialism. Without an alternative ideology of nature, environmentalism can only react to industrialism with essentially the same tools that are available to industrialism.

Two Ecological Environmentalisms

Ecological environmentalism is based on an ecologically inspired alternative to the industrial ideology of nature. It envisions nature as a relatively integrated system and seeks patterns in the variety of environmental problems, looking for underlying and less obvious causes of these problems. Both Barry Commoner and Garrett Hardin have written extensively on topics of environmental concern from an "ecological" perspective, and their works reveal interesting convergences and instructive divergences.

Commoner, in *The Closing Circle,* articulates four "laws" of ecology that reflect an ecological ideology of nature.[10] His first law is that "everything is connected to everything else." With this law, Commoner is emphasizing that ecosystems *are systems,* complexly interconnected, and stabilized through multiple feedback loops. Outside perturbations can have effects on systemic integration, sometimes leading to rapid and surprising systemic collapse. Complexity tends to give systems greater resistance to stress. His second law is that "everything must go somewhere." This means that matter in an ecosystem does not "go away" but rather is transferred from one place to another and may build up in harmful ways *within* the system. His third law is that "nature knows best." This is not meant to literally attribute cognitive capacities to nonhuman nature but is, rather, a metaphorical way of stating that human interventions into natural ecosystems are likely to be harmful to those systems. This is because living systems are products of evolution, during which various form of life have been tried out, with the successful surviving. Human interventions into ecosystems are akin to poking a pencil into the works of a watch. Man-made organic compounds are like pencil points—likely to be harmful. Commoner's fourth law is that "there is no such thing as a free lunch;" his point here is that every gain has a cost. While the payment may be delayed, it cannot be avoided, and "the present environmental crisis is a warning that we have delayed nearly too long." Such a set of laws is a view of the "web of life on earth."[11]

Garrett Hardin has also developed a perspective founded on an ecological ideology of nature. For him, the central question that an ecological understanding poses, regarding any type of action, is "and then what?"[12] Asking this question, which is the hallmark of what he calls "ecolacy," generates "caution and humility" toward any change. Under the rubric of "guilty until proven innocent," Hardin suggests a position almost identical to Commoner's "nature knows best":

> The environment is an enormously complex system of interacting elements and processes—and most of the interactions are unknown. Disrupt this web of life with a random intervention: What is the probability that harm will *not* be done? It is surely vanishingly small."[13]

Hardin recognizes that the ecological law that everything is connected to everything else can be criticized for conflating strong and infinitesimally weak connections. For this reason, he proposes a revision of Commoner's first law to read, "we can never merely do one thing."[14] Hardin suggests this revision toward modesty because the more sweeping formulation is too "poetic" and goes beyond the connectivity that can be demonstrated in the rest of nature. Moreover, the more sweeping formulation might make one "frightened by his impotence," sapping the "admirable commercial and civic energy" of the West over the past three centuries, leading people to regard the "environmental movement as an emasculating force." Hardin's more modest formulation of interconnectedness implies only that "there is at least one unwanted consequence" of our actions. It is addressed to those who are "intoxicated with dreams of technology."[15]

Hardin cautions against totalizing the ecological perspective, insisting that one must also use what he calls a "numerate" filter, as well as the "ecolate" filter. Numeracy is, for Hardin, a perspective that attends to "approximate dimensions, ratios, proportions, and rates of change in trying to grasp what is going on in the world."[16] Hardin maintains:

> Excessive ecolacy can lead to conservatism of the most stultifying sort. For prudence's sake, ecolacy must be combined with numeracy. Any action we take—and inaction is a form of action—leads to unwanted consequences. Prudence dictates that we compare the advantages and disadvantages of all proposed courses of action, choosing the one that, on balance, is *quantitatively* best.[17]

But this numerate perspective has to be applied with the recognition that we live within biological systems and that we are "part of the total system."[18]

There are, then, striking similarities in the positions of Commoner and Hardin. They both place the burden of proof on those who would change natural systems for human use, with Commoner claiming that "nature knows best" and Hardin proposing that such changes are "guilty until proven innocent." They both recognize the importance of viewing the rest of nature as a system in which actions have multiple effects. Commoner's third law, that "everything must go somewhere," leads him to ask the question "where does it go?" about any intervention into an ecosystem. In a similar vein, Hardin urges the question "and then what?" with regard to any action. While Commoner urges the broad claim that "everything is connected to everything else," Hardin's more reserved formula is "we can never do merely one thing." Although there are differing nuances within their formulations of the ecological perspective, they largely agree in the conclusions they draw.

Despite this shared ecological perspective, Commoner and Hardin have sharp differences on major social issues. They disagree fundamentally on questions of population policy, the roots of poverty, and the social changes needed to deal with ecological problems. Commoner has some faith in the possibility of a resolving of the population problem by improving living standards in the Third World. The phenomenon of a demographic transition has been observed in industrialized nations; where improvement in material standards of living has occurred, birth and death rates have declined, slowing the growth of population significantly. Commoner hopes this may occur in Third World countries, leading to a relative decline in the growth of population. The richer nations of the world should, presumably, help in raising standards of living in developing nations. Such assistance seems warranted because it would facilitate a demographic transition and because colonialism has significantly contributed to the present condition. Commoner contemplates the possible need for campaigns to reduce fertility in developing countries if birth rates remain high. This would, however, generate a political response by those countries and is "dictatorial and corrosive of human values."[19]

Hardin's views on population control are rather more notorious. He has argued that the richer countries of the world should not aid poorer countries. According to Hardin, in the absence of effective ways to coerce other nations into controlling their populations, the provision of aid will only lead to further increases in population and greater suffering further down the line. Thus, the "best" thing for the rich of the world to do about world hunger is nothing. Hardin's most chilling statement of this view is in his rejection of triage, the strategy of giving aid only to those countries where it would make a difference, allowing only the most helpless to die. According to Hardin, since *any* giving of aid will do "more harm than good, it is not necessary to decide which countries get the gift and which do not. For posterity's sake we should never send food to any population that is beyond the realistic carrying capacity of its land. *The question of triage does not even arise.*"[20]

The poor of the world, then, have the choice of accepting coercive measures of population control (which are not accepted by the rich) or starvation. They, of course, may see other options. In an increasingly integrated world, the poor might choose to respond to their starvation by trying to coerce the rich into sharing the wealth. With economies becoming increasingly interdependent, debt repudiation could make serious trouble for all economic systems. Nuclear proliferation raises the possibility of nuclear blackmail, a tactic that might get the attention of the rich of the world.[21] Commoner finds Hardin's view "barbaric".[22]

At least one of the reasons for the divergent views of Commoner and Hardin on world population stems from the difference in their positions on what causes poverty. If poverty is curable, then the problems arising out of poverty, such as high birth rates, can also be cured. On the other hand, if poverty is a necessary condition of human social life, then the problems arising from poverty must be coped with in some other way. Commoner envisions a growing alliance between those concerned with environmental issues and those concerned with social justice and peace. The problems are linked, and he believes that "as we begin to act on the environmental crisis, deeper issues emerge which reach to the core of our system of social justice and challenge basic political goals."[23] United political action can be effective in creating social change toward justice.

On the other hand, according to Hardin, the primary cause of poverty in society is that the poor are concerned only with the short term problems of survival, while the wealthy can afford to take a longer view. This difference will lead the poor to favor a present gain over a larger, but less certain, future gain. This difference between the rich and the poor will continue to grow.[24] Hardin's views on population and poverty closely parallel those of Thomas Malthus. Malthus, having concluded that the right of private property is "the most natural as well as the most necessary of all positive laws," considers whether assistance should be given to the poor. He concludes that it depends on their habits. If they are shamed by the receipt of relief and delay marriage, then perhaps some good may be done. But if they are not shamed and "many marry," then assisting them will contribute to a "general deterioration" of the masses. In either case, "it is necessary to be fully aware of the *natural tendency* of the labouring classes of society to increase beyond the demand for their labor or the means of their adequate support."[25] If poverty is inevitable, why help?

Both Commoner and Hardin believe that major social changes are needed to effectively resolve ecological problems. They disagree, however, on what those changes should be. Commoner thinks that socialism is the essential change needed to resolve the environmental crisis. This view had not yet been clearly stated in his 1971 work, *Closing Circle*. In that book, Commoner speaks of the need to govern "production by social criteria rather than private" criteria, and he advises that an economic system based on "private transactions" must be changed.[26] In *The Poverty of Power*, written in 1976, Commoner is much more explicit about the need for socialism. In this work he argues that the energy crisis and other environmental problems reveal a fundamental flaw in the way in which decisions about production technology are made. This flaw arises from the nature of capitalism, and its resolution requires viewing "the faults of the U. S. capitalist economic system from the vantage point of a socialist alternative."[27]

Hardin is less explicit than Commoner about his views of capitalism and socialism. His clearest political enemy is any system of social decision making that allows private gain at the expense of common good—this is the essence of his "tragedy of the commons." This sort of system is exemplified in the "freedom" to breed in a crowded world, as well as the free use of waters and air to dispose of wastes, whether within capitalistic or socialistic societies. Even though Hardin is not explicit about his views concerning capitalism versus socialism, he detects few problems with the system he calls "private enterprise." In this system, the decision maker bears both the cost and the benefit of his choices. This will bring his decisions in accord with the requirements of nonhuman nature. The distribution of responsibility is chancier in socialism.[28] What is clear is that Hardin is not alarmed by the inequalities inherent in "private enterprise" and, when his views on world hunger are remembered ("the question of triage does not even arise"), it is clear that he regards capitalism with far more equanimity than does Commoner.

The Necessity of Values

The important lesson to be drawn from the similarities and differences between Commoner and Hardin is that their shared ecological perspective does not lead to any specific view about how we should treat other humans nor about the best way to structure society. Hardin and Commoner do share some powerful claims about social policy based on ecological considerations. They are clear that we are now making major mistakes in our relations with the rest of nature and that the burden of proof falls squarely on those who would tamper with natural systems. For both, our environmental problems require significant social change. They both accept the idea of a managed society, assuming that sufficient knowledge is possible for such a task. Although they each criticize a reductive approach to science, they do not question the objectification of nonhuman nature. They are both totally anthropocentric in their discussion of the rest of nature, revealing no concern with it except as a human resource.

Despite these similarities, Commoner would help the poor of the world to move toward developed-nation standards of living, while Hardin would allow them to starve. Commoner would strive to end social injustice, while Hardin thinks that poverty will always be with us. For Commoner, a fundamental reason for ecological crises is the capitalistic system of production, while for Hardin, our problems are rooted in the system of the "commons," which misallocates gain and suffering. Clearly an ecological perspective does not imply a social vision.

At the conclusion of his history of the science of ecology from the eighteenth century to the present, Donald Wooster argues that "ecology is not a single approach to nature; it embraces many approaches. . . . Is it truly possible, in the light of such ambiguities, to talk about an 'ecological point of view' or 'ecological values' or an 'ecologically oriented society'?"[29] The examples of Commoner and Hardin extend this problem, for they reveal that even a shared understanding of ecology can lead to widely divergent analyses of social problems. Perhaps Langdon Winner is correct in his emphasis on the social dimension of the concept of nonhuman nature. He claims:

> Discussion about ecology and environment tell us a great deal more about the condition of society than about anything in nature as such. . . . [I]deas about things natural must be examined and criticized not only for the ways they help us understand the material world, but for the quality of their social and political counsel. Nature will justify anything. . . . It is comforting to assume that nature has somehow been enlisted on our side. But we are not entitled to that assumption.[30]

Winner may go too far in claiming that nonhuman nature will justify *anything*, but his general thesis is important. Any appeal to ecology as a sufficient ground for conclusions about how we should live or how we should structure society is bound to be incomplete. This does not mean that ecological considerations are not essential in any moral or social philosophy. Just as the ecology of our biosphere actually surrounds us and sets limits on our activities—limits we may not be aware of until we overstep them—so too must considerations of ecology permeate our thinking about how we should live. But this infusion is not a determination; we must also consider what is really of value, and this we cannot find in nonhuman nature alone.

Certain minimal conclusions drawn from an ecological perspective seem warranted. First, there is no "away," no ultimate other place to which things can be sent. Remembering that everything must go somewhere prompts an important question that must be asked and reasked about any proposed action. Keeping this caveat clearly in view might have stopped us from making some quite serious mistakes. Second, we must remember that we live within systems of ecosystems, a fact that should alert us to look for connections between problems and also open us to the possibility that we need to see some problems as symptoms of deeper mistakes.

Perhaps most importantly, an ecological perspective would lead to the recognition that the burden of proof has typically been mislocated. Industrial society has historically placed the burden of proof on those who counsel caution and would restrict actions that change nonhuman nature. An ecological ideology of nature would shift the burden of proof to those who would intervene in natural systems. But it is unclear what needs to be proved. Must one demonstrate that a food dye is harmless before it may be added to food? Surely. Must one show that the damming of a river will have no irreparable damage to humans? Probably, but must harm to other animals and plants also be considered? Even further, can the whole industrial system that we have constructed be justified? Should industrialism itself carry the burden of proof?

The claim that industrialism carries the burden of proof is so far beyond the domain of present debates that it can have no immediate practical result. There is no effective court within which the case can be presented, but the question is fundamental. Can the industrialism that steadily extends to all parts of the planet be justified? Is industrialism worth it? Has industrialism made a better world for humans? Notice that this is a much less stringent question than whether industrialism is the best path to human happiness. The evidence discussed in Chapter 3 suggests that industrialism may not lead to human happiness at all. At least beyond a certain point, the dissatisfactions of consumerism and mass society may outweigh the rewards. There is nothing within the logic of industrialism that allows a consideration of whether we already have produced too much. The pressures for growth spread throughout the system, with all sectors of society seeking more and more, yet still finding happiness elusive. Is this constant quest to acquire more worth the risk? The magnitude of the hazard need not be belabored. Suffice it to say that we have altered the global atmosphere, with largely unknown consequence. The ozone layer is now thinning, a fact that will have vast and unpredictable results. The list of problems could be much longer. Is worth it?

This seemingly inexorable expansion of industrialism raises further moral questions. By what right does the human species, however unwisely it seeks its own welfare, elbow aside countless species in their pursuit of resources? We have already seen too many species become extinct. We have encircled wilderness and threatened all rain forests. Perhaps we have ended biological history by stopping the speciation process for large animals. We now stand ready to embark on the alchemic project of manufacturing new forms of life in the pursuit of profit. By what right do we presume to remake the rest of nature according to the desires of humanity? It is to these ethical questions that we must now turn.

8 *The Critique of Anthropocentrism*

The appeals to ecology made by Commoner and Hardin do not settle questions of how one should live nor of the nature of the good society. Their ecological perspective is limited to an understanding of nature as complexes of nonhuman systems, and their counsel is one of long-range human prudence.[1] But I suggest that the limitation of their concern to human interests only, common though it may be, cannot be justified. A more expansive and less anthropocentric use of ecological insight might yield a better understanding of both nonhuman nature and society. An ecological ideology of nature that includes humans within its scope might be vital in placing humanity within nature, leading to a rejection of the anthropocentric limitation of concern to humans alone.

Notes toward a New Science

To investigate this possibility, it is first necessary to reconsider science. The minimal definition of science, as the intent to found one's views on empirical evidence instead of hope or dogma, must be maintained. But when science views nature as only inert matter in meaningless interaction, any criticism of the human domination over nonhuman nature is robbed of any grounding in fundamental reality. An alternative ideology of nature, if warranted by empirical evidence, might sever this connection between science and domination. An alternative that sees life as one essence of nonhuman nature might be the basis for a "new science." Such a science could help legitimate a respect for all of nature and would be of significant import for efforts to create an ecologically sane society.

Ecology can provide the inspiration for a new science, but only if it is freed from its current confinement. Perhaps it is not surprising that ecology has been defanged as it has been brought into the mainstream of modern science. Modern academic ecology has become entrapped in an economic metaphor for nonhuman nature, in which "producers" and "consumers" have "occupations" in ecosystems. "In their most recent theoretical model, ecologists have transformed nature into a reflection of the modern corporate, industrial system. And to a great extent, ecology has become 'bioeconomics': a cognate, or perhaps even subordinate, division of economics."[2] This is not surprising, as the science and the scientists are located within a culture that continually lapses into economic images for all dimensions of life. "Time is money," for example, suggests an unfortunate reduction of human life to economics. It is, however, possible to utilize insights derived from ecology to develop a perspective that can help humanity reorient itself toward the rest of nature. Such a perspective will not be a chunk of ecological research, nor will it be the only possible "ecological" perspective. Rather, it is a sketch of an ideology of nature that takes life as an essential aspect of existence.

The crucial conceptual change needed to free ecology from its current boundaries is an extension of ecological understanding to include humanity within its domain. When an ecological perspective is applied by humans self-referentially, then it becomes entirely plausible to see life as being, in some way, fundamental to reality. The experience of living is not foreign to us. When we think about what nature really is, we can either deny that our experience of living has a fundamental place in the nature of nature, or we can accept that the rest of nature is, in part or whole, like us in being alive. This acceptance leads to an ecologically inclusive ideology of nature.

This ecologically inclusive ideology involves a fundamental change in metaphor, portraying nature as a relatively integrated community in which each part is as it is because of its relations to the whole(s) of which it is a part. Each part of this community has standing as a participant in the larger whole, and as such is a piece of the larger whole. The image of all of nature is that of an interconnected network, where seemingly discrete things arise and decay within a larger "web of nature." From this view, a fundamental unity underlies nature's diversity.

This inclusive ecological model focuses on the relations between individuals and their environments; the relations of an individual part to its environment is essential in constituting what that individual is. The individuals are as they are because of the larger systems within which they exist. In this sense, some relations are internal to the nature of the part, although not *all* relations within ecosystems are internal. "When a bird eats a mosquito, it gets an external relation to that mosquito, but eating is an internal relation to its environment."[3] It is not that "you are what you eat," as the slogan goes, but that you are what you are within.

Although the notion of "internal relations" can be obscure and lead to murky philosophical waters, the basic meaning is, however, readily at hand. We all experience internal relations when we engage in conversations.[4] In a conversation, experience is shaped by the participatory relationship of the situation that extends beyond either individual participant's experience. A genuine conversation has a "life of its own," and the experience of each participant is internally related to the larger whole. During a conversation, my experience at any moment is internally related to the responses of the other participants. Each of our experiences is a part of a larger whole that is the conversation. An inclusive ecological image involves taking interrelatedness as the central aspect of a situation and, thus, directs attention to the larger context within which individuals exist. By noticing our essential relatedness to the rest of nature, we may increase our appreciation of the unity of humanity with the rest of nature.[5] It also facilitates an understanding of why many people experience an identification with other parts of nature, for such connections are real.

There are several reasons to favor this inclusive ecological ideology over any reductive ideology of nature. First, it can explain both the success and the limitations of the reductionist orientation toward nonhuman nature. If nature is conceived of as interconnected communities of relations, then reductive science can be understood as an attention to separate strands within those networks. The reductionist orientation involves the search for the most relevant operative factors in the simplified situations of experimental science. These factors can be understood as single threads of a complex whole. What is obscured in this approach are the interconnections among the threads, that is, the larger community *within* which those threads exist.

If nature is aptly understood as a community of communities, then one can anticipate that a reductive approach will succeed as long as there is slack in the system. Given sufficient slack, instrumental action by any element of the system may be successful for a long time. However, when that slack diminishes, continuing the instrumental action ought to generate, at an increasing rate, surprising consequences that do not follow past patterns of successful action. Types of actions that were once satisfactory might begin to generate unwanted side effects, because less slack in the network causes changes in one part to reverberate more loudly in other parts. Over time, the tempo of unintended consequence would increase. Tall smokestacks, built to eliminate local pollution, lead to the acidification of rain, with far reaching and unanticipated consequence. The use of fossil fuels for convenience and speed lead to pollution of air and unwanted changes in global climate, as well as vast changes in patterns of habitation, agriculture, and family life.[6] The accelerating rate of unintended side effects suggests serious limits of the tunnel vision of reductive science.

A second virtue of an inclusive ecological ideology is that it offers a more comprehensive image that includes humanity within nature. Ecology, understood narrowly as the study of the interrelations between nonhuman organisms and their environments, does not force any such new understanding. But when the ecological perspective is applied to humanity, it gives a more inclusive framework for comprehending humanity's relations with the rest of nature. Humanity and nature are seen as existing within one matrix. Such comprehensiveness, other things being equal, is to be preferred.

Seeing ourselves as *within* nature, itself understood as a community of life and land, directs attention to a basic blind spot in social philosophies. Historically, social thought has viewed nonhuman nature as a subsidiary of society. The rest of nature has simply been there to be appropriated through human activity. When human society is understood as a human community nested within natural communities, then the dependence of society on the rest of nature becomes noticeable. Any adequate social philosophy must include consideration of the relations between society and nonhuman nature. The reverse is also true. Any comprehensive perspective in the nature tradition must extend its concern to the social and economic structures of human societies. This is, to be sure, a difficult and unrealized ideal. But the failure even to strive for comprehension of nonhuman nature and society together means that significant elements are ignored. The larger the impact of any element on the whole, the less likely it is that such restricted vision will be fruitful. At this stage in human history, the influences of society and the rest of nature on each other are of increasing significance, a trend that is sure to continue. Both society and the rest of nature count.

A third virtue of the ecological ideology is that it provides a firm basis for understanding the limitation of *any* ideology of nature. Recognizing the embeddedness of humanity within nature implies that our knowledge of the whole is necessarily incomplete. If we understand ourselves as being embedded within nature, then all our cognitive activity happens within our bodies, within society, within nature. From these contexts, we generate mappings of our territories. The inherent incompleteness of knowledge stems from the impossibility (and undesirability) of identifying map and territory. This implies that the stance of the "disinterested" scientist, investigating a "meaningless nature," while sometimes a useful mapping, cannot be fundamental reality. Using an inclusive ecological perspective directs attention toward the ground out of which instrumental action arises. The purposes that constitute the framework, within which nature appears as meaningless, remain in view and serve to limit the unwarranted totalization of such a perspective. The instrumental orientation of science is *always* partial and involves forgetting a more fundamental unity of humanity and the rest of nature. Certainly, limiting one's perspective to small pieces of a larger integrated whole can be convenient, as well as conducive to flourishing in certain situations. The need for effective instrumental action is real. But we need to remember that the interest in instrumental action blinds as well as illuminates, just as a flashlight in the night brightens the path, but makes the forest and stars invisible. Recognizing this incompleteness forms a basis for the critique of modern hubris in our relations with nonhuman nature.[7]

Thus, an inclusive ecological ideology of nature would have at least three significant virtues. It offers a framework to explain why instrumental action, facilitated by a reductive scientific orientation toward nonhuman nature, is effective and also why it is limited. It offers a more comprehensive perspective that understands humanity as existing within nature, and it offers an understanding of the limitations of all human knowledge. These cognitive virtues suggest that such an ideology is worth developing in greater detail. Here I want only to indicate one fundamental consequence of adopting this ideology.

An inclusive ecological ideology of nature makes life one of the fundamental dimensions of nature. If we focus on the complexity of ecosystems and the interrelations of their components, various forms of life appear as centers of activity in complex interaction. This is the normal state of ecological communities. If we take life as being paradigmatic and fundamental, then the world of physics becomes the investigation of one aspect of the world from a particular perspective, not the true story about "real reality."[8] Biology does not need "reduction" to physics. If life is the norm, then meaning, striving, and freedom are regular aspects of nature, not just froth floating on a river of complexes of matter in meaningless motion.

There is, of course, the danger of unwarranted anthropomorphism in this. Within scientific modes of thought, anthropomorphism—the attribution of human characteristics to other parts of nature—has long been taboo.[9] The historical root of the ban on anthropomorphism is the struggle of modern science against the Aristotelian foundation of the medieval worldview. Aristotle's nature is filled with ends, goals, and strivings. He saw final causes spread throughout nature. Modern science sees only matter in motion—no purpose, no goals, no final causes. The triumph of modern science and its exclusion of final causes was, at first, incomplete, for it was recognized that final causes did remain operative in human life. There was, thus, a dualism of man and the rest of nature that reserved goals and purposes for humans alone. This dualism found clearest expression in Descartes, for whom only humans could be centers of activity. Animals are like the rest of nature, complexes of matter in motion.[10] But dualism has fallen into disrepute, and evolution provides a single framework for understanding humanity and the rest of nature. Hans Jonas observes that we are now confronted with a stark choice between two monisms:

> Either [we can] take the presence of purposive inwardness in one part of the physical order, viz., in man, as a valid testimony to the nature of that wider reality that lets it emerge, and to accept what it reveals in itself as part of the general evidence; or [we can] extend the prerogatives of mechanical matter . . . and oust teleology even from the "nature of

> man" . . . that is, to alienate man from himself and deny genuineness to the self-experience of life.[11]

Using an inclusive ecological ideology of nature, we can remain faithful to our own experience of ourselves as centers of action, and we can, in our approach to the rest of nature, be open to the existence of other comparable centers of experience and agency. Of course, such beliefs need evidential warrant, but purpose in nature, as well as a purposive nature, is not ruled out by a now unnecessary taboo against anthropomorphism.

Taking life within ecological communities to be a fundamental metaphor for all nature suggests interdependence, rather than domination, as a norm for relations. Ecosystems abound in cooperation and symbiosis, as well as competition and conflict. Relations involving dominance are, in fact, one type of interdependency. Seeing domination as the norm may, in part, spring from the use of physics as the paradigm for science. Within physics, laws are arranged in a hierarchical order, with laws of lesser scope "following from" the more general. Evelyn Fox Keller questions this understanding of science in which a hierarchically arranged set of laws is sought. The idea of law carries with it the idea of command, coercion, control, and hierarchy. She thinks a better metaphor might be that of order, which is more comprehensive and includes "patterns of organization that can be spontaneous, self-generated, *or* externally imposed."[12] Law implies external constraint, while order allows for self-generated activity. If we use the metaphor of order, then we might take the biological sciences, rather than physics, as the paradigm for science. Further, and most importantly,

> the conception of nature as orderly, and not merely law bound, allows nature itself to be generative and resourceful . . . nature comes to be seen as an active partner in a more reciprocal interaction to an observer, equally active, but neither omniscient nor omnipotent . . . The focus on order rather than law enlarges our vision of both nature and science . . . it suggests a science premised on respect rather than domination.[13]

Such a revisioning of the rest of nature undercuts the idea that domination is "natural."

It is significant that this use of hierarchy in our understanding of nonhuman nature has been pointed out by women in their reflections on gender bias in science. There is a unity of concern between those who question the domination over nonhuman nature and those who question the domination of women by men. Both feminism and ecology seek an understanding of all of nature that is relational, holistic, and nonhierarchical. Karen Warren has argued that the notion of higher and lower suggests a hierarchy of values that functions to legitimate domination and inequality. Quoting Elizabeth Dodson Gray, she points out that "prior to the metaphor of Up-Down, one would have said only that there existed diversity."[14]

As Patsy Hallen notes, "feminism and ecology both stress creative activity over inert matter, dynamic order over static laws, partial autonomy over determinism, relation over substance, objects as subjects over subjects as objects."[15] The development of an inclusive ecological ideology of nature might inspire more unity among the many who seek fundamental social change.

One could even try to use such a perspective to reconcile the rest of nature with Habermas's communicative ethic. John Dryzek, drawing upon the idea of agency within nonhuman nature, attempts just this.[16] In the first place, argues Dryzek, adequate ecological conditions are necessary for any human communication, so perhaps the rest of nature should be seen as a "silent partner" in all communication. Of course, Habermas might object that this is an unwarranted extension of his notion of linguistically mediated communication, but we need not try to resolve this issue here. Clearly there is abundant evidence that suggests the presence of agency in nonhuman nature, once we start to look for it. Dryzek notes the work of McClintock in genetics, of Goodall with chimpanzees, and of Griffin on animal thinking as revealing examples of agency in nonhuman nature. Accepting the fact of agency in the natural world "makes the restriction of communicative rationality to purely human communities appear arbitrary. This world is not silent and passive, but *already* full of 'values, purposes, and meanings'."[17]

It seems, then, that there is a choice about how we should regard the rest of nature. We can view it as a dead and meaningless system, if we accept physics as the paradigmatic science. But such a totalization of a perspective adapted for instrumental relations with nonhuman nature is not necessary. We could start with the primacy of life as we experience it and work outward from there. We would then regard nature, human and nonhuman, as alive and overflowing with meanings, leading us toward a kinship with the rest of life. This could open us to a more general respect for all of nature. Aldo Leopold, in the 1920s wrote this remarkable anticipation of the Gaia hypotheses:

> There is not much discrepancy, except in language, between [the] conception of a living earth, and the conception of a dead earth, with enormously slow, intricate, and interrelated functions among its parts, as given us by physics, chemistry, and geology. . . . Possibly, in our intuitive perceptions, which may be truer than our science and less impeded by words than our philosophies, we realize the indivisibility of the earth—its soil, mountains, rivers, forests, climate, plants, and animals, and respect it collectively not only as a useful servant but as a living being, vastly less alive than ourselves in degree, but vastly greater than ourselves in time and space—a being that was old when the morning stars sang together, and, when the last of us has been gathered unto his fathers, will still be young.[18]

The choice of how we shall regard both ourselves and the rest of nature is fundamental. An inclusive ecological ideology of nature would not legitimate the domination of nonhuman nature. Regarding nature as a community of purposive systems does not involve the surrender of reason nor any leap into "mysticism." We can acknowledge the importance of empirical evidence in forming belief and still take all nature as entitled to respect because of what it actually is. While empirical evidence cannot compel such a shift in understanding, such fundamental revisionings are never compelled by evidence. And the evidence that we do have, of both ourselves and at least parts of the rest of nature, surely permits an ideology of nature in which an attitude of respect for the rest of nature is grounded in the essence of nature itself.

The possibility of choice indicates an ethical dimension to ideologies of nature. There is a complex reciprocity between our values and the ways in which we understand the rest of nature. We already exist within an experiential world that is infused with values. When we distinguish, within this experienced world, between facts and values, our conceptions of each are related to the other. The values we hold and our understandings of nature develop together, complementing and amplifying each other, or giving rise to tension and change in one or the other. Understandings guide choices of value, and values guide understandings. Although values may not be determined by an ideology of nature, they are implicit in any such ideology. Thus, while for purposes of analysis we may distinguish facts and values, they ultimately intertwine.

It is not surprising, then, that trying to understand the rest of nature leads to a need for reflection on values. An ecologically based understanding of humanity that locates us *within* a community of communities composed of various centers of life, suggests that limiting concern to only human concerns is an undue, unjustified, and illegitimate bias, akin to the biases of racism and sexism. Such an understanding of nature leads us to question the anthropocentric orientation of much of modern environmentalism.

The Critique of Anthropocentrism

The question of anthropocentrism has recently been extensively discussed by environmental philosophers. In the last fifteen years or so, coinciding with a rising concern about the environment among the general public, there has been a blossoming of interest in environmental ethics among philosophers and others. This is a sharp break from the traditional concerns of moral philosophy, which has historically been almost exclusively concerned with ethical problems concerning relations between human beings. It may be, as Roderick Nash has argued, that environmental ethics represent the "farthest extension of ethical theory in the history of thought."[19] An ecological ideology of nature supports this extension of ethical concern to include the rest of nature.

The ecological ideology of Commoner and Hardin is cast in terms of human prudential action. They put their slogans in terms that are relevant to human action. By asking, "And then what?" Hardin is trying to prod decision makers into thinking more thoroughly about the many consequences of an action that must follow if nonhuman nature is understood as being an interconnected network of relations. Commoner's law that "everything is connected to everything else" is cast in the language of cybernetics and system theory. Environmental philosophers, on the other hand, tend to discuss nonhuman nature in terms of interdependent communities of the living and the nonliving, leading us beyond prudence to an ethic that includes the rest of nature.

Environmental philosophers have shown that an ethic that recognizes values in nonhuman nature is conceptually possible. Indeed, they have created several versions of such an ethic, each of which involves major revisionings of humanity's proper place within nature and requires of us significant moral restraint in our dealings with the rest of nature. There has been substantial progress in environmental ethics in just a few decades. Starting from the problem of establishing a need for an environmental ethic in the 1970s, Callicott points out that in the 1980s philosophers "have actually developed an impressive array of fairly well worked out theories of environmental ethics."[20] As he notes, at least three distinct foundations have been suggested for such an ethic: a biocentric regard for life in general; a regard for the land community; and deep ecology, with its focus on self-realization. Warwick Fox notices several other foundations for environmental ethics, including ones based on sentience in nonhuman nature or some notion of cosmic purpose.[21] Happily, some of the results of these reflections prove useful in constructing a foundation for the moral critique of industrialism.

What is now most urgently needed from ethical reflection is the dethroning of anthropocentrism. It is the anthropocentric assumption, in conjunction with instrumental science, that legitimates industrialism. Once industrialism is viewed from a nonanthropocentric perspective, then it is *obviously* a horrendous crime against the rest of nature. If we shed our anthropocentric bias, then the expanding human population, especially when coupled with environmentally destructive forms of production, appears as a vast aggression against the rest of nature. The possible loss of the majority of species in the next century constitutes a biocide of so great a magnitude as to morally require urgent radical social change toward harmony with nonhuman nature.[22]

Within industrial culture, anthropocentrism is so deeply embedded that it is hard to bring it to light. Neil Evernden offers a trenchant illustration of the problem. Imagine being at a meeting about some proposed highway that would pave over the habitat of some endangered creature. In questioning this proposal, you try to advocate for the interests of this creature. The response likely to be made by many present is, "What good is it?" How can the anthropocentric assumption buried within that question be questioned? The temptation is to meet it in a way that will pathetically reinforce the anthropocentric assumption, such as by saying, "Perhaps it will turn out to cure cancer." Evernden's suggested response, which should be used cautiously, is to reply: "What good are you?"[23] If this does not precipitate a fight, it might bring out the anthropocentric assumption that other forms of life need to be justified by their human usefulness—an assumption that underlies "What good is it?" This might provide an opportunity for a reasoned argument about the anthropocentric assumption itself. Then one could discuss whether yet another highway justifies the extinction of a form of life.

Anthropocentrism is even embedded in the way many environmentalists conceptualize the human situation. One current definition of the term "environment" reads: "All the physical, social, and cultural factors influencing the existence or development of mankind."[24] Leaving aside comment on the sexism of the word "mankind," this definition reflects an expansive and welcome inclusion of social and cultural factors into the idea of the environment. But it also is thoroughly anthropocentric. It fails to reflect an understanding that the very concept of "environment" must be relativized to the entity or species for which the rest of nature constitutes "an environment." I am part of the squirrel's environment, as it is part of mine. Each center of activity has its own environment; there is no such thing as *the* environment, unless one remains stuck within an anthropocentric bias.

One early influential critique of the anthropocentric bias of ethical theory is Richard and Val Routley's "Human Chauvinism and Environmental Ethics."[25] They articulate the influential "last man argument" to reveal clearly the anthropocentric bias inherent in traditional ethical theories. Their point is that such theories fail to account for the wrongness of the last human in the world setting out to destroy all other living things. More recently, Warwick Fox has examined the many varieties of anthropocentrism, finding them to be both dangerous and deluded.[26]

I shall here consider contemporary critiques of anthropocentrism by discussing three recent theories of environmental ethics. Paul Taylor has argued for what he calls a "biocentric outlook on nature."[27] This outlook supports an attitude of respect for the rest of nature. The biocentric outlook comprises four beliefs, two of which are close to an ecological ideology of nature. The fourth is a denial of anthropocentrism. The first belief is that humans are members of "Earth's Community of Life," like all other living things. This involves a recognition of our fundamental similarity to other biological creatures. All living beings share biological and physical requirements for well-being, with each having goods of its own. Taylor claims that all living things are free in the sense that, having goods or ends of their own, all flourish in the absence of external constraint. Humans share a common origin with all life, being equally products of evolution, and we are "members of the Earth's whole biotic community."[28] The second belief is that we are part of "a tightly woven web" of living things and environments because we are "an integral part of the system of nature."[29] His third tenet is that all living things are individuals, particular teleological centers of activity with their own individualities. Each organism is "a unique individual, pursuing its own good in its own way."[30] Finally, Taylor claims that humans are not inherently superior to other living things.

The first two of these beliefs arise naturally from an ecological ideology of nature that sees all nature as a community of communities enmeshed in a web of interdependence. The third is controversial because it restricts value to living individuals. Other environmental ethicists adopt a holistic perspective that finds value in, for example, ecosystems.

The fourth belief is a denial of anthropocentrism and makes a judgment about the relative value of different forms of life. Taylor offers a two-step argument in favor of his thesis that humans are not inherently superior to other living things.[31] He first argues that there are no good reasons for accepting human superiority and, then, that there are good reasons for rejecting any belief in such superiority. The basic claim that Taylor makes against arguments for anthropocentrism is that they beg the question at hand, assuming some human characteristic as superior in order to prove that superiority. For example, he considers the Greek idea that man is a rational animal and shows how the idea itself is used as evidence that "therefore" humans are superior to other creatures. But this criterion is, at best, a human consideration about the best life for humans. It provides no justification for applying such a criterion across all forms of life. The human capacity for reason is no more a justification for a value hierarchy among all life than is the cheetah's speed or the eagle's vision.

To justify a value hierarchy, one would have to appeal to a theological image of a Great Chain of Being. God, so it could be argued, created an order of value, descending from God, through the angels, to humanity, and thence to the "lower" animals, and then to the rocks. But, asks Taylor, even if we were to believe in such a hierarchy of existence, what reason is there to think that this order is "good"? It must be because God, the creator, is good. But how do we know this? We know through His actions, which are revealed as loving and merciful. But to see existence as embodying love and mercy in all creation is definitely anthropocentric. Is existence loving and merciful when viewed from the perspective of the animals and plants we eat and on which we experiment? Clearly not. So to infer God's goodness from creation is to import an anthropocentric perspective and to again beg the question.

Taylor also considers Cartesian dualism as a justification of anthropocentrism. For Descartes, only humans have minds and bodies, while animals have only bodies. Aside from the philosophical difficulties involved in any dualism, this understanding of humans and animals is thoroughly contradicted by our understanding of evolution. Most centrally, even if Descartes's picture of humans were accepted, why does having a mind make humans superior to other animals? What *moral* value can be attributed to the difference? To make the argument, one would have to assume what was to be proved—that some characteristic of humans, such as having a mind, is better than the excellent traits of other animals.

Finally, Taylor considers an argument for human superiority based on humans having a greater range of capacities than other forms of life. Clearly, humans do have a greater range of capacities, such as language and the ability to reflect critically on a vast spectrum of questions, as well as the capacity to create and play baseball. But, asks Taylor, why should this greater range of capacities confer superiority on humans? Taylor thinks that living things have inherent worth because each has a good of its own. "This is what having inherent worth *means*."[32] If so, the difference in capacities gives no warrant for the inherent superiority of any form of life over any other. Each living thing has inherent worth because each has a good of its own.

Taylor's positive argument for the denial of human superiority rests upon an ecological ideology of nature. To think humans superior simply does not fit with the understanding of nature that recognizes human membership in a community of life with centers of activity spread all around. Accepting the first three tenets of the biocentric outlook leads to a sense of "deep kinship with all other living things." Without some compelling reasons to support the idea of human superiority, the idea is simply "an irrational bias in our own favor," in conflict with the best evidence we have about how the world is.[33]

Unfortunately, this positive argument is weak. To be sure, Taylor does not claim to have offered any more than an informal argument, based on the idea that human superiority does not cohere with the biocentric outlook. But others have used similar biological evidence to claim that we should not think "there is anything morally . . . wrong with the human species dispossessing and causing the extinction of other species."[34] It is probably true that one would reject this view if one had a sense of "deep kinship" with other living things, but it is not at all clear that such an affective transformation will result from contemplating the first three theses of Taylor's biocentric outlook. It seems, then, that Taylor's negative arguments against anthropocentrism are strong, but his positive argument in favor of denying the inherent worth of humans is less compelling and tacitly presumes a psychological shift from aggression to kinship that might be beyond the scope of rational argument.

J. Baird Callicott has also argued extensively for an environmental ethic based on an ecological ideology of nature. Drawing upon Aldo Leopold, Callicott argues that we should understand the land as a community. For Callicott, as for Leopold, "it is the ecosystemic model of land which informs the cardinal practical precepts of the land ethic."[35] The highest good is the "complex structure of the land and its smooth functioning as an energy unit."[36] Understanding ourselves as members of the land community can draw us toward a respect for the community as such. Callicott thinks that the representation of the rest of nature as a community is the key to the *possibility* of an environmental ethic, while the *necessity* arises from our now enormous potential to destroy that community. The "twentieth-century discovery of a biotic community" shows the need for a new ethic, an "environmental ethic—founded perhaps upon love and respect, an expanded moral sentiment—[that] may be the only effective way to reestablish harmony between people and the biotic community as a whole, to which people belong."[37]

The concentration on the biotic community contrasts sharply with Taylor's focus on individual centers of life. Taylor's emphasis is on living things, such as animals and plants, which are particular centers of life, having uniqueness and individuality. For Taylor, this implies that we can have no direct duties to inanimate objects.[38] His ethic is, thus, "biocentric" instead of "ecocentric." Callicott, on the other hand, thinks that sometimes the good for individuals must be overridden by the community good.[39] The issue of holism and individualism has been the occasion for inflammatory rhetoric, with Tom Reagan, an animal rights theorist, claiming that holistic theories "might be fairly dubbed 'environmental fascism.'"[40]

Although Taylor's system seems to show that an environmental ethic does not *have* to adopt a holistic perspective, in fact Taylor's concentration on individual lives is problematic. Using the concept of "autopoiesis," coined by the biologists Humberto Maturana and Francisco Varela, Warwick Fox argues that Taylor's failure to adequately distinguish the living from the nonliving undermines the individualistic orientation of Taylor's ethic.[41] The language of cybernetics and systems theory, using notions of feedback, risks confusing living beings with complex machines, such as guided missiles, that also use feedback circuits to behave in goal-directed ways. According to Maturana and Varela, what distinguishes living from nonliving things is that living things strive to maintain their own structures; they are "autopoietic," or self-producing.[42] This is certainly a plausible way to distinguish life from nonliving systems. Autopoietic systems, for example, strive to heal themselves when subjected to outside perturbations, while machines do not. By maintaining their organization and structure, living things in practice take themselves as an end. Machines do not. Living systems are thus, in some significant sense, ends in themselves because they are ends for themselves. Of course, they may have other ends as well.

As Fox points out, this understanding of life is important for any environmental ethic concerned with distinguishing between the living and the nonliving. It implies that any system that strives to maintain its activity and structure should be understood as living. In particular, it suggests an understanding of living things that at least includes ecosystems, the ecosphere, species, and social systems.[43] Such a concept of life, based as it is on a plausible theoretical concept from biology, would require a major expansion toward holism in Taylor's biocentric outlook.

Callicott, on the other hand, advocates an ethic which is "holistic with a vengeance."[44] His holism derives from the way ecology informs an environmental ethic. As Callicott notes, "the ontological primacy of objects and the ontological subordination of relationships characteristic of classical Western science is, in fact, reversed in ecology. Ecological relationships determine the nature of organisms rather than the other way around."[45] This primacy of community implies that the principal obligation of a land ethic is to preserve the health of the community as a whole, which may involve subordinating the interests of some of its members.

The concept of autopoiesis suggests a solution to this problem. The difficulty is that any holistic philosophy, including Callicott's, might be taken as suggesting the total submersion of individuals to the larger system. Such a subordination of the individual invites the charge of fascism. Freya Matthews develops a monistic metaphysic based on Einstein's General Relativity theory. She argues persuasively that the criterion of autopoiesis can be used as a principle of individuation in such a system. Individuals are, then, those systems that maintain themselves through growth, repair, and reproduction. This amounts to a deep way to discern, define, and respect individuals within a holistic perspective.[46] The crux of such an argument lies in granting some sort of intrinsic value to systems that take themselves as an end.[47] Such a conception of the status of individuals within a larger holism is an effective counter to the charge of fascism against holistic theories.[48]

In the context of the discussion of deep ecology in the next chapter, the emphasis on relations rooted in ecology has fundamental import for understanding the self. Viewing relations as ontologically primary is a fertile insight that Callicott and other ecologically inspired philosophers have used to develop a relational concept of the self. If the self is understood as being a nest of relations, then there is no sharp line between self and other humans, nor between self and the rest of nature. From this perspective then, the world is not separate from self, but is a part of one's body.[49] Defense of the environment is then a form of self defense!

While it is true that the holism of some environmental ethics is a fundamental departure from modern philosophy,[50] practically speaking, the difference may not be as significant. Taylor, for example, does think we have obligations to preserve and extend wilderness, a conclusion that ecocentric theorists would enthusiastically endorse. The reason for the practical convergence is that Taylor understands that wilderness is the habitat of plants and animals, and that the preservation of wild animals requires the preservation of their habitat. For Taylor, because plants and animals are centers of life, we have a duty to let them be in their habitats, to share the earth with them, and to restore their habitats in compensation for our past injustice to them.[51]

There is one difference of practical significance between individualists and holists. If the bearers of value are only individuals, then harm to those individuals is clearly wrong. Those who are persuaded by theorists of animal liberation will find comfort in this. On the other hand, if value resides in the whole system, then individual members of species are of relatively lesser import, and there are situations, such as an excessive deer population endangering an ecosystem, when killing might be a "moral requirement."[52] This difference gives rise to arguments between radical environmentalists and animal rights advocates. Grounds for resolving this difference may be found in the distinction between domesticated and wild animals. Callicott argues that we have differing obligations to domesticated animals, arising from the history of domestication, that simply do not apply to animals and plants in the wild, whom we should just let be free.[53] It also seems possible to reconcile differences in the way animals in the wild should be treated—is hunting *ever* morally permissible?—by considering the health of ecosystems, either as directly valuable, or as habitats for future generations of as yet unborn individual wild animals. Ecological considerations should lead to a convergence in practice, if not in theory.

Callicott's critique of anthropocentrism is complex. He thinks all value is anthropogenic, but not anthropocentric. Even though there would be no value without human consciousness that does not mean that all values are homocentric. Just as we extend sympathy and moral concern to other humans, we may also extend moral concern to animals, species, and the land community. Callicott distinguishes between "intrinsic value," which he takes as value independent of all valuing consciousness, and "inherent value," which obtains when something is valued for itself, independently of any instrumental value that it may, or may not, have for a valuing consciousness.[54] Callicott denies that there is any intrinsic value because he thinks that there is *no* value that is not dependent on a human valuer. But if our moral sentiments can include other humans, which they obviously can, then they can also include the rest of nature, especially when it is understood as the biotic community within which we dwell. If one has such an understanding of nature, then natural entities may "own inherent value, that is, to be valued *for themselves*."[55]

While Callicott is clear that anthropocentrism is wrong, there is a tension between the confinement of value to humans and the rejection of anthropocentrism. Why reject anthropocentrism if *all* values are anthropogenic? I am not making the trivial point that, because a value (or idea or dream) originates with a human being, all values (or ideas or dreams) are human centered. Fox has dubbed this the "anthropocentric fallacy" because it fails to distinguish between the source of a value and its content.[56] Rather, the difficulty I am raising here focuses on the content of Callicott's land ethic. Callicott restricts the act of valuing something to the subjectivity of humans, yet he recommends that humans value the land for its own sake. This suggests that humans should somehow delude themselves into thinking that the land has value in itself, although, if they accept Callicott's analysis of the grounds of environmental ethics, this cannot be true.

Callicott's argument against anthropocentrism uses a problematic distinction. Although he wants an ethic that involves love and respect for the land community, he grounds such an ethic on prudential human-centered concerns. To reconcile the human genesis of all value with a valuation of the land for its own sake, Callicott distinguishes between the form of an ethic and the function of that ethic.[57] The *form* of the ethic he advocates is founded on an expansion of moral sentiment to include the biotic community, so that the ethic would issue directives involving "love, respect, and admiration for land."[58] From the "lived, felt point of view," people should have an "affective-cognitive posture of genuine love, respect, admiration, obligation, self-sacrifice, conscience, duty, and the ascription of intrinsic value and biotic rights."[59] The *function* of the ethic, however, would be to restrain humans from the destruction of the biotic communities to which they belong. This land ethic "may be the only effective way to reestablish harmony between people and the biotic community as a whole."[60] In other passages, Callicott claims that the land ethic is "necessary" because humans now have the power to destroy the integrity, diversity and stability of the rest of nature.[61] From "the outside, from the objective and analytic scientific point of view," a land ethic is "prudential."[62] Callicott recognizes that this position involves a "moral paradox" because the content of the ethic directs people to regard the land community as an end in itself, but the *reason* why they should do this is prudential, that is, for their own enlightened self-interest.

These differing ways of understanding an environmental ethic imply a morally objectionable social dualism. Those who know the real function of an environmental ethic will understand it as prudential, while those who are socialized into the ethic will regard the land with love and may be called upon to sacrifice their interests for the larger land community. Consider how this theoretical duality might be given social implementation. Someone developing a school curriculum for environmental education presumably understands the rational grounds for such education. If this person accepted Callicott's analysis, then this would mean that he or she thinks such education is necessary because humanity can no longer sustain its destruction of the biotic community. This, however, is not the content of what will be taught. Rather, the content will teach students that the biotic community should be loved for its own sake, that it has intrinsic value, and that this is a good reason for sacrificing one's interests in gratification. This duality is not entirely unnoticed by Callicott, as he quotes with approval Leopold's remark that "the path to social expediency is not discernible to the average individual."[63]

The problem is not whether there are grave practical difficulties in making complex problems widely understood in society. There surely are. It may be the case that environmental education must strive to evoke feelings about nonhuman nature, as well as cognitive understandings of humanity and the rest of nature. But to place such a dualism at the foundational level of an environmental ethic, when viewed from the perspective of the society it envisions, throws into question the whole morality of such an ethic. The dualism of a society, some of whose members know the "real" reasons for ethical rules while others are indoctrinated (the word "educated" does not truly apply), is so morally suspect as to cast doubt upon the theory which led to it.

I think the reason for this moral blind spot is Callicott's totalization of the scientific perspective. Callicott accepts reductive science as describing the reality of nonhuman nature. He sees value as "projected onto natural objects or events by the subjective feelings of observers. If all consciousness were annihilated at a stroke, there would be no good or evil, no beauty and ugliness, no right and wrong; only impassive phenomena would remain."[64] The image of "impassive phenomena," as all there really is without human consciousness, comes from an unwarranted totalization of the reductive scientific perspective. Unless such a perspective is totalized, there is no reason to think that the rest of nature would be meaningless without human consciousness. There certainly would remain much of the autopoietic activity in the land community if human consciousness were not around. If humanity is regarded as continuous with the rest of nature, then it is not extravagant to see the purposive actions of animals as embodying values. A world without humans would not be a world without value, though it would be lesser. To be sure, there would be no cognitive reflection on values and no ethical theories, no opera and no art. But there would be vastly more than only "impassive phenomena." There would still be most of the wonderful dance of life.

A puzzling note about this problem is that the position is put forward by Callicott and Leopold, who both clearly have a deep love and respect for the land. Callicott, in fact, reports his personal realization that his self was not restricted to his skin and bones, but extended outward to the Mississippi River. He also realized that the river's pollution was an injury to him. This injury was not to his personal interests, but to his person extending outward to the rest of nature.[65] The puzzle, then, is why Callicott and Leopold assume that others cannot come to such a realization without being subjected to an ethic that verges on being propagandistic.

Holmes Rolston has constructed a complex environmental ethic that defies summary, and none is attempted here. However, some of his claims about value and anthropocentrism are relevant to my argument here. He thinks Callicott's restriction of value to humans is too psychologistic. Rolston seeks a more "objective" ethic, finding value in the rest of nature. According to Rolston, Callicott refuses "to burn all humanistic bridges behind as [he] enters the wilderness of environmental ethics."[66] Rolston argues that there is, in fact, natural value *in* nonhuman nature—there to be "discovered."

Rolston approaches the question of anthropocentrism with a focus on complexity and differences within all of nature. Instead of starting, as Taylor does, from the need to recognize the similarities of humans and other forms of life, Rolston immediately involves his argument with differences as well. It is clear that there are differences between humans and others in nature, but what difference does this difference make? In the first place, Rolston notes, this is a question that only humans consider. Clearly there are significant differences between humans and other forms of life, and these differences can be understood as the result of evolution. Our capacities are well developed for the human niche, just as are the capacities of the lizard for its place. But this, according to Rolston, does not make a judgment of human superiority without foundation.[67] Rather, he argues, while each natural kind has its own integrity, only humans have personality. Even though there may be no sharp line between humans and other animals, "emergences are real."[68] One of these is the capacity to reflect critically and ethically. Given this capacity, "humans can take something more than an anthropocentric view," and this imposes duties upon us that transcend "human interests" and link us "with those of the whole natural Earth."[69] Even though Rolston conceives of humans as the "ecosystem's most sophisticated product," with the "highest per capita intrinsic value of any life form," this does not confine our moral concern to humans.[70] Our superiority carries with it responsibility, and, for Rolston, this responsibility spreads to animals, plants, trees, species, ecosystems, and nature as a whole. As we move beyond the anthropocentric view, we can find value in nonhuman nature.

It is not clear that Rolston's reservations about nonanthropocentrism are of major import. Taylor is interested in achieving a fundamental sense of biocentric equality, as a bulwark against the vicious anthropocentrism of contemporary culture. The same is true for Callicott. Neither would claim that there are not differences between humans and the rest of nature that require differences in treatment. Rolston wants to retain these differences within the discussion of anthropocentrism, while Taylor and Callicott would leave discussion of these differences until after the barrier of anthropocentrism has been crossed. Although they might come to diverse conclusions about the applications that follow from some nonanthropocentric ethic, they share the intention to include the rest of nature in ethical consideration. This is enough to morally indict industrialism.

Rolston's ethic also relies on an ecological ideology of nature. What is of value in nonhuman nature is discovered through judgments "coached by ecology." The evaluation is not ecological description, but rather a kind of metaecology.

> The injunction to maximize the ecosystemic excellence is ecologically derived but is an evaluative transition . . . [D]escription and evaluation to some extent arise together . . . Ecological description finds unity, harmony, interdependence, creativity, life support, conflict and complement in dialectic, stability, richness, community—and these are valuationally endorsed, yet they are found, to some extent, because we search with a disposition to value these things. We find in nature a mirror of what is in our minds. Still, the ecological description does not merely confirm these values; it informs them, and we find that the character, the empirical content, of order, harmony, stability, richness, community is drawn from no less than brought to nature. What is in our minds mirrors nature.[71]

This passage raises several problems, including the traditional difficulty of the relation between fact and value and the problematic metaphor of a "mirror" applied to minds in nature. I do not want here to discuss the fact/value problem, other than to note that we can no longer simply assume that facts are "out there" to be found and that values are "inside" our consciousness. Rather, we know that facts are created through the process of inquiry, and that any inquiry already embodies value. The very distinction between fact and value, assumed to make the charge of an illegitimate derivation of value from fact, is itself questionable. We now know that the world constructed through science is just that—constructed. It is not a mirror of the world.[72] And we can also be confident that the world is not a mirror of our minds.[73] In fact, one of the most promising approaches to the question of fact and value is to notice the structural similarity of scientific and ethical inquiry and to proceed from there to a reappraisal of the fact/value distinction.[74]

Using ecology to refocus our description of the world, Rolston offers a vision of a "projective nature," one that projects out all that is—stars, rocks, canyons, and seas. All life is but a piece of this projective nature.

> One cannot be impressed with life in isolation from its originating matrix. Nature is a fountain of life, and the whole fountain—not just the life that issues from it—is of value. Nature is genesis, Genesis.[75]

This image of the rest of nature as the source of all life grounds the most fundamental tenet of Rolston's complex ethic. "Before parents and the sacred, one is not so much looking to *resources* as to *sources*, seeking relationships in an elemental stream of being . . . The deepest task of an environmental ethics is this larger appreciation of nature . . . about our sources, beyond our resources."[76]

Although Rolston recognizes that his account of objective value in the world cannot be demonstrated beyond doubt to the subjectivist, no large perspective can be so demonstrated. He thinks his view can be given evidential weight by construing the experience of value as being in some way due to objective value in the rest of nature. If there is objective value in nonhuman nature, then one would predict that it would "stir up experience." Thus, the claim about objective value should be regarded as a hypothesis for which evidential warrant is given when we have experience of natural value. Without the hypothesis of objective value, Rolston thinks we would have to explain such experiences as simply being a product of subjective creativity. He admits that this is not a proof of the existence of objective values in nonhuman nature, but it is, he claims, "truer to world experience and more logically compelling."[77]

As it stands, this is a weak argument for a pivotal claim. For the *experience* of value in nonhuman nature to confirm the claim of the *existence* of natural value, one must survey the other possible sources of such an experience. If there are many possible sources that do not involve value's existence in nonhuman nature, and if some, at least, are credible on other grounds, then the evidential weight of such experiences for the hypothesis of value in nonhuman nature is thereby diminished. But clearly such experiences of value have many possible sources. For example, their source could be merely subjective, or have roots in social organization, or in education, or in taste, or in personal history. There is considerable evidence that our experience of facts are conditioned by our needs, our capacities, our emotions, our social conditions, and so on. So too with the experience of value. More generally, if we acknowledge the constructive aspect of all human experience, then it seems likely that value experience is also constructive. If we cannot so simply locate facts "in the world," why do we think we can do so for values "in the world"?

What seems clear from this brief account of three complex systems is that significant progress has been made in a short time toward unearthing the anthropocentric assumption and subjecting it to significant criticism. To be sure, there are disagreements and differences between these theorists, and some of these issues resist simple solution.[78] But beneath the disagreements, there is a certain unity of experience and thought that makes it clear that the anthropocentric assumption of human superiority cannot be given warrant. Given even a moderately informed understanding of evolution and biology, there are no rational grounds for anthropocentrism. Once life on earth is understood from an expansive ecological perspective, it becomes apparent that we are just one species among many. We are not, therefore, entitled to murder the rest of life in our pursuit of our own misconceived welfare, through the project of industrialism. Finding a positive grounding of a nonanthropocentric ethic has, however, proved more elusive.

These ethical theorists have not given much attention to social and political issues. Callicott suggests that environmental ethics is an addition to the ethics of human communities, not a replacement. He grants moral priority to interhuman obligations, but notes that the land ethic may also influence the ethics of human communities.[79] Callicott's social program, such as it is, amounts to an advocacy of environmental education in a Leopoldian vein.[80] Rolston discusses environmental ethics as it applies to business but does not do so on the basis of any analysis of economies or social dynamics. In effect, he offers a list of recommendations that he thinks businesses should follow, giving no attention to the economic systems within which they operate and that structure the behavior of business firms. In short, he never considers the structure of capitalistic economies that would make it difficult for any individual firm to adopt his moral maxims. He even seems to endorse bigness in business firms, without attending to their track record.[81] I do not mean to harshly criticize these pioneers in environmental ethics for not focusing on social issues, for their field is young and their concerns have been elsewhere. They are not alone, as theorists in the nature tradition often fail to address social issues. What I do want to stress is that the concern for the rest of nature has not forced them to consider social and economic systems, nor has it led them to advocate any significant platform for social change. This is a fateful omission, however, for by ignoring the role of social organization, they miss too much of our situation. The changes that are needed must arise within society, and they must change society. It is time to consider "deep ecology," which explicitly goes beyond ethical theory and advocates fundamental social change.

9 *Beyond Ethics to Deep Ecology*

Although the critique of anthropocentrism has established it as an unwarranted prejudice, no particular environmental ethic has yet attained wide assent from environmental philosophers, mush less among moral philosophers in general or society at large. It may be that achieving broad agreement on some nonanthropocentric ethic will only be possible after industrial society has undergone a metamorphosis.

One reason for this rests on the methodology of contemporary ethical theory. Typically ethical theories, once they pass muster as being internally consistent, are elaborated in order to compare their prescriptions with current social practices. The evidence for ethical theory is usually only the theorists intuitions about what is right and wrong. To the extent that these intuitive ideas are inconsistent, ethical theories can be useful in illuminating them and spurring reflective revision. But radical divergences between a proposed theory and typical social practice are usually taken as grounds for rejecting the theory, instead of as grounds for changing social practice. Ethical theory is thus methodologically confined to developing and explicating currently dominant conceptions of what is moral and immoral. Ethical theory of this sort simply does not have a strong enough fulcrum point to leverage a fundamental critique of actions widely regarded as legitimate.

The social dependency of ethical theory is a serious problem for any attempt to develop a nonanthropocentric environmental ethic. If the issues posed by ecological crises go to the very roots of industrial society, then it is unlikely that any ethical theory that is grounded in reflection on current social practice will penetrate deeply enough, as it remains too closely tied to such practices and the intuitions that come with them. Thus, the possibility of grounding ethical argument for any radical transformation of humanity's relations with the rest of nature requires going far beyond ordinary ethical discourse.[1]

This limitation of ethical theory explains why the negative philosophical arguments about anthropocentrism are well grounded while the positive ones are not. Given our current values about universality, impartiality, and fairness, there seems to be little reason that moral concern, in some form or other, should not be extended to at least some of the rest of nature. An inclusive ecological ideology of nature would help move us toward an adequate environmental ethic. The more the rest of nature appears to be like us—alive with striving and suffering—the more persuasive such an extension of moral concern will be. Anthropocentrism would then be seen more clearly as an illegitimate bias in favor of humans. But this negative argument only shows that the emperor has no clothes; this is no mean feat in itself, but it is essentially incomplete.

A positive nonanthropocentric ethic would involve a detailed description of the naked emperor. It would provide ways to decide if and when jobs for humans can rightfully be compared to the survival of forests, or if and when research into human disease justifies experimentation on nonhuman animals. These and many other such issues are contentious and difficult questions that will require much further discussion. As long as we assume that we are fundamentally different from the rest of nature, then we would seem to be left only with the possibility of raising a claim that there is some sort of intrinsic value in nonhuman nature as a restraint on humanity's actions. However, if we accept that we are part of nature, that we are submerged within the unfolding of life, then the need for the theoretical construct of 'intrinsic value' diminishes. Such a sense of "who we are" requires going beyond ethical discourse toward a consideration of the fundamental concepts of self and nature.[2]

Any truly fundamental critique of humanity's relation to nonhuman nature faces a dilemma. Either it must compromise its position and couch critique in appeals to principles and concepts that already have common currency, or it can be uncompromising in expression and theory, but remain idiosyncratic. A radical critique that questions society's basic belief system and also wishes to gain assent from the members of that society must confront the fact that any appeal to "common sense" or intuitions will not go deeply enough because our common sense is part of the problem. Janna Thompson clearly states this dilemma:

> To deserve the name of an ethic, a position on values must be persuasive. Either a new normative ethic of the environment will rest its appeal on

> the principles, values or ideas about their own interests that people already accept, or it will not. If it does not depart from these accepted views then it will fail to provide an adequate case for the preservation of wilderness and species. But if it does depart from traditional axioms, ways of arguing or ideas about interests, then it won't be persuasive. So traditional appeals and ways of arguing won't do and new ways seem to be ruled out.[3]

Is there any basis for a nonanthropocentric ethic that can be both reasonable and socially effective within the thoroughly anthropocentric atmosphere of industrialism? It may be that seeking reasonable arguments and solutions is a subtle reinforcement of the very style of rationality that is one root of our current situation. Neil Evernden might be right when he cautions against asking for solutions, for then the world congeals into the categories of problem and solution. If we were to abandon the framework that separates humans from the rest of nature and casts them into the role of "controllers," while the rest of the world is cast into the role of the "controlled," with what would we be left? Evernden suggests that all we can do right now is to stop and wonder, for only then can something truly new arise.

> For us wonder is a harbinger of hope, since it reminds us of our ability to suspend belief. If we were to do so, and if the new story we subsequently elaborated no longer casts us in the role of global locust, then our essence would no longer be environmental crisis. But there is no way to deliberately elaborate a new story—it is not a conscious exercise, not something susceptible of reasoned solution. One can only pull back and see what emerges to fill the void. If we wonder, what shall we believe when we emerge from reverie? That is something each of us must explore alone, before there can even emerge a vocabulary adequate to the elaboration of a new 'way the world is.'[4]

Perhaps he is right. Yet the gravity of our situation does, I think, charge us to explore the terrain of new social possibilities. Although I do not know if it is possible to question industrialism with practical effect, I am sure that the grounds for such a critique cannot be found in the waters of ordinary ethical theory, confined as it is to explicating our own ethical views. Such waters are already too contaminated.

The core hypothesis of this book is that industrialism is the hub of a set of social practices that are destructive to the rest of nature. Expansionary industrialism, in both its variants of capitalism and socialism, requires the destruction of species and ecosystems, and it now threatens the whole biosphere.[5] It encourages each of us to engage in the subtly frustrating pursuit of happiness through the consumption of the rest of nature. What is required is a perspective that takes industrialism itself as part of the problem and inspires efforts at its transformation. The development of any nonanthropocentric ethic must be part of a much larger project of radical social change. General acceptance of such an ethic requires a new society in which the experience of being related to environments that are not constructed by humans is part of everyday life. As Anthony Weston observes, "the usual categories presuppose a vision of the 'world' that is ratified below the level of consciousness by the omnipresence of noise, trash on the beaches and jet trails in the sunset, the bodies of animals available for consumption at every turn."[6] To change this daily experience of an anthropocentrized world requires creating a new society. We must create a butterfly out of the caterpillar of industrialism.

Deep Ecology

Deep ecology is, I think, one perspective that beckons in the right direction. In just two decades, "deep ecology," as a theory, has moved from a proposal in a philosophical journal put forward by Arne Naess, a Norwegian philosopher, to a position that is now a bench mark in defining varieties of environmental philosophies.[7] Over the course of its relatively short life, it has been subjected to a barrage of epithets and misunderstandings from numerous quarters, having been accused, among others, of being "self-righteous," "arrogant," "antirational," "mystical," "rubbish," and "an ideological toxic dump."[8] Clearly deep ecology has become important enough so that some people want to stamp it out.

Despite the intensity of the rhetorical wars surrounding deep ecology, most of the controversy has been misdirected. To understand why this is so, the logic of the deep ecology position must be explained because it differs in form from many other philosophical positions. Failure to appreciate this difference has led to criticisms that wholly miss the most important aspect of deep ecology.

The heart of deep ecology is its platform, which consists of a number of interrelated factual and normative claims about humans and their relations with the rest of nature. The platform has been articulated as a description of a social movement that takes "deep ecology" as its name. This platform forms the basis for a larger unity among all those who accept the importance of nonanthropocentrism and who understand that this entails radical social change.

The platform was formulated by Arne Naess and George Sessions while they were camping in Death Valley in 1984. These principles are stated "in a literal, somewhat neutral way," in the hopes that they will be "understood and accepted by persons coming from different philosophical and religious positions."[9] It is a popular and *not* a philosophically precise statement of principles around which, it is hoped, people with differing ultimate understandings of themselves, society, and nonhuman nature, might unite.

The platform itself consists of eight basic principles:

1. The well-being and flourishing of human and nonhuman Life on Earth have value in themselves (synonyms: intrinsic value, inherent value). These values are independent of the usefulness of the nonhuman world for human purposes.
2. Richness and diversity of life forms contribute to the realization of these values and are also values in themselves.
3. Humans have no right to reduce this richness and diversity except to satisfy vital needs.
4. The flourishing of human life and cultures is compatible with a substantial decrease in human population. The flourishing of nonhuman life requires such a decrease.
5. Present human interference with the nonhuman world is excessive, and the situation is rapidly worsening.
6. Policies must therefore be changed. These policies affect basic economic, technological, and ideological structures. The resulting state of affairs will be deeply different from the present.
7. The ideological change is mainly that of appreciating *life quality* (dwelling in situations of inherent value) rather than adhering to an

increasingly higher standard of living. There will be a profound awareness of the difference between big and great.
8. Those who subscribe to the foregoing points have an obligation directly or indirectly to try to implement the necessary changes.[10]

These principles are neither "ultimate" nor "basic" in a logical sense. That is, they are not intended to suggest that no further justification, by appeal to more abstract principles, is required or allowed. Rather, they are basic in being the most general views that all supporters of deep ecology hold in common.[11] There is no expectation that all would agree on some set of more abstract principles that could be used to justify the platform. In fact, disagreement on such logically ultimate principles is to be expected.[12]

From a historical perspective, the platform, because it was first articulated by Naess and Sessions, two founders of the deep ecology movement, is unique to deep ecology. However, were it to become grounds for widespread unity within a radical ecocentric movement directed toward creating a nonanthropocentric society, it might no longer be called a specifically "deep ecology" position. It could become a basis for a program of what Eckersley calls an "ecocentric" green political movement, a movement that would encompass many who might not identify themselves as "deep ecologists."[13] Thus, while it is now a "deep ecology" platform, should it achieve its intended end, it might no longer be identified as such.

If one seeks a justification for the deep ecology platform, then discussion might proceed to more fundamental principles characteristically espoused by some deep ecologists. But other justifications might arrive at ultimate principles of some other ecocentric perspective, such as ecological feminism or a variant of social ecology. There is not just one possible justification for the platform.

Alternatively, knowing what follows from adopting the platform involves elaborating the platform in the direction of greater specificity. Such elaborations ultimately lead to questions bound to the context of particular actions at specific times and places.

The essential point is that there are three relatively independent dimensions to what is now called "deep ecology."

Fundamental Justifications. There are various fundamental justifications—experiential, philosophical, aesthetic, religious, etc. They might be mutually incompatible.

Deep Ecology Platform. There are eight defining principles of the deep ecology movement. Various formulations and emphases are possible, but mutual compatibility is necessary.

Consequences of More or Less Generality. Elaborations of the principles will vary in terms of generality and context. They could range from a general party platform to specific claims about actions regarding old growth forests in the northwest of the United States or rainforests in Tasmania. They are dependent on social and historical context.

The platform is the heart of deep ecology, and it is the platform, not the various justifications for it, that should be the focus of argument about the value of deep ecology.[14]

The development of a radical ecology movement must start its collective discussion somewhere, and the deep ecology platform is a good beginning. People may come to adopt this platform from quite diverse directions and for different reasons. Those who start from the social tradition and come to believe that ecological concerns must be taken very seriously may come to the deep ecology position by understanding the ecological inadequacy of traditional social ideologies. This is the course traversed in this book. On the other hand, those who start within the nature tradition are likely to arrive at the deep ecology platform more directly by reflecting on what follows from a rejection of anthropocentrism and a recognition of the worth and the flourishing of *all* of nature.

Even the *kinds* of reasons that might persuade a person to adopt a version of the platform may range from rational to nonrational to irrational. For example, acceptance might be based on philosophical reflection, religious conviction, personal experience, intuition, mystical experience, aesthetic perception, or some other basis. Allowing for a variety of paths to the same position *is precisely* the intent of the deep ecology platform. It is not intended to be, nor is it, a systematic philosophical position; it proposes a common ground for defining an ecocentric movement for radical social change. Even the particular formulation of the platform is not intended to be final nor the only acceptable expression.[15] The point of these principles is to define the deep ecology movement, create clarity within the movement, and make clear where real disagreement might exist.[16]

When the logic of deep ecology is understood this way, much of the controversy surrounding it can be seen as irrelevant. Argument directed against one, some, or all of the eight "basic principles" is of great importance, but criticism directed to one of the underlying philosophical positions used to justify the deep ecology platform is far less relevant. Clearly, one could reject a particular philosophical or religious justification of the platform, yet still believe that the platform is correct at this point in history. I think it has been the failure to appreciate this aspect of the logic of the deep ecology position that has led to much heated but fruitless controversy. This is not to say that the views expressed in the platform do not call for justification. Surely they do. My point is simply that the alleged failure of any one justification need not lead to a rejection of the deep ecology platform.

This emphasis on the deep ecology platform is a particular reading of the deep ecology literature, not simple reportage.[17] This reading views the need for an expanded social movement aimed at replacing industrialism as the most urgent need of the moment. Thus, the focus on the platform is intended to find the basis for unity among those who may disagree on more philosophically ultimate issues.

There are some disadvantages to this approach to deep ecology. First, it does not make clear what is distinctive in the writings of deep ecologists. Warwick Fox claims that the eight-point platform should be thought of as characterizing an "ecocentric" ecology movement, rather than a specifically deep, or "transpersonal" ecology platform, to use Fox's terminology.[18] Ecocentric philosophies are those that take life or, more inclusively, life and its habitats as central.[19] Fox's point is that while all participants in an ecocentric movement would agree with the platform, many would not agree with the specific ways in which deep ecologists justify the platform. It is the appeal to specific "deeper" principles, Fox argues, that distinguishes deep ecology from other ecologically oriented philosophies.

The intention of the platform is to find a more expansive and inviting common territory than is likely to be discovered in the more rarified atmosphere of ultimate philosophical justification. A reading of deep ecology that takes the platform as central implies that a future general acceptance of the platform would make the label "deep ecology" more aptly apply to certain justifications of the platform than to the platform itself. Anticipating this hopeful prospect, I shall refer to the platform as the radical ecocentric platform when the context implies this hope for wider unity in the future.

But the platform is more than a statement of an ecocentric philosophy. It asserts that accepting the platform involves acting to change economic, technological, and ideological structures. This involves working in some form or other for social and political change. Radical ecocentrism includes both an ecocentric understanding *and* a commitment to foster radical social transformation. This requires much fuller consideration of social and political questions by ecocentric philosophers within the nature tradition. In fact, explicit consideration of social theory is rare among ecocentric philosophers. Paul Taylor, for example, calls for an "*inner* change in our moral beliefs and commitments" as "the first, indispensable step" in developing a "harmony between human civilization and nature."[20] While I commend Taylor for his willingness to move beyond the detached language of academic philosophy toward moral advocacy, he never addresses the critical question of how such an "inner" change in moral belief and commitment happens. When Taylor claims that "inner" change is an "indispensable step" prior to social and political activity, he assumes, without argument, that morality has some strategic or causal priority over politics. This assumption is dubious. Attention to the dynamics of social change would reveal that there is a dialectical relation between morality and politics, with each assuming priority in differing historical circumstances. Sometimes moral discourse may be most important, but sometimes social and political work is most important. Usually both sorts of activity are important. This exemplifies a typical weakness of the nature tradition in not attending to the dynamics of social change. The deep ecology platform, on the other hand, explicitly calls for economic, technological, and ideological change. Acceptance of the platform would shift the focus of much contemporary ecocentric philosophy toward questions of social change.

Focusing on the platform also invites the charge that deep ecology is overly eclectic. Thus, on what grounds can a thinker be included or excluded as a deep ecologist? How can one include such divergent thinkers as Heidegger and Leopold under the same banner?[21] Deep ecology, understood as a specific mode of justifying radical ecocentrism, will find such questions difficult. But when deep ecology is understood as having three distinct dimensions—a variety of justifications, a unified platform, and context-bound analyses of what follows from the program—the difficulty disappears. There may consistently be both Heideggerean and a Leopoldian justifications leading to the same platform.

Without such an understanding of deep ecology, attempts to justify the platform tend to create needless schisms. For example, the most exhaustive attempt to define what is distinctive about deep ecology is Warwick Fox's *Toward A Transpersonal Ecology*. He focuses on the nature of the self and explains deep ecology as involving an identification of self with all that is. But his specification of deep ecology, unless it is understood as one among many alternative justifications for the platform, creates unneeded friction. It leaves out others who accept the platform, but do not agree with Fox's notion of identification. Richard Sylvan and Jim Cheney, for example, both accept the platform, but are critics of Fox's version of deep ecology.[22] Which is more important, finding differences or realizing unity?

If deep ecology is understood primarily as the attempt to spark profound social change, then the question of who is and who is not a radical ecocentrist can be settled easily by referring to the platform. Disputes over possible justifications are important to the extent that they lead to differences over the platform. Several paths lead to the same place. This issue of how deep ecology should be understood is important only because there has been such intense and unproductive rhetorical wars between people who are on the same side. As Oelschlaeger puts it, "doctrinal purity serves only dogmatists."[23] Our urgent task is social change.

The Platform

What, then, do the eight points of the platform mean?

> *The well-being and flourishing of human and nonhuman Life on Earth have value in themselves (synonyms: intrinsic value, inherent value). These values are independent of the usefulness of the nonhuman world for human purposes.*

Essentially, this is a denial of anthropocentrism. It is an assertion that human *and* nonhuman life should flourish. "Life," in this context, is understood broadly to include, for example, rivers, landscapes, and ecosystems. The unreasonableness of anthropocentrism was discussed in the previous chapter, and I shall not belabor the point here. Let me just note that accepting the idea that humans are not the only valuable part of nature is the watershed perception from which a radical and ecocentric environmentalism flows.

This plank should not be taken as implying a commitment to any philosophically precise theory about intrinsic or inherent value. There are several reasons for this. One is that when deep ecologists use the language of moral discourse they are not primarily trying to construct a formal ethical theory. If one wishes to speak outside the academy, one must use language that communicates in popular contexts. That language right now uses concepts of intrinsic or inherent value and rights. A careful interpretation of deep ecology requires attention to the context within which references are made to the language of traditional ethics. To take Devall and Sessions literally, when they ascribe an "equal right" to all things and claim that all things are "equal in intrinsic worth" is to interpret them out of context.[24] In the passage in which those phrases appear, they are writing with the intent of having practical effect within the environmental movement. They are not writing with philosophical precision, and for them to do so would counter their main purpose.[25] Naess, Devall and Sessions, and Fox each explicitly deny that they are intending any philosophically precise ethical theory by the claim that nonhuman life on earth has value in itself.[26] Rather, they are using popular language to deny anthropocentrism.

The search for some sort of value in nonhuman nature, be it inherent, intrinsic, or some other sort of nonanthropocentric value seems necessary because we cannot now fully imagine an adequate environmental ethic. Such values are supposed to constrain the behavior of humans from doing what they otherwise would do. But why be concerned about whether or not there really is some sort of value in the rest of nature? As Fox points out, many ethical theorists implicitly assume that we would care about nonhuman nature "for itself" only if it has intrinsic value.[27] This is the assumption that motivates the search for the elusive intrinsic value. But this assumption may be wrong and overly constraining in the search for an environmental ethic.[28] Simply put, we *can* care for the rest of nature for reasons that have nothing to do with whether or not it has intrinsic, inherent, or any other sort of value. Such a caring can spring, for example, from a sense of being related to the rest of nature. "Thou shalt not destroy the biosphere," is as silly as "don't burn your hand," once one *feels* embedded within the rest of nature.

> *Richness and diversity of life forms contribute to the realization of these values and are also values in themselves.*

This, along with the first principle, is intended to counter the often held image of evolution as resulting in "higher" forms of life. It involves a revisioning of life and evolution and a change from understanding evolution as meaning "progress" from "lower" to "higher" forms to an understanding that sees evolution as an expression of multiple and wondrous forms of life.

Instead of scaling nature as a hierarchy of beings from bottom to top, the idea of diversity lauds difference and rejects any single standard of excellence. The widespread alarm over the extinction of many species indicates that most people do value, to some extent and for a variety of reasons, diversity in the rest of nature.

Denying the value of diversity requires some single standard of excellence. If there were such a measure, then all forms of existence, human as well as nonhuman, could be appraised according to the degree to which they manifest that excellence. Humans and other beings could then be ordered in one vast "chain of being."[29] But what single standard can one imagine that all humanity, much less the rest of nature, should exhibit?

The difference, both in concept and attitude, between seeking a single standard of excellence or valuing diversity is fundamental. Thinking in terms of some single standard of excellence is basic to much of the history of Western philosophy. One need only recall that Aristotle thought that there was one human essence, rationality, that created a standard by which human activity could be assessed. As Arthur Lovejoy points out, as late as the eighteenth century an integral part of the Enlightenment project was the belief that there was a single and universal standard of excellence, an ideal to which all should aspire. One monumental achievement of Romanticism was a reversal of this belief in a single standard, leading to the idea that not only are there "diverse excellences," but that "diversity itself is of the essence of excellence."[30] Dethroning the image of one universal ideal spawned a vast and enlivening spectrum of aesthetic expression and is now a cultural basis for resisting the trends toward uniformity in the modern world. True it is, as Lovejoy notes, that celebrating diversity does not free one from the problem of standards. "To say 'Yes' to everything" means having no character nor way of knowing how to act, for the art of living involves knowing "when to tolerate, when to embrace, and when to fight."[31] But standards in the plural encourage diversity to flourish in a way not possible when human life is forced onto the Procrustean bed of a single ideal of excellence.

The deep ecology platform emphasizes the value of diversity in both human activity and the rest of nature. Diversity is valued in the way one deals with other points of view, as well as in efforts to protect the diversity of human cultures threatened by industrial expansion and the rest of nature. This respect for difference is particularly apparent in the writings of Arne Naess. As Fox points out, Naess typically presents his views in such a way as to "*invite* the reader's interest rather than in a manner that demands the reader's *compliance*."[32] Bill Devall argues that "in intellectual discussions, a slogan for the deep ecology movement could be 'let us listen together' rather than the more common 'let us argue against each other.'"[33] Respect for all life involves respect for those with whom one disagrees.

Valuing human diversity means leaving areas of the earth free from domination by industrial economy and culture. One should remember that the very idea of wilderness is essentially an outsider's construct. Most of what seems to us to be wilderness has been steadily occupied or traversed by indigenous peoples for eons. Preserving such areas from the sphere of industrialism not only protects wilderness, but it also preserves the cultures of indigenous peoples. Thus, the struggle to protect wilderness is for the sake of both biological diversity and human diversity.

Humans have no right to reduce this richness and diversity except to satisfy vital needs.

The key point in this claim is the implied distinction between "vital" and other needs. This distinction is denied by the consumerism inherent in industrialism. To lose sight of it is to become trapped within an endlessly repeating cycle of deprivation and temporary satiation. Making the distinction opens the possibility of achieving more enduring forms of happiness and joy. Of course, the distinction cannot be drawn precisely because what is a vital need in one context may be a trivial want in another. There is a real difference between an Eskimo wearing the skin of a seal and wearing a fur coat for social status in an affluent society.

> *The flourishing of human life and cultures is compatible with a substantial decrease in human population. The flourishing of nonhuman life requires such a decrease.*

Once recognition is given to other forms of life, then it is clear that we humans are too many already. We have already jostled many species out of existence and the near future promises more of such extinctions. The continuing increase in human numbers also condemns many humans to a life of suffering. Parents within industrial societies easily recognize that having many children means slimmer life prospects for each. Consequently, many families limit themselves to fewer children, hoping thereby to give each a better life. So too we should collectively recognize that an increase in human numbers is not even in the best interest of humans, much less the rest of life.

It is to the credit of the deep ecology movement that it clearly gives priority to human population as a problem and calls for a gradual decrease.[34] There is nothing inherent in this issue that implies misanthropy or cruelty toward presently existing humans. In fact, there is considerable evidence indicating that the best way to moderate and then reverse the growth of human population is to find ways of providing a decent life for all.[35]

> *Present human interference with the nonhuman world is excessive, and the situation is rapidly worsening.*

This directs attention to current trends and claims that current levels of "interference" with the rest of nature are excessive. There are at least two sorts of such interference that need to be addressed. One sort of interference is the destruction of existing areas of wilderness, such as old-growth forests and rain forests. Such destruction is not only irreparable within any moderate time scale, but it is also wrong. In fact, the guiding principle should probably be the continuation of biological history, creating large enough wilderness areas to allow for the ongoing speciation of plants and animals. This does not mean the elimination of indigenous peoples who have found ways of living within those ecosystems without destroying them.[36]

The other form of human interference is based on particular forms of technology. Many forms of interaction with the rest of nature disrupt natural cycles far more than is necessary. For example, agricultural practices involving large scale monocropping create expanding needs for fertilizer and pesticides as crops diminish fertility and "pests" develop immunity to previously used pesticides. Such practices interfere with ecosystems more than is necessary. Multicropping, integrated pest management, and a variety of organic farming techniques interfere less with natural cycles and can enhance the fertility of soils.

Noting differences of degree in interference among various forms of technology also points to an important dimension of the population problem. Although most population growth is now projected to take place in the lesser developed countries, the populations in industrial countries have a far greater impact per person on the biosphere. The poor of less developed countries who scour hillsides for wood to cook their food certainly create serious problems, such as an increase in flooding and deforestation. But the automobiles driven by industrial peoples generate large quantities of carbon dioxide each year. In thinking about such problems, it is essential to remember that industrial patterns of life impact the biosphere much more profoundly than do those of the world's poor.

> *Policies must therefore be changed. These policies affect basic economic, technological, and ideological structures. The resulting state of affairs will be deeply different from the present.*

The scope of the changes needed is great, but significant work to create adequate models for change is underway. Although the concept remains somewhat obscure, "sustainability" is becoming a slogan in thinking about how economies should be restructured, even among those who remain within an anthropocentric perspective.[37] Taking sustainability as the criterion by which economies should be appraised is a fundamental shift away from the mindless quest for growth. As thinking along these lines develops, there may be a growing recognition that sustainability requires a decline in the human population. Rethinking economy in terms of its role in sustaining human communities leads away from industrialism toward more satisfying ways of life.[38] The interconnectedness of economies, technologies, and ideologies makes the problem large, but the very same interconnectedness implies that real change in any of these areas may facilitate change in the others.

> *The ideological change is mainly that of appreciating* life quality *(dwelling in situations of inherent value) rather than adhering to an increasingly higher standard of living. There will be a profound awareness of the difference between big and great.*

This point is especially important for industrial peoples who are enmeshed in an ultimately unsatisfying consumerism. By focusing on quality, people can see that existing patterns of labor and consumption are chronically unsatisfying. Moving toward an appreciation of the *quality* of life, instead of quantities of things, leads to an increase in happiness, not a decrease. This is quite fundamental because people are more apt to change when they experience change as improvement, rather than as a grudging submission to necessity. As long as environmentalism seems to require only denial and sacrifice, its political effectiveness will be limited. Emphasis needs to be placed on the fact that the changes sought are intended to increase the quality of life. Radical ecocentrism implies a more satisfactory way of living, an increase in vitality and joy.

> Unable to envisage any alternatives to the aims of industrial society . . . the basic presupposition at the root of the whole ecocrisis is allowed to stand unquestioned, namely, that the means to achieve human well-being lies in increased production and consumption.[39]

Even though industrialism does bring a flood of things to even the less affluent, it does not create the conditions for real human well-being.

> *Those who subscribe to the foregoing points have an obligation directly or indirectly to try to implement the necessary changes.*

Although this is clear in claiming that we must begin to act now, it is vague in not indicating particular priorities. At this point in history, priorities cannot be made more specific. No one now knows exactly what positive changes are necessary. The problems with economic growth and the emptiness of consumerism are clear enough, but they do not show precisely what needs to be done now. People who accept the deep ecology platform will continue to disagree about what is most urgent now, and there are many ways to attempt the needed changes. In light of the value of diversity, such differences should be respected and not become occasions for sectarian squabbles.

The platform, then, is a proposal for a set of general agreements among radical ecocentrists, a common ground for those who value all nature. Deep ecologists have, I think, done a valuable service in bringing such a platform to the fore. As noted above, most of the controversy about deep ecology has been over the various paths that have been used to justify the platform. Efforts to show someone "wrong," despite an underlying agreement about the platform, are of secondary importance. However, there are some debates that do have practical import. In the next chapter, I shall consider some of the disagreements that imply differences in direction for the unfolding of radical ecocentrism.

Justifications for the Platform

Having made a plea to avoid controversy over fundamentals, perhaps I should not discuss the variety of justifications that have been offered for the deep ecology platform. However, an outline of some of the justifications of the platform may dispel the suspicion that deep ecology is somehow irrational, mystical, or just unreasonable.

Several paths lead to the platform. One path appeals to prudence and epistemology. This justification involves noting the enormous risks to both human and nonhuman life entailed by industrialism. Because prudence requires a higher degree of certainty when risks are high, we need a high level of confidence that the project of industrialism can be effectively carried out. Because the knowledge required for such certainty is not available, some fundamentally new approach is necessary. Such an argument would make plausible, though not entail, something like the deep ecology platform.[40] This book is a sketch of one argument along these lines. I have offered an ecological critique of existing social forms and argued that the control of nonhuman nature is ultimately impossible. Additionally, I have claimed that it is a mistake to accept industrialism's increasing necessity for such control. An ecological ideology of nature makes reasonable relations with the rest of nature that are nondominating. An ecological ideology indicates that humans are similar in kind to other parts of nature and that the rest of nature is worthy of respect. Life itself is an unfolding out of the matrix of existence.

While an inclusive ecological ideology of nature may be important, it is not in itself sufficient to justify the deep ecology platform. Because such an ideology of nature includes humans within its domain, what "I am" is internally related to the rest of what is. Previously, we looked at the model of a conversation to clarify the notion of internal relations. This model helps us to understand that who I am and what I think I am are connected *essentially* to the rest of society and the rest of nature. It happens that I live in a culture and a time in which the social myths include a story about what "I" am, a tale which says that I am separate from everybody and everything else. This story is part of the cultural "conversation" within which I exist. But we also know that the rest of nature is also a party to our conversation, and we are internally related both to our culture and to nonhuman nature. Lately the rest of nature is becoming more outspoken in the conversations which we are. If culture is a less fundamental determinant of existence than the rest of nature, then the story of separateness is less fundamental than that of connectedness.

An inclusive ecological ideology will not, by itself, tell me which attitudes I should cultivate and which I should neglect. For that, more is needed because divergent value implications can coexist with a shared ecological ideology of nature. One might look at ecosystems, notice the different functions of various parts, agree that humanity is within nature, and yet draw conclusions about the "natural" basis of inequality.[41] On the other hand, one might notice the essential interrelatedness of all parts of an ecosystem and conclude that anthropocentrism is simply an unreasonable and unfounded bias in favor of human beings. This could motivate a reflection on values and lead to some version of the deep ecology platform. Ultimately, we all must choose what we shall stand up for.

Warwick Fox provides another way of justifying the platform. He argues that what distinguishes deep ecology from other ecocentric philosophies is its focus on the expansion of one's sense of self through the process of identification. This approach involves an analysis of the self's true nature as being fieldlike, rather than atomistic.[42] Such a view of the self allows an expansive identification with the rest of nature. Fox distinguishes three ways in which one might realize this expansion of self: personal, ontological, and cosmological.[43] Because he thinks that the personal is limited to the actual contacts people happen to have and that the ontological requires lengthy and rigorous spiritual discipline, Fox believes that the cosmological basis is most accessible for modern people. This involves experiencing "ourselves and all other presently existing entities as leaves on . . . a tree that . . . has been growing for some fifteen billion years, becoming infinitely larger and infinitely more differentiated in the process." Fox continues:

> A deep-seated realization of this cosmologically based sense of commonality with all that is leads us to identify ourselves more and more with the entire tree rather than with just our leaf (our personal, biographical self), the leaves on our twig (our family) . . . our community . . . our culture . . . the leaves on our branch (our species) . . . At the limit [there could be] . . . impartial identification with *all* particulars.[44]

Such a cosmological identification leads easily to a justification for the radical ecocentric platform. It incorporates the best story we have of the nature of the universe, and it makes obvious the bias of anthropocentrism.[45] While personal forms of identification begin with the experiences of identification with other individuals and particular places and move outward toward the rest of nature, cosmological forms of identification begin with a sense of the commonality of all existence and move inward towards an individual's identification with particular people and places. Cosmological identification might be thought of as an "outside-in" process, in contrast to the "inside-out" process of personal identification. Such an outside-in process of identification offers a fundamental reversal to the "me" or "us first" culture of industrialism.

It is worth stressing again that there are many possible justifications for the platform. Richard Sylvan is correct in claiming that the sort of consciousness advocated by Fox is neither necessary nor sufficient for someone to support the radical environmental platform.[46] However, this does not mean that such cosmological consciousness might not lead to acceptance of the platform, for some at least, and that is what is important. Even though Fox and Sylvan have engaged in heated polemics, they have each made valuable contributions to the development of radical ecocentrism. Fox's analysis of identification is valuable in showing one possible way that people might come to adopt the platform. Sylvan, on the other hand, has done some of the best thinking about the social directions for radical ecocentrism.[47]

Another sort of justification for the platform, involving the kind of identification that Fox calls "ontological," comes from an unusually profound appreciation and wonder for all of existence. This is a "mystical" path, not because it is strange or irrational, but because it insists upon the inadequacy of words and the centrality of the actual experience of nondualistic living. Buddhism is one ontological approach that seeks to develop such a consciousness through the practice of meditation. The intention in Buddhism is to experience existence before it is conceptualized. Conceptualizations are, it is claimed, subtle forms of attachment that blind one to the essential nature of reality. There is not much to be said about such a reality, since even naming it is itself a subtle falsification. As the Zen saying goes, "The finger that points at the moon is not the moon." Let me just indicate what is intended by noting that a nondualistic and preconceptual understanding of existence implies that *everything* we encounter is not different from us, just as "we" are not different from "it." There is no dualism—but then there is no monism either. Both dualism and monism are conceptual constructs, not reality. According to some schools of Buddhism, reality is interdependent: our particular existence at any moment depends on all that is. This implies a deep respect for all that is. As Francis Cook states:

> The Buddhist, in viewing things as being interdependent in this manner, comes to have, ideally, a profound feeling of gratitude and respect for all

> things, however humble they may appear to people who do not share his understanding, for in some manner that eludes the rest of us, he is aware that what he is depends utterly upon them.[48]

Other experiential paths to adoption of the platform are also possible. For example, one could become increasingly attracted to and respectful of wild nature on the basis of extended trips into the wilderness. Or aesthetic experiences of natural beauty could arouse a passion for wilderness. Such experiences could lead to an interest in the environment, ultimately leading to an acceptance of some version of radical ecocentrism.[49]

The platform can also be justified by the abstract path of metaphysics. Freya Matthews provides one such justification in *The Ecological Self*.[50] Because she believes that any new world view must have the sanction of science in order to have legitimacy within modern culture, Matthews uses an extension of Einstein's General Relativity theory called "geometrodynamics."[51] From this perspective, she articulates a monistic metaphysical theory about all reality. Such abstract terrain is difficult going, and I can offer here only the briefest of summaries. From the perspective of geometrodynamics, the only "stuff" of which our world is made is "spacetime," which is intrinsically dynamic and changeable.[52] It stretches, ripples, curves and, as a whole, expands. Matter consists of knotted regions within this spacetime, and energy is the curvature of spacetime. Spacetime itself is the principal actor, and it is the only real, self-subsisting reality. It is holistic in the sense that individual bodies cannot be localized, with each body spread out through all of spacetime. The territory of the General Relativity theory is, to say the least, counterintuitive, and the skeptical reader can only be referred to Matthews's work for an introduction to this literature.

Any monistic metaphysics requires a principle of individuation to explain the individuality apparent in our experience of ourselves and the rest of nature. Such apparently discrete individuals are not real in themselves, but are rather "functions of form, pattern, organization."[53] Rocks are forms, but being ripples of spacetime, they are not individuals in reality. So too for all other forms. But some forms exhibit distinct types of organization having intrasystemic relations that incorporate feedback loops, regulatory mechanisms, and goal directedness. Such systems manifest homeostasis, maintaining themselves within certain limits, despite changes in their environments. Vending machines dispensing cold drinks are examples of such systems. Particularly interesting are the sorts of systems that maintain themselves through external change, repairing and renewing themselves, such as living organisms. Such organisms take their own existence (although not necessarily consciously) as an end. An organism is "a system for effecting its own maintenance, repair and renewal."[54] This process of autopoiesis, Matthews suggests, is a plausible principle of individuation within her monistic metaphysics. Such a principle prevents her monism from degenerating into the claim that reality is a vast goo without important internal differentiations.

Using this analysis, Matthews argues that autopoietic systems, in taking themselves as an end, have a claim to moral considerability.[55] This, she believes, provides a metaphysically grounded justification for the idea that intrinsic value abounds in nonhuman nature. Because self-maintaining systems are open, importing energy from their environment, "the identity of a self-maintaining system is relational."[56] Such relational connectedness is generally reciprocal in ecological systems, and it is "in most cases misguided to try to assign higher and lower values to specific kinds of organisms."[57] But what of the conflict between humans and other organisms? As she notes, "the primary duty of any self [or organism] is towards itself."[58] Self-maintenance, however, only involves the satisfaction of vital needs necessary for flourishing. And what is human "flourishing"? Matthews suggests that it consists of

> a state of inner harmony and integration of the personality, which is expressed in a positive and creative attitude to life's challenges. . . . Recognition of the equality of selves then does not require that one starve, that one adopt a totally "hands-off" approach. But it does require that one refrain from thwarting the interests of other selves [human and nonhuman] if it is not necessary to one's flourishing to do so.[59]

Thus Matthews arrivers at a justification of the central tenets of the platform through a monistic metaphysics and a plausible principle of individuation.

Naess's "Ecosophy"

Finally, let me sketch some aspects of Naess's justification of the deep ecology platform.[60] As the person who originated the term "deep ecology," his position is of particular interest. Naess calls ecologically oriented philosophical world views "ecosophies." Since many ecosophies are possible, he names his own version "Ecosophy T," with the "T" referring to his mountain hut.[61]

Naess's ecosophy is explicit in putting forward certain values to guide to action in the world. However, as he points out, simply articulating a set of values is insufficient, because these values must be related to each other in some clear way.[62] This requires what he calls "hypotheses." An ecosophy, then, is an articulated set of values and hypotheses that are systematically integrated with each other. Since Naess's style of systematisation is deductive, most norms within such a system are derived from higher level norms and hypotheses. Within such a deductively elaborated system, there must at least one logically ultimate norm that cannot be justified within the system. This is a characteristic of any deductive system, whether ecosophy, geometry, or scientific theory. There is a significant difference between an ecosophy and other deductive systems. Within an ecosophy, a logically ultimate norm may not necessarily be ethically ultimate, since lower level norms may have ethical priority. Thus, the norm, "do not kill," is logically prior to "do not kill your mother," but the latter has ethically priority.[63] A virtue of formalizing an ecosophy is that it facilitates rational debate. Thus, "when the intricate interconnection between norms and hypotheses is left unarticulated, each norm tends to be taken to be absolute or ultimate. This reduces or eliminates the possibility of rational discussion."[64]

The ultimate grounding for norms is experience. Following Whitehead, Naess argues that to take the world of science as reality is to confuse a particular form of abstraction with concrete reality. Naess names this reality, the one in which we actually and immediately live, "gestalts." According to Naess, "the gestalt is a whole, self-determining and self-reliant. If we call it 'experience of the gestalt', we are easily mislead [sic] in a subjectivist direction."[65] By this, Naess means that each experience is fundamentally a whole, and only becomes broken into fragments through thinking. There is an underlying unity of experience that we only later separate into fact and value, subject and object, or I and not-I. First is the gestalt. "Gestalts bind the I and the not-I together in a whole."[66]

Naess's gestalts are strikingly similar to John Dewey's pragmatic understanding of experience, which has "in its primary integrity no division between act and material, subject and object, but contains them both in an unanalyzed totality."[67] Naess notes the similarity of his analysis to that of William James, another pragmatist who claims that there is a fundamental unity to all experience. James provides the following example in which he speaks of seeing a piece of paper:

> If our own private version of the paper be considered in abstraction from every other event, as if it constituted by itself the universe . . . then the paper seen and the seeing of it are only two names for one indivisible fact which, properly named, is *the datum, the phenomenon, or the experience*. The paper is in the mind and the mind is around the paper, because paper and mind are only two names that are given later to the one experience.[68]

According to Naess, this ontologically based approach to human existence overcomes the unwarranted dualism between thought and emotion.[69] Ordinary nonreflective experience has both a sensory and a valued dimension. Only after this experience, and on its basis, do we separate "facts" from "values," and "I" from "not-I." "Joy becomes, not *my* joy, but *something joyful* of which the I and something else are interdependent, non-isolatable fragments."[70] Thus, values are within gestalts, not projected onto a meaningless nature. The claim is that we are already immersed in a world of valuing and feeling before we analyze our experience and make distinctions between, say, thought and emotion.

In a Deweyan vein, Naess argues that although the feeling texture of experience is not mere subjective whim, such feeling tones are not final either. Rather, we need to evaluate these feelings. We must reflectively decide which of the values we will accept in living our lives.

> The transition from emotion to evaluation is not so much an actual motion, but merely a shift in emphasis based on an acceptance of feeling as a basic motivation for our diverse and actual world-views. It then remains to investigate just what feelings we can accept as guiding "stars" to justify our actions, and how to perceive these lights in a coherent

> system that articulates and explains our beliefs so as to translate them to action.[71]

Each of us must make fundamental choices about which "guiding stars" we will adopt. We all make such choices, consciously or not, and nothing could be personally more important than which we choose to follow.

Although at least one value in an ecosophy will be logically ultimate, Naess stresses that *all* must be open for revision. Ultimate premises are not open to direct test, but they can be revised, in the light of "experience and reflection," on the basis of specific instances that occasioned them and on those to which they lead. It is specific instances that are the motivation for the general norms adopted.[72] Thus, Ecosophy T is ultimately grounded on experience, but it is also a generalization from experience that is open to reflection and rational debate. The logic of Naess's system is similar to that of any deductively arrayed scientific theory in which the evidence for general laws are the confirmatory instances deduced from the laws. The structure of Naess's ecosophy bears out Wenz's claim that science and ethics share the same structure of inquiry. This implies that considerations of value are ultimately no more subjective than are questions in science.[73]

The understanding of experience, or gestalts, as fundamentally unitary provides a basis for seeing that both concepts of nature—as "all inclusive" or as "nonhuman"—arise from the same soil. First, there is experience, which is neither inside nor outside the person. Nature, as a concept, can include all there is, or it can distinguish humans from the rest of nature. Neither is "true," but either may be useful.

Pleasure, happiness, and perfection are, according to Naess, three plausible candidates for ultimate norms. After examining difficulties in each, Naess locates his own view within the tradition of Spinoza, where perfection and joy merge. This norm of perfection includes within it an increase in the quality of life as called for in the deep ecology platform. More precisely stated, the ultimate norm of Ecosophy T is *Self*-realization. In Naess's system, *Self* is not understood as being the same as *self*, but rather includes everything. To expand one's identification outward from one's self to other humans is to move toward Self. To go further toward an identification with all of nature is to identify with Self. This norm of Self-realization "thus includes personal and community self-realization, but is conceived also to refer to an unfolding of reality as a totality."[74] This all inclusive sense of realization is an endorsement of the self-realization of all—people and the rest of nature. Given a sense of the interconnectedness of all existence, the realization of each is connected to the self-realization of all others.

Such an ultimate norm cannot be supported by appeal to yet more general norms. It can, however, be made more plausible by viewing evolution as the unfolding of life within a vast matrix of existence. This is a sort of "outside-in" approach to identification.[75] An ecological ideology of nature enables but does not entail the ultimate norm of Self-realization, for it suggests a fundamental unity underlying the diversity of life. The ultimate norm of Ecosophy T focuses on the unfolding of everything in process. From this most general of norms, it is easy to move to the claim that all forms of life should flourish, that each should "unfold its specific capacities."[76] Such a norm, as Naess notes, is incomplete as a guide to conduct.[77] Because life requires some killing, this norm only means that we should limit it where possible, rather than attempt to abide by the impossible counsel to avoid it entirely. Naess acknowledges that sometimes human needs, but only vital ones, have priority over nonhuman needs.[78] Moreover, this norm does not imply a denial of the uniqueness of humanity—quite the opposite. In fact, it is the uniqueness of humans that makes us capable of being responsible.

> The uniqueness of *Homo sapiens*, its special capacities among millions of kinds of other living beings, has been used as a premise for domination and mistreatment. Ecosophy uses it as a premise for a universal care that other species can neither understand nor afford.[79]

Given this fundamental norm of Self-realization for all, one way for humans to realize themselves and move towards Self-realization is to increase their sphere of identification. Naess uses a model of human development toward maturity to explain the development of increasing identification. First, for Naess, are the early years of life when the self is narrowly restricted to the ego, a selfish center of activity. After a few years of normal development, there is an extension of self to include family and close friends. "The gradual maturing of a person *inevitably* widens and deepens the self through the process of identification. There is no need for altruism towards those with whom we identify."[80] Further expansions to include community, tribe, nation, and all of humanity are not uncommon. This process of identification can extend further. It is possible that "all-around maturity among human beings inevitably fosters a high level of identification with all life forms."[81] This is a development of identification that starts from the "inside" and works outward.

Such an expansion of identification vastly enlarges the realm of experience and opens new paths for joy and sorrow.

> The greater our comprehension of our togetherness with other beings, the greater the identification, and the greater care we will take. The road is also opened thereby for delight in the well-being of others and sorrow when harm befalls them. We seek what is best for ourselves, but through the extension of self, our "own" best is also that of others.[82]

This is clearly a powerful basis for norms of conduct. In fact, it is a counsel for a particular kind of self-perfection, from which right action flows naturally.

It is important to remember the ontological base of this ecosophy, which builds on the unity in experience of self and other. This base makes possible the cultivation of an expanded identification, but doing so requires effort and practice.[83] Asking how we widen identification, Naess claims that it is spontaneous and nonrational, but not irrational. Ecosophy T takes seriously the philosophy in which "reality consists of wholes which we cut down rather than of isolated terms which we put together. In other words: there is not, strictly speaking, a primordial causal process of identification, but one of largely unconscious alienation which is overcome in experiences of identity."[84] As we overcome this alienation by becoming more aligned with what really is, we change our ways of acting. "Through the wider Self every living being is connected intimately, and from this intimacy follows the capacity of *identification* and as its natural consequences, [sic] practice of non-violence. No moralizing is needed, just as we need not morals to make us breathe."[85] Thus, the process of expanding identification is not merely psychological but is grounded in reality. The process of identification is possible because there *is* an underlying whole of which we are, each of us, a part.

Ecosophy T is not intended or presented as a compulsory metaphysics. Rather, it is like advice one might give to a friend, an invitation to use such norms as "guiding stars" in thinking about how to live. This ecosophy is open to the only sort of test such a recommendation can be given—how does it feel when tried? Does cultivating such a way of being lead toward greater joy and less alienation? Is one's life fuller and richer when one acts out the story of separateness or the story of connectedness? Ecosophy thus leads us back to the very ground of all philosophy and advises us to carefully examine who we are and to ponder well how we should live.

However one responds to this invitation, at the very minimum Naess's ecosophy has two important virtues. First, it does support the deep ecology platform and thus should put to rest the charge of irrationality that is sometimes leveled against deep ecology. Certainly one might disagree with Ecosophy T; disagreement is normal in philosophical discussion and the most one can ask is an articulated and systematically developed statement of a plausible set of norms and connecting hypotheses.[86] Further, Naess's ecosophy shares ontological foundations with other major philosophies that can by no means be charged with irrationality. Thus, while one might conclude that Ecosophy T is wrong, it is not reasonable to claim that it is irrational, unreasonable, or mystical. Second, the articulation of Ecosophy T and other ecosophies should help to further discussion about how we ought to regard ourselves and the rest of nature. Reason might be able to help us in working through the ecological crises that, I fear, will define our children's epoch. What seems important is that we begin to act on the understanding that we have worked our way into a profound misadaptation with the rest of nature.

The platform of deep ecology constitutes a basis for creating a balanced way for humanity to live well within nature. We humans urgently need wider and wiser agreement on what needs to be done, and we need to work together from there. Without profound social change, the platform will remain a mere "ought to be" on the fringes of industrial society. It is time, then to examine the social implications of a deep ecological perspective.

10 *For a Radical Ecocentrism*

The need for social movements to redirect the trajectory of industrial society is urgent. An inertial tendency toward the expanding the domination over the rest of nature is built into the culture and politics of industrial society. The convergence of the various ideologies of nature implicit in political economy, industrialism, and reductive science provide a powerful support for industrial culture. To an ever-increasing degree, the rest of nature is transformed into resources and commodities by industrial societies. Many want to accelerate this process.

The expansion of industrialism is honored as "economic growth," a process demanded by politicians and populace alike, appearing as if it is the only road to "prosperity." This enchantment with economic growth sprawls across most of the political spectrum, uniting conservatives, moderates, liberals, and many progressives. The political realities of industrial societies create this unity. Under conditions of economic expansion, all sides can get more of what they want, as the fruits "trickle down" even to the most disadvantaged. In times of economic contraction, struggles over the distribution of social wealth intensify. Progressives call upon the state to expand public sector expenditures that meets considerable resistance from conservatives. Since increasing social discontent threatens the control of those in power, all factions unite in calling for economic growth. But such progress is cancerous from the perspective of the rest of nature.

Ecologically sensitive progressives point to ways in which economies can be restructured, arguing that certain changes benefit both humanity and its environment. For example, retrofitting houses with insulation both generates employment and lessens the demand for energy. While this is true and, therefore, worthy of support, such win-win proposals do not get to the root problem of industrialism. The social addiction to economic growth is one of the tap roots of the tension between the ecological good and industrialism, and it will remain an addiction as long as the human good is conceived as an increase in material consumption. Changing our conception of the human good involves fundamentally transforming industrialism.

Recently, some streams within the nature and social traditions are creating a significant confluence. Some within the nature tradition now recognize that creating satisfactory relations with the rest of nature requires changing society, and some within the social tradition are realizing that the creation of a just society requires resolving the ecological crises of industrial society. Each stream sees that this requires radical social change—their confluence is radical environmentalism. Radical environmentalism has five main branches: human centered environmentalism calling for radical social change, social ecology, ecological feminism, bioregionalism, and deep ecology.[1] Human-centered radical environmentalism usually starts from the fact of ecological crisis and argues that human interests require radical social transformation.[2] This approach appeals to those who have not yet seriously questioned the assumption of anthropocentrism.[3] The limitations of such an approach become apparent when it tries to deal with questions about other species, wilderness, and the proper size of the human population. In any case, human centered radical environmentalism is not ecocentric. Social ecology emphasizes the need to abolish society's hierarchies in order to create the possibility of ecologically harmonious relations between society and the rest of nature.[4] Ecological feminism, a part of the feminist movement, stresses the connections between the domination of women and the domination of nature.[5] It sees that at least one basic cause of the crises is rooted in patriarchy and the masculine worldview. Deep ecology grows out of a nature tradition extending back to John Muir and Henry David Thoreau. In this chapter I want to show the value of deep ecology for the project of transforming of industrial society. It has significant contributions to make to what I believe is a rapidly growing international radical environmental movement. I shall also briefly consider some unresolved questions which this movement must ultimately resolve.

Of these perspectives in radical environmentalism, only human-centered environmentalism accepts anthropocentrism. The others are ecocentric. Each grows out of its own history of concerns and each continues to reflect a partiality rooted in its history.[6] As the radical ecocentric movement matures, hopefully the differences between these perspectives will become only differing emphases within a larger unity. There are some signs that this understanding of a deeper unity underlying diversity is developing. Marti Kheel, an ecological feminist, argues that the differences in the ways men and women now typically form their identities makes a gender-neutral concept of the self suspect. This suggests that ecofeminism, in its ability to speak specifically to women and the ways that they currently form their identities, has a unique importance to women. But she sees that this does not lead to any fundamental opposition between ecological feminists and deep ecologists.[7]

Such a unity must be based on clarity about the necessity for social change. Within the United States, at least, there is a recurrent fantasy that some kind of technological invention will suffice to resolve all our problems. One could sense this reaction sweep through the United States a few years ago when it appeared that the process of "cold" fusion would offer unlimited energy in the not too distant future. Almost no one pondered whether such a development would be good; its virtue was assumed. There was almost no awareness that access to unlimited energy by this society might be catastrophic for the good of humans and certainly would be so for other forms of life. Is giving a drunk an automobile that runs on air a good idea? Even now, as we become more enmeshed in problems created by technological "solutions," we continue to yearn for the technological fix. Environmentalists are not immune to this fever.

Efforts to design with ecological sensitivity are good, but the limits of this approach are severe. Fluorescent light bulbs and superinsulated houses are design innovations that offer light and shelter with reduced environmental impact. To think that real solutions lie in this sort of tinkering is naïve, dangerously so if it directs attention away from the complex, necessary, and often frustrating path of social change. Langdon Winner crisply points out that the end of appropriate technology as a social movement can be precisely located on the evening of November 4, 1980 when Ronald Reagan was elected President. His regime ended the favorable climate for appropriate technology created by the Carter administration and the movement ended.[8] The moral is that changing the direction of industrial society requires attending to the social and economic institutions of that society. Social struggle to restructure society must be part of the solution.

It should also be said, but perhaps not emphasized, that the changes needed are *radical*. Without discussing the Earth's ills at length, it needs to be said that we, all of us, face very profound problems. We have a world that threatens significant climate change with attendant mass migrations of people in a nuclearized and politically unstable system of nation states. Massive species extinction is in progress now and will continue. Agricultural lands are being turned into deserts. We have done this with somewhat over five billion people. One-quarter of those people have life styles that are vastly more destructive to the ecology than the other three-quarters. The same one-quarter is responsible for two-thirds of the global warming and almost the entire threat to the ozone layer. If we had a stable population, the spread of the life style of the rich to the poor would create a great additional strain on the environment. But we do not have a stable population. The United Nations now projects population stabilization at around eleven billion.[9] "For today's rich-country consumption levels to be achieved by a whole world that size would mean multiplying today's ecological impacts some 20 or 30 times over."[10] This simply cannot come to pass—some sort of break with our recent past is on its way.

Radical social change does not come about all at once. Michael Harrington's phrase "visionary gradualism" aptly characterizes the perspective on social changes that we need.[11] Social change must be guided by a vision of a place truly worth creating, but the changes only come about gradually, step-by-step, and require steady effort. The relevant time frame is not a few years or a decade, but generations. We should understand ourselves as living in a "transitional epoch" of several generations. A long view helps us know what should be done now.

What Deep Ecology Offers Social Progressives

The success of deep ecology or any other social movement aimed at restructuring humanity's relations with the rest of nature depends on the latent dissatisfaction of life in industrial society. If almost everyone were getting happier and happier as a result of accumulating more and more things, then calls for radical change would have little prospect of being widely heeded. In fact, as discussed, people within industrial societies do not experience increasing levels of satisfaction as they accumulate more. People become addicted to getting new things, entranced with the process of acquiring. When economies contract, people become angry, scared, insecure, and nervous about any limitation on their consumption. Industrial life swings through moods of excitement, boredom, anger, and fear. It is not a recipe for human joy or excellence.

This pattern of experience endures, not because the pattern is inherently satisfactory, but because people do not notice it. Certainly there is an awareness of the series of individual experiences, but the larger pattern exists mainly on an unconscious level. It is as if a trance has been induced by mass media, and people aimlessly graze the malls armed with credit cards, seeking *something*, though they know not what. Lacking a clear vision of a better alternative, they continue down the consumerist path. Life within industrialism is, I believe, supersaturated with latent discontent. Social progressives seem to lack a vision of the good society that does not involve spreading consumer goods around more equally. The collapse of so called socialism into a form of market economy has not helped in envisioning an alternative to the ethos of capitalism. Although it is hard now to discern what will arise out of East Europe and the dissolution of the Soviet Union, it seems that socialism, of the state capitalist variety, will be discarded in favor of the dream of shopping malls with parking lots big enough for all to come.

Perhaps, then, the most distinctive and important contribution of deep ecology to the prospect of radical change is its vision of a joyful alternative to consumerism. Environmentalism often casts itself as doomsayer, with nature as the avenging angel for industrialism's excesses. From the perspective of the dutiful consumer, this version of environmentalism speaks only of deprivation and loss. Deep ecology, on the other hand, is explicit in offering a vision of an alternative way of living that is joyous and enlivening.

This seems paradoxical, because deep ecologists have been the strongest critics of anthropocentrism, so much so that they have often been accused of a mean-spirited misanthropy. Although some who accept the deep ecology platform may have such a misanthropic streak, deep ecology is actually vitally concerned with humans realizing their best potential.[12] Naess remarks, near the beginning of his major work on deep ecology that his "discussion of the environmental crisis is motivated by the unrealized potential human beings have for varied experience in and of nature: the crisis contributes or could contribute to open our minds to sources of meaningful life which have largely gone unnoticed or have been depreciated."[13] Even though Naess's Ecosophy T recommends that people transcend their isolation from the natural world and identify with the rest of nature, his view is, in some sense, centered on humans. The reason for this apparent paradox is that deep ecology is a recommendation about how *humans* should live, and it recommends that they identify with all life, that they live nonanthropocentrically. "The change of consciousness referred to consists of a transition to a more egalitarian attitude to life and the unfolding of life on earth. This transition opens the doors to a richer and more satisfying life for the species *Homo sapiens*, but not by focussing on *Homo sapiens*."[14] Deep ecology's conviction that this is a path toward a more joyful existence is important for any movement that would change society. "We can hope that *the ecological movement will be more of a renewing and joy-creating movement*."[15] This emphasis changes the fundamental message of radical ecocentrism from deprivation to one of a more satisfying way of being fully human.

A second major contribution of the deep ecology platform and any ecosophy that leads to it is the critique of human needs. Certainly deep ecologists are in the company of many other social theorists who distinguish between vital human needs and wants of lesser or trivial importance. One of the moral insights of social progressives is the evil of a society in which some have much and others have so little. Although the rich and the poor each have unmet needs, there is a fundamental difference between the relatively trivial dissatisfactions of the rich and the absolute deprivations of the poor. This sense of injustice, arising from an identification with the suffering of the downtrodden, was a strong element in the now dormant socialist project. "With an emphasis on this perspective, environmentalists might restore the cutting edge to socialism, restoring a sense of the absolute to perceptions of deprivation."[16]

A third contribution is deep ecology's focus on the process of identification. This is strategically critical in unraveling the knot of consumptive materialism. The relation between one's sense of identity and the impulse toward consumerism has been discussed earlier in the context of expansionary industrialism. I argued that one of the driving forces of consumerism is the loss of traditional ways of forming one's identity and their replacement by material possessions. Some sense of self-identity is a vital need for humans. Deep ecology's emphasis an alternative mode of creating one's identity through an expansion of identification goes to the very core of one of the engines driving industrialism. An expansion of personal identification to *all* humans is a basis for rejecting consumerism in a world of desperately unmet human needs. It also leads to rejecting militarism.

Deep ecology's emphasis on the further expansion of identification carries an experientially based rejection of consumptive materialism. The message is not that we must "give up" some of what we want. Rather, the claim is that consumptive materialism could be lost without significant reduction in human happiness. The aim is a good quality of life, which is not equivalent to material consumption. The dominance of economic ways of talking and thinking about happiness fosters the illusion that consumption and happiness are equivalent. The experience of an expanded identification, along with some critical reflection, shows that they are not. Such an expanded identification is perhaps more akin to an increase in vitality and sensitivity. Increased sensitivity is a more vital way of being, but it carries a price. If one identifies with the possibly never seen rain forest, then a mahogany table, for example, beautiful in texture, grain, and craftsmanship, becomes ugly and offensive as a part of the rain forest wherein other peoples and a multitude of species once abided. Aldo Leopold is correct when he notes that "One of the penalties of an ecological education is one lives . . . in a world of wounds."[17] Social progressives know a similar pain from their identification with the suffering of the poor of the world.

The expansion of identification and the ensuing reduction of the urge to consume would be helpful in alleviating some of the suffering in the Third World. If one accepts the reasonable hypothesis that overconsumption and militarism are two of the fundamental causes of the degradation of the environment, then deep ecology provides a most fundamental critique of each of these. As David Johns points out, the very concept of overconsumption changes when it is placed within the context of deep ecology. Within any human-centered social perspective, overconsumption "is primarily seen as a social relationship, a problem of distribution between the wealthy and the poor, a problem of economic ownership." On the other hand, when nonhuman nature is taken as a community and valued for its own unfolding, "then human consumption which disrupts it is wrong; it would constitute overconsumption."[18] Stemming the consumerist impulse in industrial countries would slow the transfer of wealth—both in the form of material and in human life for cheap labor—from the poor of the Third World to industrial nations. If industrialism were to slow down and reverse itself, there would be much more economic and cultural room for countries of the Third World to find their own unique ways of unfolding.

Finally, the first plank of the platform calls for the flourishing of all life, human and nonhuman. If the idea of letting *every thing* flourish is powerful when applied to nature, it is even more so applied to human societies—let *every* person flourish. This fundamental norm is continuous with the ideals of all progressive social movements, going beyond them by including nonhuman life. Implicit in this ideal is the goodness of each human developing to his or her fullest. It would be hard to overestimate the impact of this ideal of human development in progressive social change. It is at the very root of political democracy and calls for economic democracy. Socialism and anarchism stand resolutely for the right of each person to realize their best potential. So then, what is wrong with capitalism? Would there be anything wrong with it if it were successful in bringing home the bacon for everyone? Yes, at least from a Marxist perspective. Capitalism promotes a systematic and deepening inequality, both economically and, more profoundly, in terms of human dignity. For Marx, the increase of wages for the worker is "nothing but *better payment for the slave,* and would not conquer either for the worker or for labour their human status and dignity."[19] Naess, too, sees the evils of economic class, noting that most of the people in industrial countries are a "global upper class" and that the core of "class suppression" is the repression "of life fulfillment potentials in relation to fellow beings."[20] Imperialism and colonialism promote a systematic inequality among humans of differing countries and inequality within each of those countries. Racism promotes a systematic inequality of equals. Sexism promotes a relationship of domination and inequality between men and women. And notice that in each of these—capitalism, racism, and sexism,—the "victors" are degraded in their "victory." The racist and the sexist lose their full human potential as they enact the role of oppressor. So too with humanity and nature. The domination of nature presumes the moral irrelevance of the rest of nature, and this "victory" diminishes humans.

Bioregionalism

The bioregional movement in the United States articulates an alternative vision of human society that would both be more humane and offer the prospect of a tenable symbiosis between society and the rest of nature.[21] The bioregional vision is one of relatively self-sufficient communities defined by their bioregions. This involves a radical decentralization of human society on both the political and the economic level. This would enable both genuine democracy and local control of economic activity.

Decentralization is necessary to achieve meaningful political democracy. The scale of industrial states is such that their versions of political democracy, while better than other alternatives at the level of the nation state, enable little effective rule by citizens. This is due, in part at least, to the size and complexity of the domain of sovereignty. The process designed to choose national candidates requires a life of seeking and maintaining power for those who devote themselves to politics. Moving upward in the hierarchy of political parties, one finds increasingly that the only participants are those whose prime interest is power. Politics on the scale of the nation state thus becomes a contest between professionals. Unfortunately, these are exactly the people who a wise society would keep out of power! A further distortion of effective democracy arises from the costs of a modern political campaign for state or national office. Such campaigns, tied as they are to mass media, are expensive. Consequently, the political process is corrupted by concentrations of wealth. Thus, some form of decentralization is desirable for any genuine political democracy.

Politically smaller units cannot become sovereign without a corresponding devolution of economies. Without control over its economy, a community cannot have effective political control of itself. This devolution of economies into bioregions requires the creation of local forms of livelihood and the minimizing of imports and exports. Chain stores, for example, are economic extensions of distant corporations, and they undermine local control of local resources. Just as national political autonomy is lost to blind markets when economies become global, so too local communities become subject to markets when they become involved with nonlocal economies and lose local sovereignty.

Even though economic exchange between communities might be minimized, some exchange seems unavoidable. Val and Richard Routley (now Plumwood and Sylvan) state the problem well: "If communities are large enough to satisfactorily produce entirely for themselves everything which might be needed at a non-simple level of life, they will be *too* large and *too* anonymous to operate a free anarchist communist system satisfactorily."[22] This need for exchange leads to serious difficulties, for exchange often leads to money, to the state, and to a loss of community autonomy. Practical solutions, given the will to find them, are being created. The Mondragon cooperatives in northwestern Spain incorporate economic decentralization and political democracy. There are more than 150 worker-owned cooperatives that are democratically governed and produce a wide variety of products. They also have schools, housing, and banks. The movement started in 1943 as a school to train workers and now involves more than 21,000 people.[23] The fundamental need is to prevent economic relations from dominating social relations. The economy must be submerged into society, instead of being a force that governs society.

The bioregional movement in the United States should be given credit for beginning to think through the problem of cities. Cities are now the dominant form of habitat for North Americans and constitute a fundamental ecological problem. If current trends continue, "more than half of humanity will reside in urban areas shortly after the turn of the century."[24]

It is neither plausible nor desirable to imagine the dispersal of city populations into surrounding countrysides, at least within any foreseeable future. There are advantages to city life in terms of available energy for heating and transportation, as well as other advantages. However, cities as currently organized are imperial centers reaching out great distances, drawing in food, water, and energy, and dispersing their wastes outward. A new vision of what cities might become is needed to start rethinking and reconstructing urban life. The bioregional movement has taken some small but important first steps toward this. A tactic has been devised whereby urban citizens can articulate a bioregional vision and work toward its implementation. This could lead to effective political action aimed at moving municipal governments toward creating programs for ecologically sound transportation, renewable energy, recycling and reuse, community cooperatives, and even wild life habitats within cities.[25]

Political and economic decentralization would tend to move society toward more ecologically rational forms of life. When economies spread outward, approaching the whole planet as a limit, feedback from mistakes is hidden, unnoticed, or forgotten. The consequences of our economies now extend outward into distant and unknown places. This global economic network results in vast and unwanted ecological degradation that is hard to see because the feedback loops are so extensive. Such ecological degradation is hard to contest because the centers of decision making are remote and often unknown. When the links between economic choices and consequences can be seen, for example, by walking along a river and observing a local business polluting it, then understanding and effective action become possible. You can see the harm to the river, you know who is doing it, and the polluters are neighbors open to persuasion or other effective political action. Decentralization, by shortening the feedback loops between economic choice and consequence, facilitates social learning and the possibility of ecological wisdom. Both knowing the consequences of actions and having effective local control makes it more likely that people will act to prevent harm to themselves and their neighbors, as well as other forms of life.

It is care for other forms of life, engendered by an identification with place, that is one of the reasons for the affinity between deep ecology and bioregionalism. One can truly love what one knows. Attachment to place grows out of living and working in a community, amongst friends and neighbors, and it can lead to an understanding of the local ecology and make effective care possible. This understanding of place is central to the bioregional vision. "The kinds of soils and rocks under our feet; the sources of the waters we drink; the meaning of the different kinds of winds; the common insects, birds, mammals, plants, and trees; the particular cycles of the seasons; the times to plant and harvest and forage—these are the things necessary to know."[26] This emphasis on place is one basis for an expanded identification with all forms of life.

One of the most interesting considerations favoring bioregionalism as a social vision is that it represents a chance to continue cultural evolution. Lewis Mumford observes:

> One of the great benefits of individualized national and regional cultures is that, if the opportunities are consciously seized, these potential alternatives can be experimented with under varied conditions and their advantages compared. Any philosophy of history that takes account of natural and human diversity must recognize that selective processes in nature have reached a higher stage in man, and that any mode of organizing human activities, mechanically or institutionally, which limits the possibilities of continued trial, selection, emergence, and transcendence, in favor of a closed and completely unified system, is nothing less than an effort to arrest human cultural evolution.[27]

One shudders to contemplate how little would be left of human cultural diversity if the project of industrializing the earth is completed.

There are, of course, problems with bioregionalism. The precise definition of specific bioregions among the intersections of water and biota and culture may be difficult. There are watersheds, communities of plants and animals, and human communities. Currently, these are usually not mutually congruent, and they raise questions about how specific bioregions should be delimited. The need to resolve such theoretical problems is, unfortunately, not now at hand.

A more urgent problem is that the existence of decentralized communities is no guarantee that its members will behave responsibly toward the land, the flora, and the fauna. If newspaper reports are to be believed, many in the Pacific Northwest think that employment in the logging industry is more important than the preservation of old-growth forests. Almost half the voters in West Valley, a community in New York State, favor making their community a dump site for nuclear waste. Of the seven communities in the United States that chose to accept a grant to study the possibility of becoming a site for high-level nuclear waste, five were Indian tribal communities. As one Native American notes, "five hundred years of colonization has done a real job on us. It makes us targets of cash and poverty politics."[28] Bribery, either in the form of money offered or of threatened job losses, builds upon preexisting social inequalities and lack of local autonomy. Radical ecocentrists must incorporate an understanding of social injustice into their tactics if they are to deal with such problems. But even if localism does not guarantee ecological wisdom, it would make mistakes more visible and cause the burdens of those mistakes to fall closer to those who make them. Communities can then learn from these mistakes, and this would make them more likely to behave responsibly towards "their" places in the future. National governments are far more ready than local residents to devastate a local area in the name of "national interest."

There is also the danger of violence in the process of devolution, as recent devolutions of nation states into smaller regions demonstrates. Religious and ethnic sectarianism has led, not infrequently, to the massacres of immigrant populations. Unfortunately, humans (most often, men) are capable of relishing violence, and ethnic and religious sectarianism can inflame people in awful ways. However, even though localism may have its outbreaks of violence, such outbreaks pale beside those of the nation state. The largest slaughters have been carried out by nation states in pursuit of national interests. When the might of national armies and modern technology is brought to bear, the results can be unspeakably gruesome. A full-scale nuclear war would likely end civilization. The roots of violence go rather deep, and although the movement toward decentralization does unleash sectarian furies, the sovereign nation state is hardly a cure.

It may be that the loss of local autonomy on some issues is desirable. Bioregions can act in ways that negatively affect other regions, as wastes flow downstream. Further, some choices must be made collectively and must span bioregions. For example, the protection and expansion of wilderness, desirable from a global perspective, may involve significant social and economic costs to particular bioregions. Some problems, such as the protection of whales and the avoidance of ozone-depleting chemicals, require global cooperation of some sort for their resolution. These and other problems require ways in which interregional disputes can be discussed and effectively resolved. Thus, just as there is need for more local autonomy, there is also need for political avenues of collective decision making that are global in scope.

The need for national and global political structures raises serious difficulties for the ideal of local autonomy. If the problems of genuine democracy are already difficult at the level of the nation state, effective democratic processes in the context of global government are almost impossible.

Thus, the devolution into local communities needs to be supplemented with means of regulating and coordinating relations between localities. How this can be done democratically is by no means clear.

The bioregional vision is just that now—a vision, and it is incomplete. The short-term reality involves a world carved into political sovereigns that have little bioregional logic and which will not be easily or immediately dissolved. But the vision is useful because it guides visionary gradualism now. Although bioregionalism is not a subset of deep ecology, there is a significant convergence between these two movements which needs to be noticed and encouraged. As will be noted below, there are some differences which can, perhaps, be worked out within a context of fundamental agreement.

Problems for Deep Ecology

Two criticisms that some have made of deep ecology are that it counsels passivity and that it proposes a spiritual basis for radical ecocentrism. The first charge is simply wrong, as deep ecology is anything but passive in theory or practice. In fact, it is a platform that unites many radical ecocentrists in their numerous and various struggles. Deep ecologists have often encouraged and been active in a wide range of environmental struggles. Bill Devall's recent book, for example, counsels a broad spectrum of activities as ways of "practicing deep ecology." He mentions, among others, the following: actions for experiencing one's bioregion; criteria to guide choices about what one consumes; using Naess's slogan, "simple in means, rich in ends," to focus attention on quality of life; silence as a practice; rituals; councils of all beings; intentional communities; direct action, including monkey-wrenching and "ecotage," as well as guidelines for taking direct action; political support for the politically oppressed peoples of the Third World; participation in Green movements; and much more. In fact, Devall claims that "a basic thrust of the deep, long-range ecology movement is transformation of the masses into a new kind of society."[29]

But there is still a problem. Some social activists are uneasy about deep ecology's so-called spiritual approach to social change.[30] To some extent, this charge is obviated when the distinction between the platform and the various justifications for it is emphasized. The platform is no more "spiritual" than other programs for change. On the other hand, some deep ecology writers have focused much attention on spiritual and psychological transformation. Devall, for instance, claims that the movement is "primarily a spiritual-religious movement."[31] Warwick Fox focuses his analysis on the psychological dimension of deep ecology, discussing several forms of identification without relating them to social and political questions.[32]

The problems with spiritual or psychological approaches to social change are twofold. On the one hand, they risk becoming sectarian in activity and expression, drawing lines around the "true believers," and excluding "heretics." On the other hand, it simply defies credibility to think that a spiritual or psychological foundation can support a social movement of sufficient weight to transform society. For ordinary religious movements, this limitation is not fundamental, as their primary concern is with other worlds, not the social transformation of this world. But the deep ecology movement does aim to transform society, and it is not clear that spiritual conversions or transformational psychologies are foundations that can effectively support this goal in a broadly based social movement.

This uneasiness is strengthened by the fact that there has been relatively little emphasis on social issues by deep ecologists. Sylvan is fair in claiming that deep ecology has not yet developed an adequate political theory.[33] To some extent, this neglect of social issues can be attributed to the personal interests of deep ecology's founders, rather than to any deficit in deep ecology itself. It can also be explained by the relative youth of the movement whose first task has been to provide a rationale for a deep and joyful concern for all of nature. The updating and publication in English of Naess's book on deep ecology is a step toward clarifying some of the social and political dimensions of deep ecology. Further developments along these lines can be expected.

As to the danger of sectarianism, many deep ecology writers explicitly attempt to be inclusive in presenting their views. This attempt, especially if emphasized, can be a check on the tendency, by no means exclusive to deep ecology, toward sectarianism. Naess is emphatic about the need to approach questions nondogmatically and to avoid sectarianism. *"Devaluation of each other's efforts within the total movement is an evil which must be avoided at all costs. No sectarianism!"*[34] Humans have a tendency to define themselves in opposition to something else. The devil is a useful persona for the true believer. This tendency seems to be exacerbated within oppositional movements, and the tendency of leftists to beat each other up in scholastic bickering is extreme. Although deep ecologists no doubt share this tendency with others, at least they have a theoretical basis for a self-definition that is inclusive instead of oppositional. Their positive valuation of diversity, both human and nonhuman, is explicit. This is a useful check on the tendency to needlessly create enemies—there are already enough real ones.

Real Divisions within Radical Ecocentrism

I have argued that some version of the deep ecology platform has the potential to become a basis for unity among radical ecocentrists and have stressed the importance of not creating divisions where none need exist. Unfortunately, there are some issues that involve substantive differences in the nature of a future society and will require thoughtful and friendly debate. In particular, questions dealing with the correct balance between the needs of humans and of the rest of nature, the extent of wilderness, and the optimal human population will have to be addressed as the radical ecocentrist movement matures.

Discerning a just balance between human needs and the needs of the rest of life will involve deciding which human needs are vital, and balancing these needs with the needs of the rest of nature. This involves more clarity about the "interests" of the rest of nature. This difficulty has been put starkly by James Lovelock, whose Gaia hypothesis posits the Earth as a living creature. "Gaia theory forces a planetary perspective. It is the health of the planet that matters, not that of some individual species of organisms. This is where Gaia and the environmental movements, which are concerned first with the health of people, part company." Problems like the depletion of the ozone layer, acid rain, or nuclear radiation are "seen as real and potentially serious hazards but mainly to the people and ecosystems of the First World—from a Gaian perspective, *a region that is clearly expendable.* It was buried beneath glaciers, or was icy tundra, only 10,000 years ago."[35] Many radical ecocentrists will not comfortably accede to such a view, which writes off large expanses of human habitation.

Lovelock's view of the "health of the planet" poses sharply the problem of weighing the needs of humans against those of other forms of life. This difficult question is not open to simple solution and requires much further debate within radical ecocentrism. Deep ecology does, I think, begin the discussion in appropriate if understated terms: "Present human interference with the nonhuman world is excessive, and the situation is rapidly worsening."[36] Before we can find reasonable means of weighing human life and suffering against the continued existence of other life forms, we must first explicitly acknowledge that other forms of life do count. Only then can we hope to find a just balance. Agreement in this area will not be easy.

Connected to the problem of finding a proper balance is the question of the preservation and expansion of wilderness. We may have already ended biological history, at least for large mammals.[37] The best we can do now is to preserve patches of biological diversity, and we are not even doing well at that. Deep ecology is the clearest and most forceful of all radical ecocentrisms about the need for the preservation and expansion of wilderness.

The concern for wilderness is a divisive issue for radical ecocentrists. At least one Third World environmentalist, Ramachandra Guha, has argued that "the emphasis on wilderness is positively harmful when applied to the third world."[38] His position is that establishing wilderness areas in the Third World will involve the displacement of local inhabitants and is, in effect, a transfer of wealth from the poor to the rich. "The wholesale transfer of a movement culturally rooted in American conservation history can only result in the social uprooting of human populations in other parts of the globe."[39] Moreover, according to Guha, this concern distracts attention from the environmental problems of the poor, such as fuel and water shortages, soil erosion, and air and water pollution. Interestingly, if one imagines such a debate occurring while Europeans were overwhelming Native Americans, the Native Americans could have forcefully argued that "wilderness" was a European concept, not theirs. The very concept of wilderness is ethnocentric.

Unfortunately, industrialism has placed the problem of wilderness in a new context, one in which the continued existence of many species is in question. Native Americans co-existed with diverse forms of life for centuries, but the spread of industrialism around the globe, with its displacement of other forms of life, forces an explicit focus on the preservation and expansion of areas free from the tentacles of industrialism.

Perhaps the basis for thinking through the problem of wilderness is a dedication to the continuation of biological history. Such a continuation implies preserving the speciation process. Taking the norm of continuing biological history seriously might lead to a change in emphasis from preserving species to preserving biological lineages, since such lineages are the source of biological diversity.[40] At this time in history, with the current human population, we must disinhabit significant portions of the Earth, leaving them with many fewer humans.[41] Although this does not mean that indigenous peoples cannot live in such areas, it does mean that they cannot pursue industrial paths within those areas. There may be ways to do this that can lead to win-win solutions for local inhabitants and other life forms. It is not a degrading livelihood to care for the boundaries of areas that have been largely freed of human settlement and to guide visitors gently into such biological reserves. But solutions of this sort *must* take cognizance of the human needs involved in any plan for desettlement. Such burdens as do arise from creating and preserving enough wilderness to allow for the continuation of biological history should be born by those most able to bear them; the rich of the world must compensate the displaced poor. If such win-win solutions are not found, then poaching and other forms of human encroachment will be difficult or impossible to stop. The situations around the planet are complex and varied, but the evolutionary process, which produced life, must be respected as we seek creative solutions. As Michael Soule points out, "there is too much at risk to gamble on any one social ideology, theory, or approach. . . . Opportunism and tolerance must be the watchwords of the science, politics, and the art of nature protection."[42]

Questions of the extent of wilderness and the preservation of biological history may well represent an area in which there is a fundamental and irreconcilable difference between deep ecology and social ecology. Murray Bookchin sometimes claims that humanity should take control of the direction of biological evolution, but only after it has shed itself of the onus of social hierarchies. Thus, he has recently written that it is part of the human potential to intervene in evolution and, in some sense, move it forward.

> Nature, due to human rational intervention, will thence acquire the intentionality, power of developing more complex life-forms and capacity to differentiate itself. . . . Social ecology advances a message that not only calls for a society free of hierarchy and hierarchical sensibilities, but for an ethics that places humanity in the natural world as an agent for rendering evolution—social and natural—fully self-conscious and as free as possible in its ability to make evolution as rational as possible in meeting human and non-human needs.[43]

Since Bookchin does not directly address the question of biological history, it is not clear where he stands on the issue of whether wilderness should be expanded to enable speciation to continue. In any case, this dispute will remain theoretical for some time to come. His proposal of making evolution "rational" only comes into play after a nonhierarchical society has been created. Under such conditions, unfortunately somewhat in the future, reasoned debate between people may settle the issue wisely. Such a debate might lead to an agreement to create large biological reserves where evolution could progress free from human interference and other reserves where experiments to make evolution more "rational" could be undertaken. At least under present social conditions, Bookchin is clear that wilderness should be preserved.[44]

The wilderness issue also has the potential for divisiveness between the deep ecology and the bioregional movement. If one imagines a future North America "reinhabited" with small groups of agriculturally and largely self-sufficient communities, then, as Roderick Nash points out, "wilderness has disappeared" into communities of shepherds, farmers, and woodcutters.[45] The creation of sufficiently large areas of wilderness may imply a concentration of populations in cities. But will people wander off into the wilds, first perhaps to hunt, but then to settle?[46] It is to the credit of deep ecology that the question of wilderness is now one of the major issues for radical ecocentrism. Whether there can be any good answer to the question depends on solving an even more intractable problem.

The preservation of any significant wilderness and biological history depends on human numbers. Aren't we *already* too many? The question of the proper human population inflames passion and unreason among all parties. In the debate between Hardin and Commoner noted previously, people can easily come to self-serving and nasty positions about "other" people being too numerous. To claim that over population is the only problem is simple-minded. Considering only human numbers overlooks the importance of styles of life that humans adopt. A person living in an industrial area places far greater stress on the biosphere than does a person living in the Third World. But it is also simplistic to ignore that there are over five billion of us—more than enough—and we are growing rapidly toward another doubling! Solutions to the population problem will vary with location and culture, but the problem *must* be addressed by anyone interested in progressive social change. Unless we find effective ways of curtailing our numbers, all hopes of creating decent human societies, much less ones that allow the rest of nature to flourish, will be frustrated. Even though the percentage of people living in absolute poverty declined somewhat between 1970 and 1985, the actual numbers of people living in such conditions *increased*. Combining social justice with an increasing population is like running down the up escalator. Increasing effort is required just to stay in place.[47] We are in danger of becoming a lonely but numerous species, scratching away at an increasingly harsh and dusty Earth, eking out a livelihood that is increasingly more difficult to secure.

Deep ecology is to be commended for giving priority to the population problem and for putting forth the claim that the flourishing of nonhuman life requires a substantial decrease in human population. Richard Sylvan has argued the deep ecology case for a reduction of population in Australia, pointing out a whole set of desirable outcomes for both humans and nonhumans if such a course is pursued.[48] Other versions of radical ecocentrism have not confronted the problem of human numbers as clearly.

The Problem of Agency

The requirement of agency derives from Marx's critique of utopian socialism. He criticized attempts at social change that appeal to "society at large" rather than to the proletariat, who had a definite interest in overthrowing capitalism.[49] Marx may have been wrong in his hope that the industrial proletariat would be the agent to transform capitalism, but his attention to the question of agency is important. The urgent question now is, who will dare to make radical ecocentric change? Insistence on this question is a contribution that theorists of social change can make to radical ecocentrism. This is just the sort of consideration that a social activist would continuously ponder, asking: Who would be my ally in this or that struggle? How can we make the movement broader and deeper? Who will act to create a solution? The problem of agency has not been a focus of deep ecology or bioregionalism, but it is arguably *the* "fundamental political question of the balance of this century and beyond."[50] How will such changes come about? Failure to focus on this question has been a deficit of the nature tradition. Failure to find an answer will be our common tragedy.

Perhaps there is no effective social agency for the needed transformations. Such a conclusion has practical implications. At least some activists in the Norwegian ecophilosophy movement have become convinced that industrial society cannot be effectively reformed, and that it will last only a few more decades. Therefore they decided to redirect their efforts. "After a few years, we stopped having as our aim the diversion of IGS [Industrial

Growth Society] onto a socio-ecologically sound track. Instead, we started investing our activist energy into inspiring as many people as possible to experiment with a basis for a viable society to replace the one that is now step by step cracking up at its base."[51]

If there is no effective human agency, then the agent of change is the rest of nature. Naess gently suggests this when he says that "significant deterioration of ecological conditions may well colour the next few years in spite of the deepening ecological consciousness. The situation has to get worse before it gets better."[52] The sense that it may not be possible to find a social agent is not restricted to deep ecologists, Earth First, or Norway. Herman Daly, a senior economist at the World Bank and an outstanding theorist of steady-state economics, in discussing how a transition to such a steady-state economy might occur, says:

> It will probably take a Great Ecological Spasm to convince people that something is wrong with an economic theory that denies the very possibility of an economy exceeding its optimal scale. But even in that unhappy event, it is still necessary to have an alternative vision ready to present when crisis conditions provide a receptive public. Crisis conditions by themselves, however, will not provide a receptive public unless there is a spiritual basis providing moral resources for taking purposive action.[53]

Unfortunately for us, there may be no effective social agency for the transformation of industrialism.

But there are some reasons for hope. Morality might deepen, and its causality could become more effective than is now apparent. I remember driving west out of Philadelphia through the normal cluttered honky-tonk atmosphere of many American highways: car lots, fried chicken stores, neon lights offering cheap gasoline, liquor stores, and supermarkets housed in cinder block buildings with no aesthetic connection to place. Place itself had been displaced. This scene repeats itself endlessly all over North America. But coming over a rise and descending into a valley, it was suddenly different. Spread out below were green fields coming forth with crops, well-kept homes and barns sparsely spread among the fields, and some people in a cart drawn by a horse. I had unexpectedly wandered into Amish country, and it had a beauty that, I imagine, was common in the last century. I was seeing a healthy agricultural community of small homesteads. The Amish, having a religiously grounded moral unity, preserve their own way of life, despite the pressures and enticements of the industrial society which surrounds them. With such unity, the agency of morality is great indeed.

If morality can be effective enough to allow the Amish to flourish in their way of life, then there may be significant parallels between the Abolitionist movement and radical ecocentrism. After all, despite the complexities of the history leading up to the Civil War, the Abolitionist movement is an example of the efficacy of moral agency. Roderick Nash, in exploring parallels between the Abolitionist movement and radical environmentalism, notes some significant similarities and draws a hopeful conclusion.[54] Political compromise was too limited for the abolitionism, as it is for radical environmentalism. "Moral suasion" helped the Abolitionists, as it helps the radical environmentalists. The separatist option is limited because it leaves the problem behind. What was finally effective for the Abolitionist movement was, as we know, coercion. This is becoming part of the environmental movement as well, with the liberation of animals from laboratories, civil disobedience, Ghandian-style campaigns to save old-growth forests, and various forms of "ecotage" against the machines that would open the wilds to loggers.[55] And the state has responded with undercover agents, arrests, and charges of "conspiracy," a pattern familiar to activists of the 1960s. Some radical ecocentrists have not only been bombed, they have been arrested. As Nash points out, the possibility of freedom for slaves once seemed as remote as an ecocentric society does today. Surely the recent changes in Eastern Europe and what was once the Soviet Union indicate that major social change, even if unlikely, can happen—and rapidly.

Radical ecocentrism intends fundamental changes both in the consciousness of industrial peoples and the economic structures of industrial society. The intention toward such transformation does not make it untenable as a foundation for a broad-based social movement, but it does raise the question of how consciousness changes. Marx recognized the necessity of fundamentally transforming the consciousness of the working class in order to realize communism. Marxism approaches this problem dialectically, insisting on a constant interrelation between theory and practice and anticipating a transformation of the working class through struggle against the capitalistic class. Struggle and new forms of society lead to new forms of consciousness. In this way, Marxism offers insight into the ways in which experience leads to changes in the working-class consciousness, which in turn increase the effectiveness of the working class in its struggle against capital. This increased effectiveness leads to further social change, setting conditions for further transformations of workers, and so on. The problem for radical ecocentrism is to identify the kinds of people within the present social order who might be likely to effect the needed changes.

How can the needed consciousness arise? Clearly it does arise sometimes in some people, but it is not always clear why, even to the person affected. John Cobb remarks that "it is an exaggeration to say that I chose to become an environmentalist. On the contrary, as I became aware of the situation in new ways, I discovered that I had become an environmentalist."[56] The prospects for fundamental change exist only if such forms of consciousness become more general. But how can this happen?

If there is a developmental dialectic between the environmental activism and radical ecological consciousness, such that an increase in one tends to foster growth in the other, then there is hope for the future effectiveness of radical ecocentrism. It seems almost certain that more and more people will become aware of increasingly severe environmental problems, if only because they are personally touched by them. At least some people will act on that awareness through various forms of social protest. As citizens become involved in environmental problems of direct concern to them, they find that other issues are connected and also require attention. Resistance to a proposed incinerator or concern about toxic wastes in the community's drinking water can lead rather directly to larger questions about the production of garbage or industrial processes that generate toxic wastes. Such concerns can easily develop into doubts about the larger production and distribution systems that generate both garbage and hazardous wastes. It is a small step from here to a view of the whole mode of industrial production as the problem. This opens the door to the radical ecocentric platform. Of course not every person who becomes involved in a local problem will be led to radical ecocentrism, but the potential is there. People can make connections between their problems and larger issues because the connections are really there.

Similarly, workers' concerns about their health leads unions to demand the right to know what their members are exposed to on the job. They might then demand the right to refuse to work, without the loss of wages, when workers would be exposed to hazardous substances. Community activists might organize for similar rights to know and refuse in their community. When labor *and* community activists lend support to each other on these issues, there arises a powerful basis for effective movements to confront and change current modes of production.[57]

Interestingly, such movements can be particularly effective when they follow a two-pronged strategy of political action to force governmental regulation of hazardous substances and community action to compel the enforcement of these regulations.[58] This strategy leads to the possibility that the contested action might be prevented entirely. The fact that there are problems in getting approval for incinerators, dump sites, and nuclear power stations, exemplifies the effectiveness of a combination of governmental regulations—necessitated by environmental political pressure—and community activism at the proposed sites. As Andrew Szasz notes, such activism "pits people against capital and state regulators, provides the empowering experience of collective action, and radicalizes participants."[59] Such a model of the dialectic between activism and consciousness gives grounds for hopes of success both in specific struggles and in the spread of a radical ecocentric consciousness—not certainty, but hope.

On a more national scale, the Green movement within the United States is a seed of radical ecocentrism which might blossom into a significant social and political force. Their recently adopted program spans many areas, including positions and policies on arts and education, economics, direct action, energy, agriculture, and biological diversity.[60] This program was only developed after long discussion within local chapters and between those chapters, and it reflects consensus in the movement. Throughout the program, ecocentric values are affirmed, including the respect for nature, plants, animals, and species diversity, and there are calls for the expansion of wilderness and the preservation of native cultures. These values are combined with an understanding of the bankruptcy of both capitalistic and state socialistic regimes and an advocacy of decentralized and regionalized economies. They call for public control of banking and energy but intend such control to be held by a "decentralized public sector." Such public control would not prohibit individuals, small cooperatives, and small companies from free economic activity. Rather it seeks to resubmerge local economies into a social context that puts human development and ecology before profit. Thus the Greens seek to reverse the dominance of the economy over all other aspects of society, which is a central trait of industrialism. The emergence of the Green movement in the United States will, no doubt, continue to face difficulties similar to those of Europe, but there is hope in the fact that such movements have achieved the degree of success they have in what is, in proper perspective, a very short time.

The importance of feminism in helping to create the social agency for change is vast. As Ynestra King argues, "potentially, feminism creates a concrete global community of interests among particularly life-oriented people of the world: women."[61] However, as she notes, feminism does not, necessarily, lead to an ecological feminism. It is possible for feminism to accept the project of domination over nature, which is, she says, the position of many socialist-feminists. What is needed is a specifically ecological feminism that can "integrate intuitive, spiritual, and rational forms of knowledge, embracing both science and magic insofar as they enable us to transform the nature-culture distinction and to envision and create a free, ecological society."[62] If ecological feminists were to be effective in shifting the direction of feminism in an ecological direction, the hopes for an effective radical ecocentrism would increase enormously.

Anticipating the development of radical ecocentrism into a major political force, we should note three contributions from radical social theory. First, the value of equality within society is extremely important, both as an element of social justice and as an antidote to the social demand for economic expansion. If material equality becomes recognized as a social good, then the process of trying to achieve status through material possession would be weakened. In a society where having more than others is regarded as rude and tasteless, rather than as a mark of merit or status, demands for economic growth would be muted.

Second, until such social equality is attained, there will be a tendency for divisive conflict between social progressives and radical ecocentrists. There is a latent fracture line between social progressives and ecocentrists when environmental reform involves economic costs. In such situations, the distribution of the burdens of such reforms will be a politically important question. When such reforms seem unavoidable, the rich will seek to place their costs on the backs of the poor.[63] Social progressives will resist this, perceiving its fundamental injustice. But where will the radical ecocentrists stand? They may be tempted to endorse the reform, despite the fact that it increases social inequality, because it might abate some serious environmental problem.

To decide where they should stand when this type of immediate reform increases inequality, they must understand the real causes of the destruction of nature. If they understand that capitalism and industrialism must be undone, then the dangers of expedient alliances with the wealthy will be clear. Minor reforms are to be welcomed, to be sure, but *not* if they are carried out at the expense of the poor. To accede to such socially regressive reforms, even if environmentally desirable, corrodes the possibility of political alliances between radical ecocentrists and social progressives. If radical ecocentrists do not stand consistently on the side of the poor, they will lose one of their major allies for the changes that *really* need to be made. Only a clear understanding of industrialism's determinative role in the rape of the Earth can foster resistance to this division. To change industrialism, radical ecocentrism must make common cause with the oppressed of the world.

Finally, just as humanity and nature need to be understood within a holistic perspective, so too does modern social reality require a holistic understanding.[64] The various forms of oppression include economic exploitation, racism, sexism, patriarchy, heterosexism, nationalism, authoritarianism, and the domination over nature; each exists in overt and subtle forms. Each of these forms of oppression requires struggle, but struggle against only one probably cannot be effective. The systemic integration of modern society makes them intertwined. Concern for any oppression requires concern for all oppression. This implies an objective basis for a broad-based political unity, and in this there is hope.

The real problem is the behemoth of industrialism ever expanding its grip, around the globe, beneath the earth, and into the skies. The seeds of an effective and radical ecocentrism live in those who somehow awaken to the exhilaration of being human in harmony with the rest of nature. Some may choose to stand for the forests, and that is good. Others, however, must reach out to the oppressed of the world and build bridges between the poor who live within the industrial world and those at the periphery. This requires political organization and action. It is another essential path.

Although grounds for despair are all around, there are also signs of hope. The environmental movement has broadened and deepened with astonishing rapidity. The Green movement is a significant presence in the national politics of many countries. Environmental groups supporting direct action, such as Earth First, Sea Shepherd, and Greenpeace often have significant support from the general public. Feminism, both in theory and in practice, has become an important force for social change, and ecological feminism will probably increase in importance within feminism.

It is hard to know now whether such movements can gain sufficient strength in numbers to force a reversal of the structure of industrialism. We do not know how much time we have. We may be in a transitional epoch and not the closing hours of industrialism—no one really knows. If there is time, then building an effective radical ecocentric movement founded on the desire for community life, on a rejection of social domination and sexual oppression, on an empathy for other animals, and on a love for all of nature may be able to effectively challenge and restructure industrialism.

We have recently taken a few steps back from the nuclear abyss. Should demilitarism spread, as it can if citizens continue to press for a real peace, this will release massive social resources for social and ecological reconstruction. Numerous projects must be funded, including: reforestation, stopping desertification, controlling and reversing population growth, developing energy efficiency and eventually ceasing the use of fossil fuels, stopping the loss of rain forests, expanding wilderness, ending the human extinction of animal and plant species, protecting the ozone shield, dealing with climate change, and many other tasks. Since the world military budget is some $900 billion each year, the financial resources are there if we can demilitarize society. The point is not that it is easy, but that it is possible. Peace action remains critical.

The struggle will extend beyond any of our lifetimes, and it is important to live now in a way that enables one's spirit to flourish. Humility, humor, and compassion are necessary to stay on the path. It is important to remember that mistakes are part of the way and results are often ambiguous. While the search for purity is admirable, its attainment is impossible and the fruits of action are uncertain. The point is the action, not its fruit. Such an understanding can sustain us through the hard times with a joy in all existence and an appreciation of our fellow travelers. As Norman Cousins put it, none of us "knows enough to be a pessimist."[65]

NOTES

Chapter 1.

1. See, for example, Barry Commoner's discussion of the "Third Law of Ecology," *The Closing Circle* (N.Y.: Bantam Books, 1972), 37–41.

2. Such a social ideal has been depicted aptly by Aldous Huxley in *Brave New World* (N.Y.: Harper, 1989) and received advocacy by some, notably B. F. Skinner. See particularly Skinner's *Beyond Freedom and Dignity* (N.Y.: Knopf, 1971) and also his popular novel *Walden Two* (N.Y.: MacMillan, 1976). The real nightmare is that the fear of disorder would lead people to positively desire such an "orderly" world. Some now praise the orderliness of Disneyland, which is rather thoroughly managed.

3. There is another and less common way to develop the inclusive concept of nature. If we understand ourselves as parts of nature, then our attempts to describe nature must always be incomplete. Whatever the merits of the cognitive maps we devise, they are only maps, created by parts of a terrain that is vastly greater in expanse than the maps which represent them. This use of the inclusive concept of nature pushes toward a profound change in our self-understanding and could ground a radical critique of the hubris of modern humanity. Rigorously developing this approach goes beyond description, understood as a cognitive mapping of some larger reality, to an experiential identification with this larger reality. This understanding of our connectedness to the rest of nature leads toward an ecologically inspired philosophy and will be discussed in the concluding chapters of this book.

4. See Peter A. Fritzell, "The Conflicts of Ecological Conscience," in *Companion to A Sand County Almanac: Interpretive and Critical Essays*, edited by J. Baird Callicott (Madison: University of Wisconsin Press, 1987) for a sensitive exposition of the tension between these two concepts of nature in Aldo Leopold's *A Sand County Almanac*. There is a nonconceptual relation to nature which is more fundamental than either the inclusive or dualistic concepts of nature. In my ninth chapter, I shall return to these two concepts in the context of suggesting that "gestalts," or experience, underlies both concepts.

5. Many other living creatures also live within their versions of the world—worlds that are constituted in part by the structure of their sensory organs. See "A

Stroll through the World of Animals and Men" by Jakob von Uexküll in *Instinctive Behavior*, translated and edited by Claire H. Schiller (N.Y.: International Universities Press, 1957).

6. See Chapter 1 of *Political Ideologies and Political Philosophies*, edited by H. B. McCullough (Toronto: Wall & Thompson, 1989) for a sample of the diversity of concepts of "ideology."

7. Roderick Nash, *Wilderness and the American Mind*, 3rd. ed. (New Haven: Yale University Press, 1982), xiv.

8. Max Oelschlaeger, *The Idea of Wilderness*, (New Haven: Yale University Press, 1991), 28.

9. Of course, social ideologies that attempt to justify the status quo need seek no agents of change and rarely distance themselves sufficiently from their contexts to ponder how the existing social system manages to reproduce itself over time. The analog to the requirement of agency for such theories would be an explanation of why people conform to structures of domination.

10. For one view of this, see World Commission on Environment and Development, *Our Common Future* (N.Y.: Oxford University Press, 1987), especially 15–17. For a more radical view, see Saral Sarkar, "Accommodating Industrialism: A Third World View of the West German Ecological Movement," *The Ecologist* 20, 4 (July/August 1990).

Chapter 2.

1. For examples of the first view, see William R. Catton, *Overshoot: The Ecological Basis of Revolutionary Change* (Chicago: University of Illinois Press, 1980), and Donella Meadows, Dennis L. Meadows and Jørgen Randers, *Beyond the Limits: Confronting Global Collapse, Envisioning a Sustainable Future*, (Post Mills, Vt.: Chelsea Green Publishing Co., 1992). The second attitude can be found in the annual Worldwatch Institute reports, such as Lester R. Brown et al., *State of the World 1990* (N.Y.: Norton, 1990). The Worldwatch Institute's sense of urgency is increasing. They now see this as the "decisive decade." See Sandra Postel, "Denial in the Decisive Decade," in Lester Brown et al., *State of the World 1992* (N.Y.: Norton, 1992). The third view is represented in *The Resourceful Earth*, edited by Julian Simon and Herman Kahn (Oxford: Basil Blackwell, 1984). For a useful discussion of the difficulties involved in adjudicating disputes about the seriousness of ecological problems, see John Dryzek, *Rational Ecology: Environment and Political Economy* (N.Y.: Basil Blackwell, 1987), chap. 2.

2. The most important locus for discussion of these topics is the scholarly journal *Environmental Ethics*, which has now been published for over a decade. There is almost no discussion in this journal of economic systems and their connection to environmental problems. Using a very loose criterion, I estimate that fewer than 15 percent of the articles and discussion papers over the decade have considered the role of economics in any form. Although there has been some discussion of Marx, not one paper has directly addressed the importance of capitalism in understanding environmental problems. Of late, there has been an improvement, and social and political analysis is becoming more common in the journal.

3. See Warwick Fox, "The Deep Ecology-Ecofeminism Debate and Its Parallels," *Environmental Ethics* 11, 1 (1989): 5–25.

4. *New York Times*, 23 March 1989. This figure, based on data from the Environmental Protection Agency, is low because it does not include emissions from automobiles, releases from toxic dumps, or emissions from companies that produce less than 75,000 pounds of toxic substances per year. These are substantial omissions and, if included would raise these numbers considerably.

5. Of course, some individuals can psychologically free themselves from the dominion of an economic system by becoming less attached to the rewards of conformity and the pains of nonconformity. If such nonconforming behavior becomes commonplace, the socioeconomic system will collapse, but unless this sort of disengagement becomes general, the system will continue.

6. Raymond Dasmann, "National Parks, Native Conservation and 'Future Primitive,'" *The Ecologist* 6, 5 (1976).

7. Roy A. Rappaport, "Ritual Regulation of Environmental Relations among a New Guinea People," in his *Ecology, Meaning, and Religion* (Berkeley: North Atlantic Books, 1979).

8. Robert Heilbroner notes that defining capitalism is a "profound and perplexing" problem to which he devoted a recent book, *The Nature and Logic of Capitalism* (N.Y.: Norton, 1985).

9. William Cronin, *Changes in the Land* (N.Y.: Hill & Wang, 1983), 63.

10. Both statements are quoted in Peter Mathiessen, *Indian Country* (N.Y.: Viking Press, 1984), 45–46 and 119.

11. John Locke, *Second Treatise of Government*, edited by C. B. Macpherson, ed., (Indianapolis: Hackett Publishing, 1980), paragraph 25.

12. Locke, paragraph 27.

13. Robert Nozick, *Anarchy, State, and Utopia* (N.Y.: Basic Books, 1974), 174–75.

14. Warwick Fox, personal communication, July 1990.

15. Locke, paragraph 31.

16. Locke, paragraph 32.

17. Locke, paragraph 33.

18. Locke, paragraph 51.

19. Locke, paragraph 48.

20. Locke, paragraph 50.

21. Thus, Robert Nozick, in *Anarchy, State, and Utopia,* recognizes that some principle of rectification is required to correct past injustices in the acquisition of property, but he pays scant attention to the principle (see 152–53) and does not acknowledge that the history of property acquisition is one of force, not of justice. This makes his theory of entitlement totally inapplicable until some principle of rectification is developed sufficiently to apply it to contemporary societies. It is indicative of Nozick's lack of interest in past injustice that he devotes little attention to the idea of rectification. Peter Wenz makes the point that all such theories of property rights simply ignore the actual history of the acquisition of private property and consequently cannot honestly legitimate present reality. See Peter S. Wenz, *Environmental Justice* (Albany: State University of New York Press, 1988), 75–76.

22. The question of ownership in modern capitalism is complex because many corporations are legally owned by stockholders who can exercise no effective control over the actions of the corporation. The classic study of this divorce of ownership and control is Adolf A. Berle and Gardiner C. Means, *The Modern Corporation and Private Property* (N.Y.: Macmillan, 1933).

23. See Commoner, *The Closing Circle* chap. 9, for development of the theme that industrial production, with its products and by-products that are outside the natural cycles of decay and cannot fit into ecological cycles.

24. Tibor Machan, "Pollution and Political Theory" in *Earthbound,* edited by Tom Reagan (N.Y.: Random House, 1984), 98.

25. Many economists attempt to solve the problem of environmental regulation by a "cost-benefit" analysis of various courses of action. The cost-benefit approach and the political approach are fundamentally incompatible. The political process with its norms (ideal, at least) of discussion and consensus presumes a primacy of the political over the economic. The political approach presumes that the process proceeds through rational argument about ultimate goals regarding nature and then moves on to agreements reached on the basis of that discussion. Property rights are thus subordinated to political determination. The cost-benefit approach assumes the stance of benevolent technocracy, within which the questions are resolvable through the determination and allocation of costs and benefits. The

cost-benefit approach turns the process into a technical problem of ascertaining costs and benefits, from which a decision to minimize costs and/or maximize benefits follows with no need for argument over goals. An excellent discussion of this incompatibility is found in Mark Sagoff, *The Economy of the Earth* (N.Y.: Cambridge University Press, 1988). For a more concise discussion of the same point, see Wenz, *Environmental Justice*.

26. See Karl Polanyi's classic analysis of this process in *The Great Transformation* (Boston: Beacon Press, 1957). "The economic advantages of a free labor market could not make up for the social destruction wrought by it. Regulation of a new type had to be introduced under which labor was again protected, only this time from the working of the market mechanism itself" 77. The response to the extreme abuse of humans that has been created by the labor market arose far more quickly than did the attempt to stop the abuses that have been created by the "nature market." This latter process has only recently begun.

27. Polanyi, *The Great Transformation*, 42.

28. Michael H. Best and William Connolly, "Nature and Its Largest Parasite," in *The Capitalist System*, 3rd ed., edited by Richard C. Edwards, Michael Reich, and Thomas E. Weisskopf, (Englewood Cliffs: Prentice Hall, 1986). See also Barry Commoner, *The Poverty of Power* (N.Y.: Knopf, 1976), 189ff.

29. The problem of the necessity for capitalistic rationality to discount the future is discussed by William Ophuls, *Ecology and the Politics of Scarcity* (San Francisco: W.H. Freeman & Co., 1977), 168–169, and John Dryzek, *Rational Ecology*, 74–75.

30. The actual situation is more complicated. Holders of vast resources, such as oil corporations or large timber corporations, realize that they can disrupt their own markets if they do not pace their activities in relation to the demand for their products. I am indebted to David Orton for pointing this out to me.

31. Charles A. S. Hall, "Sanctioning Resource Depletion: Economic Development and Neo-Classical Economics," *The Ecologist* 20, 3 (May/June 1990) 101. He is referring to C. Clark, *Mathematical Bioeconomics: The Optimal Management of Renewable Resources* (N.Y.: Wiley-Interscience, 1976).

32. Fred Hirsch, *Social Limits to Growth* (Cambridge: Harvard University Press, 1976). I discuss this topic is more extensively in Chapter 4.

33. See Paul Wachtel, *The Poverty of Affluence* (Philadelphia: New Society Publishers, 1989) chap. 2, for a discussion of this phenomenon.

34. Of course, those who are regulated in this way tend to take control of the

agencies of regulation. See Murray Edelman, *The Symbolic Uses of Politics* (Urbana: University of Illinois Press, 1964).

35. In this regard, see Jürgen Habermas, *Legitimation Crisis* (Boston: Beacon Press, 1975).

36. Hugh Stretton, *Capitalism, Socialism and the Environment* (N.Y.: Cambridge University Press, 1976), 6.

Chapter 3.

1. *National Geographic* 179, 6 (June 1991) 65.

2. Hillary F. French, "Restoring the East European and Soviet Environments," in *State of the World 1991*, edited by Lester Brown et al. (N.Y.: Norton, 1991), 94. Some of the more extreme claims in this essay should be treated with caution, as they come from Radio Free Europe and Radio Liberty, not on-site information.

3. Simon and Kahn, *The Resourceful Earth*, 3.

4. E. Federov, *Man and Nature: The Ecological Crisis and Social Progress* (N.Y.: International Publishers, 1981), 31, 64, 130.

5. Federov, *Man and Nature*, 125.

6. Norberto Bobbio, *Which Socialism? Marxism, Socialism and Democracy* (Minneapolis: University of Minnesota Press, 1987), 119.

7. For an excellent analysis of socialism along these lines, see Michael Luntley, *The Meaning of Socialism* (La Salle: Open Court, 1989).

8. The idea of democracy "more or less" is developed and defended in Frank Cunningham, *Democratic Theory and Socialism* (N.Y.: Cambridge University Press, 1987).

9. For valuable ideas concerning such an economy, see *Economics, Ecology, Ethics: Essays Toward A Steady-State Economy*, edited by Herman E. Daly (San Francisco: W. H. Freeman & Co., 1980) and Herman E. Daly and John B. Cobb, Jr., *For the Common Good: Redirecting the Economy Toward Community, the Environment, and a Sustainable Future* (Boston: Beacon Press, 1989).

10. Douglas R. Weiner, *Models of Nature: Ecology, Conservation, and Cultural Revolution in Soviet Russia* (Bloomington: Indiana University Press, 1988), 28.

11. Weiner, *Models of Nature*, 32.

12. Weiner, *Models of Nature*, 36, 37.

13. Weiner, *Models of Nature*, 61–62.

14. Weiner, *Models of Nature*, 99.

15. Richard Levins and Richard Lewontin, *The Dialectical Biologist* (Cambridge: Harvard University Press, 1985), 182.

16. Weiner, *Models of Nature*, 219.

17. Levins and Lewontin, *The Dialectical Biologist*, 180–81. This is only one element of a complex issue. For a brief discussion of the ideological, material, and political elements involved in the Lysenko case, see chap. 7 of Levins and Lewontin. They argue that there is no evidence that in fact Soviet agricultural output was damaged by the acceptance of Lysenkoism. Clearly the same case cannot be made for the degradation of the nature preserves.

18. Boris Komorov, *The Destruction of Nature in the Soviet Union* (White Plains: M.E. Sharpe, 1980), 60.

19. The climatologist Veitsman, quoted in Weiner, *Models of Nature*, 225.

20. Weiner, *Models of Nature*, 227.

21. Weiner, *Models of Nature*, 228.

22. Komorov, *The Destruction of Nature*, 81–90.

23. Raymond F. Dasmann, *Planet in Peril: Man and the Biosphere Today* (N.Y.: World Publishing, 1972), 148.

24. This a major consideration in Komorov, *The Destruction of Nature*.

25. Edelman, *The Symbolic Uses of Politics*.

26. Komorov, *The Destruction of Nature*, 70–71.

27. Charles E. Ziegler, *Environmental Policy in the USSR* (Amherst: University of Massachusetts Press, 1987), chap. 5.

28. "East Meets West," *E: The Environmental Magazine* 2, 3 (May/June 1991): 41, 43.

29. Max Weber, *The Theory of Social and Economic Organization*, translated by A. M. Henderson and Talcott Parsons (N.Y.: Free Press, 1964), 338.

30. This discussion draws on Dryzek, *Rational Ecology*, chap. 8.

31. See Komorov, *The Destruction of Nature*, for a discussion of the secrecy surrounding the vast pollution of Soviet waters with PCBs by Soviet military. The extensive release of radioactive wastes and other toxic wastes by the United States military is closely analogous. See Brown, *The State of the World 1992*, 52–53.

32. Some Marxists are trying to create a theoretical space within which some regard for nature can be recognized. See the journal *Capitalism, Nature, Socialism*, especially John Ely, "Lukac's Construction of Nature" in Vol. 1 (Fall 1988).

33. "The Puritan wanted to work in a calling; we are forced to do so. [The modern economic order] is now bound to the technical and economic conditions of machine production which today determine the lives of all individuals who are born into this mechanism, not only those directly concerned with economic acquisition, with irresistible force. Perhaps it will so determine them until the last ton of fossilized coal is burnt. In Baxter's view the care for external goods should lie on the

shoulders of the 'saint like a light cloak, which can be thrown aside at any moment.' But fate decreed that the cloak should become an iron cage." Max Weber, *The Protestant Ethic and the Spirit of Capitalism*, trans. by Talcott Parsons (N.Y.: Scribner's, 1958), 181.

Chapter 4.

1. This oversimplifies, as one aim of technical innovation within capitalism is to maintain or increase control over the labor force. The relations between capitalism and technology are rather complex. See Andrew Feenberg, "The Critical Theory of Technology," *Capitalism, Nature, Socialism* No. 5 (October 1990).

2. "Critique of the Gotha Program," in *The Marx-Engels Reader*, 2nd edition, edited by Robert C. Tucker (New York: Norton, 1978), 531.

3. See Herbert Marcuse, *Eros and Civilization* (N.Y.: Vintage Press, 1962) for the possibility of replacing work with play.

4. Tucker, *Marx-Engels Reader*, 441, emphasis added.

5. The complexity of determining "the" start of the industrial revolution and the multidimensional nature of the industrial revolution is well developed by Lewis Mumford in *The Myth of the Machine: The Pentagon of Power* (N.Y.: Harcourt Brace Jovanovich, 1970), chaps. 6–7.

6. Fernand Braudel, *The Wheels of Commerce*, Vol. II of *Civilization and Capitalism: 15th-18th Century* (N.Y.: Harper & Row, 1982), 300–302.

7. Braudel, *The Wheels of Commerce*, 247 emphasis in original. This is not Braudel's final word on this complex issue. See *The Perspective of the World*, Vol. III of *Civilization and Capitalism: 15th-18th Century* (N.Y.: Harper & Row, 1984), 536–587, for a discussion of the "dialectic between the long and the short-term" issues in understanding the industrial revolution.

8. Polanyi, *The Great Transformation*, 41.

9. John Kenneth Galbraith, *The New Industrial State* (N.Y.: New American Library, 1968), chap. 2.

10. The extension of planning into the political realm dictated by the capital expenses that are involved in industrial production can be illustrated by a current controversy involving the phasing out of the use of chlorofluorocarbons (CFCs), known to deplete the ozone layer. One candidate for replacing CFCs are hydrochlorofluorocarbons (HCFCs). Although HCFCs are less destructive to the ozone layer than are CFCs, they are still harmful. Industrial producers demand to know how long substitutes for CFCs will be used before they would be willing to produce them. The chemical industry claims that sixty years of the use of HCFCs is

necessary to repay their capital investment, according to John Holusha, "Ozone Issue: Economics of a Ban," *New York Times*, 11 January, 1990. Of course, no one now knows how dire the state of the ozone layer may be in twenty years, much less sixty years. Despite this, large investments of capital require that corporate planning extends into the control of state decisions.

11. Martin Heidegger, "The Question Concerning Technology" in *The Question Concerning Technology and Other Essays* (N.Y.: Harper & Row, 1977), 17, 24.

12. "Manifesto of the Communist Party" in Tucker, *The Marx-Engels Reader*, 477.

13. Richard Barnet, *The Lean Years: Politics in the Age of Scarcity* (N.Y.: Simon and Schuster, 1980), 239.

14. Richard J. Barnet, "Defining the Moment," *The New Yorker*, 16 July, 1990, 59.

15. Steven Shrybman, "Selling the Environment Short," *Earth Island Journal* (Spring 1991): 31–34. Shrybman documents the impact of the Free Trade Agreement of 1989 on Canadian environmental regulations, leading to the "lowest common denominator." This is also likely to happen with such agreements with Mexico, leading to a leveling downward of United States regulations. See also *The Ecologist* 21, 2 (March/April 1991) for several articles discussing the role of the Food and Agriculture Organization of the United Nations in promoting "internationalism" and the consequent creation of local poverty and the destruction of sustainable agriculture and local ecosystems.

16. Commoner, *The Closing Circle*, chap. 9.

17. For a critique of Commoner along these line see Charles T. Rubin, "Environmental Policy and Environmental Thought: Commoner and Rukelshaus," *Environmental Ethics*, 11, 1 (Spring 1989).

18. Theodore Roszak, *Person/Planet: The Creative Disintegration of Industrial Society* (Garden City: Anchor Books, 1979), 243.

19. Lester R. Brown et al., *State of the World 1987* (N. Y.: Norton, 1987), 38.

20. Jean Baudrillard, quoted in Tom Birch, "The Incarceration of Wildness," *Environmental Ethics* 12, 1 (Spring 1990): 18.

21. Frederick Engels, "On Authority" in Tucker, *Marx-Engels Reader*, 731.

22. Locke, *Second Treatise*, paragraphs 48–50.

23. This theme is developed in Nicholas Xenos, *Scarcity and Modernity* (N.Y.: Routledge, 1989).

24. Thorstein Veblen, *The Theory of the Leisure Class*, quoted in Xenos, *Scarcity and Modernity*, 20.

25. Galbraith, *The New Industrial State*, 228.

26. Bill Devall, *Simple in Means, Rich in Ends* (Salt Lake City: Gibbs-Smith, 1988); also *Less is More: The Art of Voluntary Poverty*, edited by Goldian Vanden Broeck (N.Y.: Harper & Row, 1978).

27. See the review of survey evidence within and between societies reported by Richard A. Easterlin, "Does Economic Growth Improve the Human Lot?" in *Nations and Households in Economic Growth*, edited by Paul A. David and Melvin W. Reder (Stanford: Stanford University Press, 1972).

28. This phenomenon has been discussed from different perspectives at some length. For economic perspectives, see Tibor Scitovsky, *The Joyless Economy* (N.Y.: Oxford University Press, 1976) and Fred Hirsch, *The Social Limits to Growth*. See Paul Wachtel, *The Poverty of Affluence* for a psychological perspective and Albert Borgmann, *Technology and the Character of Contemporary Life* (Chicago: University of Chicago Press, 1984), 130ff, for a philosophical perspective on consumerism.

29. "The average person today is four-and-a-half times richer than were his or her great-grandparents at the turn of the century." Alan Durning, "Asking How Much is Enough" in Lester R. Brown et al., *State of the World 1991*, 153.

30. See Hirsch, *Social Limits to Growth*.

31. Hirsch, *Social Limits*, 1.

32. See Wachtel, *Poverty of Affluence*, particularly chap. 4.

33. Wachtel, *Poverty of Affluence*, 79.

34. Marshall Sahlins, *Stone Age Economics* (Chicago: Aldine, 1972), 1–2. See also Colin Turnbull's lyrical description of the lives of rain forest pygmies in *The Forest People* (N.Y.: Simon and Schuster, 1961).

35. Jonathon Porritt, *Seeing Green: The Politics of Ecology Explained* (Oxford: Basil Blackwell, 1985), xiii.

36. Nafis Sadik, *The State of World Population 1990* (N.Y.: United Nations Population Fund, n.d.), 12, emphasis in original.

37. In Saral Sarkar, "Accommodating Industrialism," 151–152.

Chapter 5.

1. The need to control subjectivity is based on the necessity of maintaining social order in increasingly dense, complex, and integrated societies. Per capita expenditures for advertising in the United State rose from $198 in 1950 to $498 in 1989. The typical American teenager sees 100,000 TV ads between birth and high school graduation. Durning, "Asking How Much Is Enough," 163.

2. The United Nations has recently raised its population projections because the rate in the reduction of birth rates has fallen in the last few years. This is

because fertility rates have unexpectedly stabilized at four rather than two children per woman. See Sadik, *The State of the World Population: 1990*.

3. Langdon Winner, *The Whale and the Reactor: A Search for Limits in an Age of High Technology* (Chicago: University of Chicago Press, 1986).

4. "Any discussion of the reorganization of technology to serve human needs seems, at this point, so utopian that it robs one of the conviction necessary to shape a believable vision." John McDermott, "Technology: The Opiate of the Intellectuals," *New York Review of Books* 31 July, 1969, 34.

5. This situation is often used to describe situations where a high degree of social control is imputed, as when some "ruler" is claimed to be a puppet of others. To say someone is a puppet is to claim that they are controlled by someone else—that they are not autonomous.

6. Lewis Mumford, "Technics and the Nature of Man," in, *Philosophy and Technology*, edited by Carl Mitcham and Robert Mackey (N.Y.: Free Press, 1972), 82.

7. Max Horkheimer, *Critical Theory* (N.Y.: Herder and Herder, 1972), 57.

8. Stanley Diamond, *In Search of the Primitive* (New Brunswick: Transaction Books, 1974), 1.

9. See Sahlins, *Stone Age Economics*.

10. Gregory Bateson, *Steps to an Ecology of Mind* (N.Y.: Ballantine Books, 1972), 434.

11. This line of discussion has been pursued over the years by C. West Churchman. See *Prediction and Optimal Decision* (Englewood Cliffs: Prentice Hall, 1961), *Challenge to Reason* (N.Y.: McGraw Hill, 1968), and *The Design of Inquiring Systems* (N.Y.: Basic Books, 1971).

12. See Herbert A. Simon, *Models of Man* (N.Y.: Wiley and Sons, 1957), especially part 4. This idea of getting through has been applied to environmental problems by Warren Johnson in *Muddling Toward Frugality* (Boulder: Shambala, 1978).

13. Donella Meadows, "Systems Paradigm," *Co-Evolution Quarterly*, No. 34 (Summer, 1982): 101.

14. Alasdair MacIntyre, *After Virtue: A Study in Moral Theory*, 2nd ed. (Notre Dame: University of Notre Dame Press, 1984), 106–107.

15. E. Federov, *Man and Nature*, 125, 128.

16. John Perlin, *A Forest Journey: The Role of Wood in the Development of Civilization* (N.Y.: Norton, 1989).

17. See Birch, "The Incarceration of Wilderness," 22. See also Bill McKibben, *The End of Nature* (N.Y.: Doubleday, 1989), for a similar insight.

Chapter 6.

1. Hans Jonas, *The Imperative of Responsibility: In Search of an Ethics for the Technological Age* (Chicago: University of Chicago Press, 1984).

2. Two common grounds for such an extension are being a subject of a life and the capacity to suffer. For the first approach, see Tom Reagan, *The Case For Animal Rights* (Berkeley: University of California Press, 1983); Peter Singer's *Animal Liberation* (N.Y.: Avon Books, 1975) is an example of the second approach.

3. Lynn White, Jr., "The Historical Roots of our Ecological Crisis," *Science* 155, 3767 (10 March 1967): 1203–7. This essay has been widely reprinted. The quotes above are from *Environment and Society*, edited by Robert T. Roelofs et al. (Englewood Cliffs: Prentice Hall, 1974), 11, 13.

4. Robin Attfield has argued for this position. See, for example, "Western Traditions and Environmental Ethics" in *Environmental Philosophy*, edited by Robert Elliot and Arran Gare (University Park: Pennsylvania State University, 1983), and Robin Attfield, "The Prospects for Preservation" in *Philosophical Inquiry* 8, 1–2 (Winter/Spring 1986).

5. Carolyn Merchant, *The Death of Nature: Women, Ecology, and the Scientific Revolution* (San Francisco: Harper & Row, 1990), 193.

6. Robert Heilbroner, *The Nature and Logic of Capitalism*, 135.

7. C. S. Peirce "The Fixation of Belief," in *Pragmatism: The Classic Writings*, edited by H. S. Thayer (Indianapolis: Hackett, 1982), 74.

8. "How To Make Our Ideas Clear" in Thayer, *Pragmatism*, 97.

9. The only problem with Peirce's "solution" is that we can give no meaning to the end of inquiry. How would we know that we had reached the end of inquiry? If we cannot know this, then of what use is the idea of ultimate agreement? It is as suspect and useless as the idea of correspondence. Peirce displaces the problem of truth, but it might be best to simply dispose of it. This point is developed by Richard Rorty, in "Pragmatism, Davidson and truth," in *Objectivity, Relativism, and Truth: Philosophical Papers* Vol. 1 (Cambridge: Cambridge University Press, 1991). He acknowledges that the point was made by Michael Williams.

10. This point has received emphasis and development by both Jürgen Habermas and Richard Rorty. See particularly chapter 6 in Habermas, *Knowledge and Human Interests* (Boston: Beacon Press: 1971) and Rorty, *Objectivity*.

11. See, for example, Carolyn Merchant, *Death of Nature*, Evelyn Fox Keller, *Reflections on Gender and Science* (New Haven: Yale University Press: 1985), and Sandra Harding, *The Science Question in Feminism* (Ithaca: Cornell University Press: 1986).

12. For good discussions of the development of the modern image of nature from rather different perspectives, see E.J. Dijksterhuis, *The Mechanization of the World Picture* (London: Oxford University Press, 1961), William Leiss, *The Domination of Nature* (Boston: Beacon Press, 1974), Morris Berman, *The Reenchantment of the World* (Ithaca: Cornell University Press, 1981), and Carolyn Merchant, *Death of Nature*.

13. For a useful discussion of these experiments, along with much illustrative material, see *Explorations in Transactional Psychology*, edited by Franklin P. Kilpatrick (N.Y.: New York University Press, 1961).

14. Kilpatrick, *Explorations*, 3.

15. Kilpatrick, *Explorations*, chap. 10.

16. This shift in focus can be dated with the publication of Thomas Kuhn's *The Structure of Scientific Revolutions* (Chicago: University of Chicago Press, 1962), although this oversimplifies a complex history.

17. For a very good summary of the debates leading to the general rejection of positivism as an adequate understanding of science, see Frederick Suppe, "The Search for Philosophic Understanding of Scientific Theories" in *The Structure of Scientific Theories*, 2nd. ed., edited by Frederick Suppe (Urbana: University of Illinois Press, 1977), and Richard Bernstein, *Beyond Objectivism and Subjectivism: Science, Hermeneutics and Praxis* (Philadelphia: University of Pennsylvania Press, 1983), part 2.

18. For a more extended development of these points, along with examples, see my "Method and Factual Agreement in Science," *Boston Studies in the Philosophy of Science* Vol. 8 (Dordrecht: Reidel, 1971), 459–469.

19. Rene Descartes, *Discourse on Method and Meditations*, trans. by Laurence J. Lafleur (N.Y.: Bobbs-Merrill, 1960), 15.

20. For further discussion of reasons why physics should not be taken as paradigmatic of science, see Sandra Harding, *The Science Question*, 44–47.

21. Indeed, the roots precede Plato and include the Ionian philosophers and Pythagoras. See J. Baird Callicott, "Traditional American Indian and Western European Attitudes Toward Nature: An Overview," *Environmental Ethics* 4 (1982): 293–318, for a brief discussion of this.

22. E.A. Burtt, *The Metaphysical Foundations of Modern Science* (Garden City: Anchor Books, 1954), 238–39.

23. Ragnar Granit, "Reflections on the Evolution of Mind and Its Environment" in *Mind in Nature*, edited by Richard Q. Elvee (San Francisco: Harper & Row, 1982), 106.

24. Jürgen Habermas has developed a powerful understanding of the nature of science and attempted a quasi-transcendental justification for the instrumental ori-

entation. In particular, see *Knowledge and Human Interests* and his "Introduction" to *Theory and Practice* (Boston: Beacon Press, 1973).

25. I am grateful to William Pohle for this point. See also Dijksterhuis, *Mechanization of the World Picture*, 17.

26. George Sessions, "Ecocentrism and the Greens: Deep Ecology and the Environmental Task," *The Trumpeter* 5, 2 (Spring 1988): 67.

27. Warwick Fox, *Toward a Transpersonal Ecology: Developing New Foundations for Environmentalism* (Boston: Shambala, 1990), 252.

28. Freya Matthews, *The Ecological Self* (Savage, MD: Barnes and Noble: 1991).

29. McKibben, *The End of Nature*, 213.

30. For example, see Bruce Holbrook, *The Stone Monkey* (N.Y.: William Morrow and Co., 1981) for a description of science within a Chinese cultural context.

31. John Dewey, *The Quest for Certainty* (N.Y.: G. P. Putnam, 1960), 14.

32. Robert Persig, *Zen and the Art of Motorcycle Maintenance* (N.Y.: William Morrow and Co., 1974).

33. Dewey, *Quest*, 130.

34. Dewey, *Quest*, 128.

35. See Max Horkeimer and Theodor Adorno, *The Dialectic of Enlightenment* (N.Y.: Herder and Herder, 1972) for a complex and intriguing critique of the Enlightenment.

36. Gregory Bateson, "Ecological Flexibility in Urban Civilization" in *Steps to an Ecology of Mind*, 495.

37. See, for example, Jürgen Habermas, *The Philosophical Discussion of Modernity: Twelve Lectures*, translated by Frederick Lawrence (Cambridge: MIT Press, 1987).

38. These passages are from Marx, "Economic and Philosophic Manuscripts" in *The Marx-Engels Reader*, edited by R. Tucker, 84–85.

39. The question of nature in Marx is complex because Marx did not have only one view on this issue. For a fuller discussion of some of these issues and a discussion of controversies among later Marxists, see Alfred Schmidt, *The Concept of Nature in Marx* (London: NLB, 1973), especially chap. 4.

40. Herbert Marcuse, *One Dimensional Man* (Boston: Beacon Press, 1964), 166–167.

41. Marcuse, *One Dimensional Man*, 235.

42. Marcuse, *One Dimensional Man*, 236–238.

43. C. Fred Alford, *Science and the Revenge of Nature: Marcuse and Habermas* (Tampa: University of Florida Press, 1985), 64. Alford's nuanced discussion of both Marcuse and Habermas on their views of nature is valuable and extends over the whole corpus of Marcuse's writings.

44. Habermas, *Knowledge and Human Interests*, 32–33.

45. Henning Ottman, "Cognitive Interests and Self-Reflection" in *Habermas: Critical Debates*, edited by John B. Thompson and David Held (Cambridge: MIT Press, 1982), 89, emphasis in the original.

46. Joel Whitebook, "The Problem of Nature in Habermas," *Telos* No. 40 (Summer 1979): 53.

47. Habermas, "A Reply to my Critics," *Habermas: Critical Debates*, 243–44, emphasis in original.

48. These phrases are drawn from Whitebook, "The Problem of Nature," 61, but the argument is endorsed by Habermas, *Critical Debates*, 247.

49. A similar point is made by Warwick Fox, "The Deep Ecology-Ecofeminism Debate and Its Parallels," 17–18.

50. Habermas, "A Reply," 248.

51. Alford, *Science and The Revenge of Nature*, 151. This work is a valuable critical discussion of Habermas, incorporating his replies to these critics.

52. Alford, *Science and the Revenge of Nature*, 147.

53. Jonas, *The Imperative of Responsibility*, 8.

54. Whitebook attempts a sketch of this in a discussion of biology, and Alford considers medical anthropology's discoveries of effective means of healing among tribal cultures.

55. Robyn Eckersley, *Environmentalism and Political Theory* (Albany: State University of New York Press, 1992), chap. 5.

Chapter 7.

1. *New York Times*, 30 May 1991, advertisement in Opinion/Editorial section.

2. See Patrick McCully, "A Message to the Executives and Shareholders of E. I. DuPont de Nemours and Co. and Imperial Chemical Industries, Ltd.," *The Ecologist* 21, 3 (May/June 1991): 114–116.

3. *The SEQR Handbook* (Albany: New York State Department of Environmental Conservation, 1982), B-36.

4. Lester Milbraith, *Environmentalists: Vanguard for a New Society* (Albany: State University of New York Press, 1984), 82, Table C-6 on 123, Table C-7 on 124.

5. Milbraith, *Environmentalists*, Table C-2 on 120.

6. A number of studies articulate two different paradigms to describe environmentalism. Thus, William R. Catton Jr. and Riley E. Dunlap distinguish between a "human exemptionalist" paradigm and a "new ecological" paradigm in their "A New Ecological Paradigm for Post-Exhuberant Sociology," *American Behavioral Scientist* 24, 1, (September/October 1980): 15–47. Lester Milbraith distinguishes between a

"dominant social" paradigm and a "new environmental" paradigm in *Environmentalists*. Arne Naess distinguishes "shallow" from "deep" ecology in "The Shallow and the Deep, Long-Range Ecology Movements," *Inquiry* 16, 1 (March 1973): 95–100. The most comprehensive survey of types of environmentalism is in Fox, *Toward a Transpersonal Ecology*, 22ff.

7. Langdon Winner, *The Whale and the Reactor*, chap. 8.

8. Winner, *The Whale and the Reactor*, 139, 149.

9. John Dryzek, *Rational Ecology*, 23. See also Mark Sagoff, *The Economy of the Earth*, chap. 2.

10. Barry Commoner, *The Closing Circle*. His laws are explained in chap. 2.

11. Commoner, *The Closing Circle*, 42.

12. Garrett Hardin, *Filters Against Folly*, (N.Y.: Penguin Books, 1986), 24.

13. Garrett Hardin, *Exploring New Ethics for Survival: The Voyage of the Spaceship Beagle* (Baltimore: Penguin, 1973), 62, emphasis in original.

14. Hardin, *Filters*, 58. See also Hardin, *Exploring New Ethics*, 38.

15. Hardin, *Filters*, 58–59. The sexual metaphors are suggestive of a masculine orientation toward domination.

16. Hardin, *Filters*, 41.

17. Hardin, *Filters*, 65, emphasis added.

18. Hardin, *Filters*, 52.

19. Commoner, *Closing Circle*, 240.

20. Garrett Hardin, "Carrying Capacity as an Ethical Concept," in *Lifeboat Ethics: The Moral Dilemmas of World Hunger*, edited by George R. Lucas, Jr. and Thomas W. Ogletree (N.Y.: Harper and Row, 1976), 131, emphasis added.

21. Robert Heilbroner suggests this possibility in *An Inquiry into the Human Prospect* (N.Y.: Norton, 1980).

22. Commoner, *Closing Circle*, 296.

23. Commoner, *Closing Circle*, 209.

24. Hardin, *Filters*, 76–80.

25. Thomas Malthus, "A Summary View of the Principle of Population," reprinted in *On Population: Three Essays* (N.Y.: New American Library, 1960), 56–58, emphasis added.

26. Commoner, *Closing Circle*, 286, 287.

27. Barry Commoner, *The Poverty of Power* (N.Y.: Knopf, 1976), 262.

28. Hardin, *Exploring New Ethics*, chap. 13.

29. Donald Wooster, *Nature's Economy: The Roots of Ecology* (Garden City: Anchor Books, 1979), 347–348.

30. Winner, *Whale and the Reactor*, 135, 137.

Chapter 8.

1. Commoner neither discusses nor tries to justify his anthropocentrism, but Hardin is explicit in limiting his concern to humans, noting that his view is "definitely homocentric." Hardin, "Carrying Capacity," in *Lifeboat Ethics*, 134.

2. Wooster, *Nature's Economy*, 292.

3. Arne Naess, *Ecology, community and lifestyle: Outline of an Ecosophy*, translated and revised by David Rothenberg (N.Y.: Cambridge University Press, 1989), 36.

4. This illustration is used by Charles Birch and John B. Cobb, Jr., *The Liberation of Life: From the Cell to the Community* (N.Y.: Cambridge University Press, 1981), 104–105.

5. Michael E. Zimmerman, "Quantum Theory, Intrinsic Value, and Pantheism," *Environmental Ethics* 10, 1 (Spring 1988): 17.

6. For more examples, see David Ehrenfeld, *The Arrogance of Humanism* (N.Y.: Oxford University Press, 1978).

7. In this regard, see Gregory Bateson, *Steps to An Ecology of Mind*, especially "Conscious Purpose versus Nature" and "Effects of Conscious Purpose on Human Adaptation."

8. For two extended arguments, from diverse perspectives, for dethroning physics as the paradigm of knowledge, see Sandra Harding, *The Science Question in Feminism* and Nicholas Maxwell, *From Knowledge to Wisdom: A Revolution in the Aims and Methods of Science* (N.Y.: Basil Blackwell, 1984).

9. This discussion draws heavily on Hans Jonas's discussion of anthropomorphism in *The Phenomenon of Life* (Chicago: University of Chicago Press, 1966), 33–37.

10. It is worth noting that Habermas, as discussed in Chapter 6, preserves a dualism in his analysis of human reason.

11. Jonas, *The Phenomenon of Life*, 37.

12. Evelyn Fox Keller, *Reflections on Gender*, 132, emphasis in original.

13. Keller, *Reflections on Gender*, 134–35.

14. Karen Warren, "Feminism and Ecology: Making Connections," *Environmental Ethics* 9, 1: 6.

15. Patsy Hallen, "Making Peace with Nature: Why Ecology Needs Feminism," *The Trumpeter* 4, 3 (Summer 1987): 6.

16. John Dryzek, "Green Reason: Communicative Ethics for the Biosphere," *Environmental Ethics* 12, 3 (Fall 1990): 192–210.

17. Dryzek, "Green Reason," 206, emphasis in original.

18. Aldo Leopold, "Some Fundamentals of Conservation in the Southwest,"

Environmental Ethics 1, 2 (Summer 1979): 140. For an explanation of the Gaia hypothesis, see James Lovelock, *Gaia: A New Look at Life on Earth* (N.Y.: Oxford University Press, 1979) and *The Ages of Gaia: A Biography of Life on Earth* (N.Y.: Norton, 1988).

19. Roderick Frazier Nash, *The Rights of Nature: A History of Environmental Ethics* (Madison: University of Wisconsin Press, 1989), 122; see chap. 5. for a brief history of the "greening of philosophy."

20. J. Baird Callicott, "The Case Against Moral Pluralism," *Environmental Ethics* 12, 2 (Summer 1990): 101.

21. Fox, *Towards a Transpersonal Ecology*, chap. 6.

22. The estimate is by Michael Soule, "Conservation Biology and the 'Real World'" in *Conservation Biology: The Science of Scarcity and Diversity* (Sunderland: Sinauer Associates, 1986), 4.

23. Neil Evernden, *The Natural Alien: Humankind and the Environment* (Toronto: University of Toronto Press, 1985), 11–12.

24. Full page advertisement on the back cover of *E: The Environmental Magazine* 2, 3 (May/June 1991). It has run more than once.

25. Richard and Val Routley, "Human Chauvinism and Environmental Ethics," in *Environmental Philosophy*, edited by D. S. Mannison, M. A. McRobbie, and R. Routley, (Canberra: Australian National University, 1980). The paper was written in 1973. The Routleys subsequently changed their names to Richard Sylvan and Val Plumwood. See also R. and V. Routley, "Against the Inevitability of Human Chauvinism," in *Ethics and the Problem of the 21st Century*, edited by K. E. Goodpaster and K. M. Sayre, (Notre Dame: University of Notre Dame Press, 1979).

26. Fox, *Toward a Transpersonal Ecology*, 13–22.

27. Paul Taylor, *Respect for Nature: A Theory of Environmental Ethics* (Princeton: Princeton University Press, 1986), chap. 3.

28. Taylor, *Respect*, 115.

29. Taylor, *Respect*, 116–117.

30. Taylor, *Respect*, 128.

31. For Taylor's arguments concerning anthropocentrism, see *Respect*, 129–156.

32. Taylor, *Respect*, 149, emphasis in original.

33. Taylor, *Respect*, 154–155.

34. Richard A. Watson, "A Critique of Anti-Anthropocentric Biocentrism," *Environmental Ethics* 5, 3 (Fall 1983): 253.

35. J. Baird Callicott, *In Defense of a Land Ethic* (Albany: State University of New York Press, 1989), 89. This book is a collection of his essays written over a decade.

36. Callicott, *In Defense*, 91, quoting Leopold.

37. Callicott, *In Defense* , 70, see also 83.

38. Taylor, *Respect*, 123.

39. Callicott, *In Defense*, 84.

40. Tom Regan, *The Case for Animal Rights*, 362. Later in this same work, Regan notes that at the level of practice, there may be more harmony than such a label would indicate.

41. Warwick Fox, *Toward a Transpersonal Ecology*, 169–175.

42. "An autopoietic machine . . . has its own organization . . . as the fundamental value it maintains constant." Humberto R. Maturana and Francisco J. Varela, *Autopoiesis and Cognition: The Realization of the Living* (Dordrecht: Reidel, 1980), 79. They do mean "machine," at least in the sense that they intend their approach to be "mechanistic," appealing only to forces "found in the physical universe," 75.

43. Fox, *Toward a Transpersonal Ecology*, 172.

44. Callicott, *In Defense* , 85.

45. Callicott, *In Defense* , 87.

46. Freya Matthews, *The Ecological Self*, 98ff. She notes that while Maturana and Varela use the concept to dissolve the need for any *telos* in living systems, she is using it as being definitive of *telos*, see *Ecological Self*, note 9, 173.

47. Matthews claims that this is "analytic," or necessarily true, *The Ecological Self*, 118. Warwick Fox has made a similar argument using the concept of autopoiesis; see *Toward a Transpersonal Ecology*, 169–178.

48. See Fox's reversal of this charge by claiming that holism more aptly suggests "environmental democracy" than it does "environmental fascism," *Toward a Transpersonal Ecology*, 178–79.

49. Callicott, *In Defense*, 114.

50. Callicott, *In Defense*, 84.

51. Taylor, *Respect*, 305–306.

52. Callicott, *In Defense*, 21.

53. See Callicott's essay "Animal Liberation and Environmental Ethics: Back Together Again" in *In Defense*, 49–59, where the important distinction between wild and domesticated animals is used to find common ground between the animal liberation and the environmental movements. However, there is a wide divergence between Taylor and another environmental philosopher on the issue of hunting. See Taylor, *Respect*, 179–86 and Holmes Rolston III, *Environmental Ethics: Duties to and Values in the World* (Philadelphia: Temple University Press, 1988), 91–93.

54. Callicott, *In Defense*, 161. He rightly points out that the distinction between these two types of value is not consistent in philosophical discussion. For a

different stipulation of these terms, see Taylor, *Respect*, 73–74. In fact, Callicott himself is inconsistent in his own usage, claiming in 1986 that species have intrinsic value (see *In Defense*, 153), while rejecting intrinsic value in favor of inherent value in 1985 (see *In Defense*, 161).

55. Callicott, *In Defense*, 163, emphasis in original. Callicott goes on in the same article to use a conservative version of quantum mechanics to push this question into difficult terrain. He notes that quantum mechanics erases the distinction between primary and secondary qualities because all properties, including velocity and location, require observation for their realization. This implies that there can be no intrinsic value in nature, but this is a concession of no consequence, "since *no* properties in nature are strictly intrinsic, that is, ontologically objective and independent of consciousness," 169.

56. Fox, *Toward a Transpersonal Ecology*, 21. See also Paul Taylor, "In Defense of Biocentrism," *Environmental Ethics* 5, 3, (Fall 1983): 237–243, for a distinction between content, practical significance, and psychological explanation to show that a nonanthropocentric outlook cannot be dismissed as impossible on the basis that it is put forward by humans.

57. Callicott, *In Defense*, 70; see also 99.

58. Callicott, *In Defense*, 70, quoting Leopold.

59. Callicott, *In Defense*, 99.

60. Callicott, *In Defense*, 70.

61. Callicott, *In Defense*, 83; see also 96.

62. Callicott, *In Defense*, 99.

63. Callicott, *In Defense*, 70; the quote is from Leopold's *Sand County Almanac*, 204. Interestingly, Habermas concurs with a similar conclusion when he agrees with Whitebook that regardless of what might be shown theoretically about anthropocentrism, "a question would still remain at the level of social psychology." See Whitebook, "Nature in Habermas," 64 and Habermas, "Reply to My Critics," 247.

64. Callicott, *In Defense*, 147. "The *source* of all value is human consciousness," 133 (emphasis in original). In fairness to Callicott, it should be noted that he indicates an understanding of the limits of Newtonian science and has written papers on the implications of quantum mechanics for a new world view. For example, in *In Defense* he seems to accept the idea that, within a quantum mechanical understanding of reality, "physics and ethics are . . . equally descriptive of nature," 170. This, of course, seems to lead in quite a different direction. I think that Michael Zimmerman has correctly located the difficulty of making appeals to quantum mechanics in his argument that such appeals will not give any experiential grounding in overcoming anthropocentrism. He also suggests, for a different rea-

son, that Callicott has an excessive attachment to a "scientific" perspective. See Zimmerman, "Quantum Theory, Intrinsic Value, and Pantheism."

65. Callicott, *In Defense*, 114.

66. Rolston, *Environmental Ethics*, 115.

67. Rolston, *Environmental Ethics*, 67.

68. Rolston, *Environmental Ethics*, 68, and 70.

69. Rolston, *Environmental Ethics*, 72.

70. Rolston, *Environmental Ethics*, 73.

71. Rolston, *Environmental Ethics*, 231.

72. See Richard Rorty, *Philosophy and the Mirror of Nature* (Princeton: Princeton University Press, 1979).

73. Rolston's use of the metaphor of a mirror requires further development for its appraisal. The metaphor of a dual mirroring for understanding the relation between mind and nature is suggestive, but difficult to understand. If we combine an understanding of the impossibility of any simple objectivist analysis of knowing with the suggestion, arising out of quantum mechanics, that the world as we experience it only arises when we look at it, we are left without any place to rest. The metaphor of a dual mirroring suggests understanding the relation between knowing and nature as *two* mirrors, each reflecting the other with no concrete image between them, mutually crystallizing explicit images only when consciousness focuses on some particularity. But then why does this *particular* particularity appear? Such speculations wander too far from the path of current interest.

74. In this regard, see Wenz, *Environmental Justice*, chap. 12.

75. Rolston, *Environmental Ethics*, 197.

76. Rolston, *Environmental Ethics*, 31, emphasis in original.

77. Rolston, *Environmental Ethics*, 215.

78. There is, for example, an argument that ecofeminism provides a deeper and richer critique of anthropocentrism than any discussed above. See Val Plumwood, "Nature, Self, and Gender: Feminism, Environmental Philosophy, and the Critique of Rationalism," *Hypatia* 6, 1 (Spring 1991): 3–27.

79. Callicott, *In Defense*, 94.

80. Callicott, *In Defense*, 223–237.

81. Rolston, *Environmental Ethics*, 322.

Chapter 9.

1. Of course, it is possible to articulate an ethic that makes claims that widely diverge from ordinary social practices. Utilitarianism, for example, claims that

those acts are good that maximize happiness for the greatest number. Recently, Peter Singer has used arguments appealing to this principle to establish a strong obligation for peoples in industrial societies to provide massive aid to the hungry of the world and to radically change the way animals are treated. See Peter Singer, *Practical Ethics* (N.Y.: Cambridge University Press, 1979). But such arguments do not often lead people to fundamentally change their life styles. I am not arguing against advancing reasoned argument in ethical matters. Rather, I am simply noting that the actual effectiveness of such argument is quite limited. Ethical beliefs, although not necessarily philosophical arguments, are nested within societies, and social change is necessary to create the conditions for any radical change in conduct guided by morality.

2. Val Plumwood notes that, "instrumentalism is generally viewed by mainstream philosophers as a problem in ethics, and its solution is seen as setting up some sort of theory of intrinsic value. This neglects a key aspect of the overall problem that is concerned with the definition of the human self as separate from nature." "Nature, Self, and Gender," 10.

3. Janna L. Thompson, "Preservation of Wilderness and the Good Life," in *Environmental Philosophy: A Collection of Readings*, edited by Robert Elliot and Arran Gare (University Park: Pennsylvania State University Press, 1983), 87.

4. Evernden, *The Natural Alien*, 141.

5. For another useful analysis of our predicament that takes industrialism as central, see Joel Jay Kassiola, *The Death of Industrial Civilization: The Limits to Economic Growth and the Repoliticization of Advanced Industrial Society* (Albany: State University of New York Press, 1990).

6. Anthony Weston, "Non-Anthropocentrism in a Thoroughly Anthropocentrized World," *Trumpeter* 8, 3 (Summer 1991): 110.

7. For support of this characterization of the importance of deep ecology, see Warwick Fox, *Toward a Transpersonal Ecology*, 44–45 and the works referenced there. It is important to note that deep ecology as a social movement has origins which predate Naess's formulation of deep ecology as a theory.

8. Since deep ecology is controversial, it is important to examine what deep ecologists actually say, rather than accepting their critics' characterizations of the position. This can be difficult, for the writings of deep ecologists are spread throughout various journals, some of which are hard to locate. Fortunately, there are now three books available which articulate versions of deep ecology from three different perspectives. The most accessible formulation is Bill Devall and George Sessions, *Deep Ecology: Living as if Nature Mattered* (Salt Lake City: Gibbs Smith, 1985). The popular accessibility of this work means that it sometimes lacks philo-

sophical precision. The most elaborate and theoretically sophisticated statement of deep ecology is by its founder, Arne Naess, in *Ecology*. This work is a not simply a translation of the book of the same title by Naess, which was in its fifth Norwegian edition in 1976. It is, rather, a "new work in English" written in collaboration with the translator. This is not only an authoritative summary of deep ecology, but is also a systematic and theoretical elaboration of Naess's own personal version of ecology and philosophy—what he calls an "ecosophy." The most comprehensive philosophical discussion of both deep ecology and other philosophies influenced by deep ecology is Warwick Fox, *Toward a Transpersonal Ecology*. Fox's book is an exhaustive summary of much of deep ecology, as well as a sophisticated argument for a particular foundation for deep ecology. It is extensively footnoted and includes a history of the development of the deep ecology. Fox examines a number of meanings of the "deep" metaphor in deep ecology and proposes the name "transpersonal ecology" as a substitute for "deep ecology." While I sympathize with his attempt at linguistic reform based on defects in the metaphor of "deep," my sense is that the label has gained too wide a currency within environmental philosophy to make the effort worth the confusion. See chap. 5 of his *Toward a Transpersonal Ecology* for Fox's arguments about "deep" versus "transpersonal" ecology. For references to the various charges and responses by deep ecologists through 1989, see Fox, *Toward a Transpersonal Ecology*, 43–50 and the endnotes to these pages. Murray Bookchin has recently claimed that deep ecology was "spawned among well-to-do people" raised on "Eastern cults mixed with Hollywood and Disneyland fantasies," and that it goes "hand-in-hand with a pious formula for human oppression, misery, and even extermination." *Remaking Society* (Boston: South End Press, 1990) 11–12. Bookchin's claims are given no documentation and bear no relation to what such theorists have actually written. The only deep ecology source that Bookchin notes is Devall and Sessions.

9. Devall and Sessions, *Deep Ecology*, 69–70.

10. These principles have been widely reprinted. For example, see Devall and Sessions, *Deep Ecology*, 70; Naess, "The Deep Ecological Movement: Some Philosophical Aspects," *Philosophical Inquiry* 8, 1–2 (Winter/Spring 1986): 14; Naess, *Ecology*, 29; Fox, *Toward a Transpersonal Ecology*, 114–115; Devall, *Simple in Means*, 14–15.

11. Naess, *Ecology*, 28–29.

12. "It does not follow that supporters of deep ecology must have, on ultimate issues, identical beliefs. They do have common attitudes about intrinsic values in nature, but these can . . . be derived from different, mutually incompatible sets of ultimate beliefs." Naess, "The Deep Ecological Movement," 25.

13. See Robyn Eckersley, *Environmentalism*.

14. The centrality of the platform has been claimed by a number of deep ecology writers. See, for example, Arne Naess, "The Deep Ecological Movement," 23–26; Arne Naess, *Ecology*, 27–32; Bill Devall, *Simple in Means*, 12–18.

15. Other sketches are possible, even encouraged. Naess regards his own formulation as tentative, *Ecology*, 31. He expects that others who identify with the deep ecology movement "will work out their own alternative formulations," *Ecology*, 28. Bill Devall, one of the founders of deep ecology, prefers the concept of "worth" to "value." Devall, *Simple in Means*, 14.

16. Naess, *Ecology*, 32.

17. Scanning the pages of one of the main journals of the movement, *The Trumpeter*, shows a wide diversity of concerns and interests. Fox's main concern is showing the distinctiveness of deep ecology as a philosophical position, *Towards a Transpersonal Ecology*, 44. Thus, he is working at the level of justification. Devall's *Simple in Means* is concerned with elaborating ways of "practicing" deep ecology and also with developing what follows from accepting the platform.

18. Fox, *Towards a Transpersonal Ecology*, 144.

19. For further explanation of this term and its relation to philosophy and social movements, see Eckersley, *Environmentalism*, chap. 3 and Fox, *Towards a Transpersonal Ecology*, 117–18.

20. Taylor, *Respect*, 312, emphasis in original. Taylor would call his position "biocentric," but this difference is not significant here.

21. Max Oelschlaeger makes this point. See *The Idea of Wilderness: From Prehistory to the Age of Ecology* (New Haven: Yale University Press, 1991), 304.

22. See Richard Sylvan, "A Critique of (Wild) Western Deep Ecology" (unpublished manuscript), 2; Jim Cheney, "The Neo-Stoicism of Radical Environmentalism," *Environmental Ethics* 11, 4 (Winter 1989), 295.

23. Oelschlaeger, *The Idea of Wilderness*, 308.

24. Devall and Sessions, *Deep Ecology*, 67.

25. See Warwick Fox, *Approaching Deep Ecology: A Response to Richard Sylvan's Critique of Deep Ecology*, Environmental Studies Occasional Paper 20 (Hobart: University of Tasmania, 1986), 37ff, and *Toward a Transpersonal Ecology* for extended discussions of why Fox thinks it is an error to interpret deep ecology as an alternative axiology. He provides ample references for the claim that the principle of biocentric equalitarianism is not primarily a philosophical claim about intrinsic value in nature. There may be, however, real differences among deep ecologists on the philosophical tenability of concepts such as the intrinsic or inherent worth of nature. For example, recently Bill Devall has explicitly accepted the inherent worth

of nature, a concept that posits natural objects as having value that is "not dependent on a human observer," *Simple in Means*, 15. However, Devall's focus in that book is not philosophical; his intention is to inspire others to adopt and implement deep ecology. Naess himself, in what is perhaps his most precise formulation of deep ecology, accepts the claim that all forms of life have a "right" to live, although he acknowledges that this concept is problematic, *Ecology*, 166–67. Part of the problem may be linguistic. Naess's translator, David Rothenberg, claims that the Norwegian term for "intrinsic value" does not translate precisely into English. As he puts it, "what, then, actually exists independent from us? The value is not so much independent from us as independent from our valuation," *Ecology*, 11. Although such a claim may not really clarify the issue, it does hint at a complexity in precisely rendering Naess's view in English. I think the question of values and rights in nature is now an issue about which deep ecologists differ. In any case, it is clear that the technical philosophical question of value in nature is not a primary interest of deep ecologists.

26. Warwick Fox cites passages from Naess, Sessions, Devall, myself, Alan Drengson, Michael Zimmerman, Neil Evernden, John Livingston, John Rodman, and Joanna Macy that indicate agreement among these radical environmentalists that the issue is *not* intrinsic or inherent value in a technical, philosophic sense. See Fox, *Toward A Transpersonal Ecology* 215 ff.

27. Fox, "Approaching Deep Ecology," 79. Plumwood made the same point in a different context. See note 2.

28. See Anthony Weston, "Beyond Intrinsic Value: Pragmatism in Environmental Ethics," *Environmental Ethics* 7, 4 (Winter 1985): 321–339.

29. This phrase is the title of Arthur Lovejoy's fertile study of this notion's history in Western philosophy and literature. See *The Great Chain of Being: A Study of the History of an Idea* (Cambridge: Harvard University Press, 1936).

30. Lovejoy, *The Great Chain of Being*, 293.

31. Lovejoy, *The Great Chain of Being*, 312.

32. Fox, *Toward a Transpersonal Ecology*, 243, emphasis in original. This is rather out of step with the usual philosophical practice, which is to show what is wrong with other views so as to clear the stage for an exposition of one's own views. In part, this style is an artifact of typical graduate education in philosophy, which tends to be highly argumentative, with an emphasis on reading texts for what is wrong with them, instead of what is right with them. In part, this style reflects the conception of a single standard of rationality.

33. Bill Devall, "Deep Ecology and its Critics," *The Trumpeter* 5, 2 (Spring 1988): 55.

34. "Population reduction towards decent levels might incidentally require a thousand years." Naess, *Ecology*, 127.

35. "Almost any activity that increases well-being and security lessens people's desires to have more children than they and national ecosystems can support." World Commission on Environment and Development, *Our Common Future*, 98. This is sometimes referred to as the "Brundtland Report."

36. For example, see Colin Turnbull, *The Forest People*.

37. World Commission, *Our Common Future*.

38. Herman E. Daly and John B. Cobb, *For the Common Good*.

39. Bhikkhu Bodhi, the foreword of *Buddhist Perspectives on the Ecocrisis*, edited by Klaus Sandell (Kandy, Sri Lanka: Buddhist Publication Society, 1987), vi.

40. Arguments along this line, although not terminating in radical ecocentrism, might be constructed from Hans Jonas, *The Imperative of Responsibility* and Gregory Bateson. See his *Steps to an Ecology of Mind* and *Mind and Nature: A Necessary Unity* (N.Y.: E. P. Dutton, 1979). See also Morris Berman's excellent discussion of Bateson in *The Reenchantment of the World*, chaps. 8 and 9.

41. See Richard A. Watson, "A Critique of Anti-Anthropocentric Biocentrism," and "A Note on Deep Ecology," *Environmental Ethics* 6, 4, (Winter 1984): 377–379 for what may be an example of this. I am not sure what Watson's real position is.

42. *Toward a Transpersonal Ecology*, 215ff.

43. See chap. 8 of *Toward a Transpersonal Ecology*.

44. Fox, *Toward a Transpersonal Ecology*, 255–56, emphasis in original.

45. Fox, *Toward a Transpersonal Ecology*, 258. For a critical response to this sort of identification and an advocacy of a more personal form of identification, see Val Plumwood, "Nature, Self, and Gender." Plumwood indicates no disagreement with the platform. She does not address the problem Fox raises for those who emphasize a personal basis for identification, which is that such personally based forms of identification can easily become narrow and the basis for exclusion and aggression, *Toward a Transpersonal Ecology*, 262–63. If one allows a diversity of modes for justifying the platform, such a dispute has lesser import than it might otherwise have.

46. Routley has changed his last name to Sylvan. Richard Sylvan, *A Critique of Deep Ecology*. Discussion Papers in Environmental Philosophy, no. 12 (Canberra: Australian National University, 1985), 31–32.

47. See Val and Richard Routley, "Social Theories, Self Management, and Environmental Problems," in D. S. Manison, M. A. McRobbie, and R. Routley,

Environmental Philosophy (Canberra: Australian National University, 1980), 217–232. He has also made a deep ecological analysis of the population problem. See David H. Bennett and Richard Sylvan, *Over Population Resources Environment: Focus Australia*. Discussion Papers in Environmental Philosophy, no. 15 (Canberra: Australian National University, 1987).

48. Francis Cook, *Hwa-yen Buddhism* (University Park: Pennsylvania State University Press, 1971), 15. The interested reader can find a slightly longer discussion of this in my "Images and Ethics of Nature," *Environmental Ethics* 7, 4 (Winter 1985): 316–18.

49. See Alan Drengson, "Developing Concepts of Environmental Relationships," *Philosophical Inquiry* 8, 1–2 (Winter/Spring 1986): 50–63, for one such scenario.

50. Freya Matthews, *The Ecological Self*.

51. Matthews, *The Ecological Self*, 49.

52. Matthews, *The Ecological Self*, 60ff.

53. Matthews, *The Ecological Self*, 93.

54. Matthews, *The Ecological Self*, 98.

55. Matthews, *The Ecological Self*, 118.

56. Matthews, *The Ecological Self*, 123.

57. Matthews, *The Ecological Self*, 125.

58. Matthews, *The Ecological Self*, 128.

59. Matthews, *The Ecological Self*, 128.

60. The following discussion draws heavily on Naess's *Ecology*, which his most complete articulation to date of his own ecosophy.

61. So his translator states. *Ecology*, 4.

62. This and the surrounding discussion draws heavily on his *Ecology*, 40–44. See also chap. 4 of Fox, *Toward a Transpersonal Ecology* for three systematizations of Naess's views.

63. Naess, *Ecology*, 75.

64. Naess, *Ecology*, 42–43.

65. Naess, *Ecology*, 66.

66. Naess, *Ecology*, 60.

67. John Dewey, *Experience and Nature* (N.Y.: Dover Publications, 1958), 8.

68. William James, "The Tigers in India," in *Pragmatism: The Classic Writings*, edited by H. S. Thayer (Indianapolis: Hackett Publishing Co., 1982), 247, emphasis in original.

69. Naess, *Ecology*, 63.

70. Naess, *Ecology*, 60–61, emphasis in original.

71. Naess, *Ecology*, 67.

72. Naess, *Ecology*, 69.

73. Wenz, *Environmental Justice*, chap. 12.

74. Naess, *Ecology*, 84.

75. The outside-in metaphor is from Fox, *Toward a Transpersonal Ecology*, chap. 8.

76. Naess, *Ecology*, 166.

77. Naess, *Ecology*, 167–68.

78. Naess, *Ecology*, 170.

79. Naess, *Ecology*, 171.

80. Arne Naess, "Identification as a Source of Deep Ecological Attitudes," in *Deep Ecology*, edited by Michael Tobias (San Diego: Avant Books, 1984), 263–264, emphasis in original.

81. Arne Naess, "Intrinsic Value: Will the Real Defenders of Nature Please Stand Up?" in *Conservation Biology: The Science of Scarcity and Diversity*, edited by Michael Soule (Sunderland: Sinauer Associates, 1986), 511.

82. Nacss, *Ecology*, 175.

83. See Bill Devall, *Simple in Means* for an extended discussion of ways of practicing deep ecology.

84. Naess, "Identification," 262.

85. Naess, "Self-Realization: An Ecological Approach to Being in the World," *The Trumpeter* 4, 3 (Summer 1987): 39, emphasis in original.

86. I have here given only a sketch of Naess's system. The interested (or skeptical) reader should consult his *Ecology* for his extensive elaboration of Ecosophy T.

Chapter 10.

1. The best comprehensive discussion of ecofeminism, social ecology, bioregionalism, and ecocentric political theory in general is in Robyn Eckersley's *Environmentalism*.

2. For an excellent anthropocentric radical environmentalism, see Lester Milbraith, *Envisioning a Sustainable Society: Learning Our Way Out* (Albany: Sate University of New York, 1989). See also John Dryzek, *Rational Ecology*, Joel Jay Kassiola, *The Death of Industrial Civilization*, and William Ophuls, *Ecology and the Politics of Scarcity*.

3. I do not mean to characterize the beliefs of these authors, as they do not directly address the question of anthropocentrism. Dryzek uses an anthropocentric perspective, but he does not claim that it is adequate. He uses it as a minimal assumption and adopts it because such an assumption is embedded in the perspectives which he wishes to meet on their own ground, *Rational Ecology*, 35.

4. Murray Bookchin has generated numerous books and articles in his long and consistent advocacy of social ecology, an ecologically informed variant of anarchism. The main work is *The Ecology of Freedom* (Palo Alto: Cheshire Books, 1982). His most recent statements of his position are *Remaking Society* and *The Philosophy of Social Ecology: Essays on Dialectical Naturalism* (Montreal: Black Rose Books, 1990).

5. A good discussion, though not easily accessible, is Val Plumwood, "Ecofeminism: An Overview and Discussion of Positions and Arguments," *Australasian Journal of Philosophy*, Supplement to vol. 64 (June 1986): 120–138. A less theoretical but lively expression of ecofeminsim is *Healing the Wounds: The Promise of Ecofeminsim*, edited by Judith Plant (Philadelphia: New Society Publishers, 1989). See also *Hypatia* 6, 1 (Spring 1991), which is a special issue on ecological feminism.

6. The human-centered environmentalists rarely argue for their anthropocentrism. Social ecologists focus on social hierarchy, ecological feminists focus on gender rooted causes, and deep ecologists emphasize anthropocentrism.

7. See Marti Kheel, "Ecofeminism and Deep Ecology: Reflections on Identity and Difference," *The Trumpeter* 8, 2 (Spring 1991): especially 70. See also Karen Warren's discussion of the "boundary conditions" of ecofeminist ethics. She includes "descriptions and prescriptions of social reality that do not maintain, perpetuate, or attempt to justify social 'isms of domination' and the power-over relationships used to keep them intact." "Ecological Feminism and Ecosystem Ecology," *Hypatia* 6, 1 (Spring 1991): 181. Although she does not mention it, this would clearly include deep ecology within ecofeminist ethics. I think the perception of unity will spread to most radical environmentalists as the movement develops further.

8. Winner, *The Whale and the Reactor*, 80.

9. Sadik, *The State of World Population: 1990*.

10. James Robertson, "Toward a Multi-Level One-World Economy," *New Options* 63: 2.

11. Michael Harrington, *Socialism: Past and Future* (N.Y.: Penguin Books, 1990), chap. 9.

12. Naess is clear that his view is not misanthropic. His "negative reaction towards the increase of human population is not to foster any animosity towards

humans as such—on the contrary, human fulfillment seems to *demand* and *need* free nature." *Ecology*, 141, emphasis in original.

13. Naess, *Ecology*, 24.

14. Naess, *Ecology*, 91.

15. Naess, *Ecology*, 91, emphasis in original. He also states: "Human nature may be such that with increased maturity a *human* need increases to protect the richness and diversity of life for *its own sake*. Consequently, what is useless in a narrow way may be useful in a wider sense, namely satisfying a human need." Naess *Ecology*, 177, emphasis in original.

16. Robert C. Paelke, *Environmentalism and the Future of Progressive Politics* (New Haven: Yale University Press, 1989), 168.

17. Aldo Leopold, *A Sand County Almanac: With Essays on Conservation from Round River* (N.Y.: Ballantine Books, 1970), 197.

18. David M. Johns, "The Relevance of Deep Ecology to the Third World," *Environmental Ethics* 12, 3 (Fall 1990): 242.

19. Karl Marx, "Economic and Philosophic Manuscripts," in *The Marx-Engels Reader* edited by Robert C. Tucker, 80, emphasis in original. Interestingly, Marx also recognizes the process of extending identification when he claims that when workers unite in struggle, they acquire a new need for society: "The brotherhood of man is no mere phrase with them, but a fact of life." "Manuscripts," 100–101.

20. Naess, *Ecology*, 138.

21. For one recent overview of bioregionalism, see Kirkpatrick Sale, *Dwellers in the Land: The Bioregional Vision* (San Francisco: Sierra Club Books, 1985). For a less radical, but meticulously developed, perspective focusing on community instead of bioregion, see Herman E. Daly and John B. Cobb, Jr., *For the Common Good*.

22. Val and Richard Routley, "Social Theories," 284.

23. Roy Morrison, *We Build the Road We Travel* (Philadelphia: New Society, 1991).

24. Lester R. Brown et al., *State of the World, 1987* (N.Y.: Norton, 1987), 38.

25. The Planet Drum Foundation brought together community activists to articulate the notion of a "Green City" for the San Francisco Bay area. They put this together in a pamphlet called *A Green City Program* which is useful for urban activists in any city. See Peter Berg, Beryl Magilavy, and Seth Zuckerman, *A Green City Program for San Francisco Bay Area Cities and Towns* (San Francisco: Planet Drum Books, 1989). Further information about this program and bioregionalism in general is available from Planet Drum Foundation, P.O. Box 31251, San Francisco, CA 94131, Shasta Bioregion.

26. Sale, *Dwellers*, 42.

27. Lewis Mumford, *The Myth of the Machine,* 159.

28. "Grants Open Doors for Nuclear Waste," *New York Times,* 9 January 1992.

29. Bill Devall, *Simple in Means,* 128.

30. See Richard Sylvan, "A Critique of Deep Ecology," 30ff.

31. Devall, *Simple in Means,* 160.

32. See Warwick Fox, *Towards a Transpersonal Ecology.* I should note that Fox's concern in this book is with what is philosophically distinctive about deep ecology, 43. Although he recognizes the political dimensions of deep ecology, that is not the subject of his book.

33. Richard Sylvan, "A Critique of Deep Ecology," 39.

34. Naess, *Ecology,* 91, emphasis in original.

35. Lovelock, *The Ages of Gaia,* xvii, emphasis added.

36. Point 6 of the deep ecology platform; see Chapter 9 for the complete platform.

37. Bruce A. Wilcox, "Insular Ecology and Conservation," in *Conservation Biology: An Evolutionary-Ecological Perspective,* edited by Michael E. Soule and Bruce A. Wilcox, (Sunderland: Sinauer Associates, 1980).

38. Ramachandra Guha, "Radical American Environmentalism and Wilderness Preservation: A Third World Critique," *Environmental Ethics* 11, 1 (Spring 1989): 75.

39. Guha, "Radical American Environmentalism," 76. There are other parts of Guha's argument that spring from a misunderstanding of deep ecology. It simply is not true that "deep ecology runs parallel to the consumer society without seriously questioning its ecological and socio-political basis," (79) even though it may be true that this has not been emphasized enough by deep ecologists.

40. Terry L. Erwin, "An Evolutionary Basis for Conservation Strategies," *Science* 253, 5021 (August 1991).

41. Johns, "The Relevance of Deep Ecology," 235.

42. Michael Soule, "Conservation Tactics for a Constant Crisis," *Science* 253, 5021 (August 1991): 749.

43. Murray Bookchin, *Remaking Society,* 203–204; also see 42 and his *The Philosophy of Social Ecology,* 179ff, especially 182. I cite here only the most recent writings of Bookchin. The interested reader should consult Robyn Eckersley, "Diving Evolution: The Ecological Ethics of Murray Bookchin," *Environmental Ethics* 11, 2 (Summer 1989): 99–116 and Bookchin's reply, "Recovering Evolution: A Reply to Eckersley and Fox," *Environmental Ethics* 12, 3 (Fall 1990): 253–274. There are a number of references in both of these articles to many of Bookchin's other writings on this subject, as well as some heated rhetoric. The reader of this exchange must pay close attention to the arguments therein to separate the wheat from the chaff.

Bookchin has a tendency to be vituperative in responses to criticism, and his recent books reflect little extended attention to what deep ecology writers actually have written. On the basis of his reply to Eckersley, I believe that once society is rid of hierarchy, Bookchin would be willing to "give evolution a helping hand," but he does not think that we should "seize the helm of evolution." "Recovering Evolution," 273. In the same article, Bookchin suggests that, with a new social context, it would be alright, using "prudent, nonexploitative, and ecologically guided" means to transform the "Canadian barrens" into "an area supporting a rich variety of biota," 272. He does not mention the native inhabitants of these areas.

44. "Recovering Evolution," 261.

45. Nash, *Wilderness and the American Mind*, 382.

46. Devall and Sessions mention this possibility in *Deep Ecology*, 176.

47. The metaphor and statistics are from Sadik, *The State of World Population*, 4.

48. David H. Bennett and Richard Sylvan, "Over population."

49. Tucker, *Marx-Engels Reader*, 498.

50. Paelke, *Environmentalism*, 203.

51. Sigmund Kvaloy, "Norwegian Ecophilosophy and Ecopolitics and Their Influence from Buddhism" in *Buddhist Perspectives on the Ecocrisis*, edited by Klas Sandell (Kandy, Sri Lanka: Buddhist Publication Society, 1987) 62. Dave Foreman, a founder of the Earth First movement, has argued that the movement is a holding action to save species and old growth forests until industrialism collapses.

52. Naess, *Ecology*, 211.

53. Herman E. Daly, "The Steady-State Economy: Postmodern Alternative to Growthmania," in *Spirituality and Society: Postmodern Visions*, edited by David Ray Griffin, (Albany: State University of New York Press, 1988).

54. See Nash, *Rights of Nature*, the epilogue.

55. See Christopher Manes, *Green Rage: Radical Environmentalism and the Unmaking of Civilization* (Boston: Little, Brown & Co., 1990) for a sympathetic and up-to-date account of the activities of radical ecocentrists.

56. John B. Cobb, Jr., "Postmodern Social Policy," in Griffin, *Spirituality and Society*, 102.

57. Such was the outcome of the Third New York State Environment and Labor Conference, November 1991, which had delegates from a wide spectrum of labor and community groups.

58. See Andrew Szasz, "In Praise of Policy Luddism: Strategic Lessons From the Hazardous Waste Wars," *Capitalism, Nature, Socialism* 2, 1 (February 1991): 17–43.

59. Szasz, "In Praise of Policy Luddism," 43.

60. Copies of the program are available for $4.00 from The Greens Clearinghouse, P.O. Box 30208, Kansas City, MO 64112, 816–931–9366.

61. Ynestra King, "The Ecology of Feminism and the Feminism of Ecology," in *Healing the Wounds*, edited by Judith Plant, 19.

62. King, "The Ecology of Feminism," 23.

63. Hugh Stretton, *Capitalism, Socialism, and the Environment*, 48–49.

64. See Michael Albert, Leslie Cagan, Noam Chomsky, Robin Hahnel, Mel King, Lydia Sargent, and Holly Sklar, *Liberating Theory* (Boston: South End Press, 1986) for an attempt to articulate a holistic theory that links various forms of oppression. This book does not question its own anthropocentrism.

65. *Whole Earth Review* No. 61 (Winter 1988): 20.

BIBLIOGRAPHY

Albert, Michael, Leslie Cagan, Noam Chomsky, Robin Hahnel, Mel King, Lydia Sargent, and Holly Sklar. *Liberating Theory*. Boston: South End Press, 1986.

Alford, C. Fred. *Science and the Revenge of Nature: Marcuse and Habermas*. Tampa: University of Florida Press, 1985.

Attfield, Robin. "The Prospects for Preservation." *Philosophical Inquiry* 8, (1986): 140–147.

———. "Western Traditions and Environmental Ethics." In *Environmental Philosophy: A Collection of Readings*, edited by Robert Elliot and Arran Gare. 201–230. University Park: Pennsylvania State University, 1983.

Barnet, Richard J. "Defining the Moment." *The New Yorker*, 16 July 1990, 46–60.

———. *The Lean Years: Politics in the Age of Scarcity*. N.Y.: Simon and Schuster, 1980.

Bateson, Gregory. *Mind and Nature: A Necessary Unity*. N.Y.: Dutton, 1979.

———. *Steps to an Ecology of Mind: A Revolutionary Approach to Man's Understanding Himself*. N.Y.: Ballantine Books, 1972.

Bennett, David H., and Richard Sylvan. *Over Population Resources Environment: Focus Australia*. Discussion Papers in Environmental Philosophy, no. 15. Canberra: Australian National University, 1987.

Berg, Peter, Beryl Magilavy, and Seth Zuckerman. *A Green City Program for San Francisco Bay Area Cities and Towns*. San Francisco: Planet Drum Books, 1989.

Berle, Adolf A., and Gardiner C. Means. *The Modern Corporation and Private Property*. N.Y.: Macmillan, 1933.

Berman, Morris. *The Reenchantment of the World*. Ithaca: Cornell University Press, 1981.

Bernstein, Richard. *Beyond Objectivism and Subjectivism: Science, Hermeneutics and Praxis*. Philadelphia: University of Pennsylvania Press, 1983.

Best, Michael H., and William Connolly. "Nature and Its Largest Parasite." In *The Capitalist System*, 3rd ed., edited by Richard C. Edwards, Michael Reich, and Thomas E. Weisskopf. Englewood Cliffs: Prentice Hall, 1986.

Birch, Charles, and John B. Cobb, Jr. *The Liberation of Life: From the Cell to the Community*. N.Y.: Cambridge University Press, 1981.

Birch, Tom. "The Incarceration of Wildness." *Environmental Ethics* 12 (1990): 3–26.

Bobbio, Norberto. *Which Socialism? Marxism, Socialism and Democracy*. Minneapolis: University of Minnesota Press, 1987.

Bookchin, Murray. *The Ecology of Freedom*. Palo Alto: Cheshire Books, 1982.

———. *The Philosophy of Social Ecology: Essays on Dialectical Naturalism*. Montreal: Black Rose Books, 1990.

———. "Recovering Evolution: A Reply to Eckersley and Fox." *Environmental Ethics* 12 (1990): 253–274.

———. *Remaking Society: Pathways to a Green Future*. Boston: South End Press, 1990.

Borgmann, Albert. *Technology and the Character of Contemporary Life: A Philosophical Inquiry*. Chicago: University of Chicago Press, 1984.

Braudel, Fernand. *The Perspective of the World*. Vol. 3 of *Civilization and Capitalism: 15th–18th Century*. N.Y.: Harper & Row, 1984.

———. *The Wheels of Commerce*. Vol. 2 of *Civilization and Capitalism: 15th–18th Century*. N.Y.: Harper & Row, 1982.

Broeck, Goldian Vanden, ed. *Less is More: The Art of Voluntary Poverty*. N.Y.: Harper & Row, 1978.

Brown, Lester R., and Jodi Jacobson. "Assessing the Future of Urbanization." In *State of the World 1987*, edited by Lester R. Brown, et al. 38–56. N. Y.: Norton, 1987.

Brown, Lester R. et al. *State of the World 1991*. N.Y.: Norton, 1991.

———. *State of the World 1992*. N.Y.: Norton, 1992.

Burtt, E. A. *The Metaphysical Foundations of Modern Science*. Garden City: Anchor Books, 1954.

Callicott, J. Baird. "The Case Against Moral Pluralism." *Environmental Ethics* 12 (1990): 99–124.

———. *In Defense of A Land Ethic: Essays in Environmental Philosophy*. Albany: State University of New York Press, 1989.

———. "Traditional American Indian and Western European Attitudes Toward Nature: An Overview." *Environmental Ethics* 4 (1982): 293–318.

Catton, William R. *Overshoot: The Ecological Basis of Revolutionary Change*. Chicago: University of Illinois Press, 1980.

Catton, William R., and Riley E. Dunlap. "A New Ecological Paradigm for Post-Exhuberant Sociology." *American Behavioral Scientist* 24 (1980): 15–47.

Cheney, Jim. "The Neo-Stoicism of Radical Environmentalism." *Environmental Ethics* 11 (1989): 293–325.

Churchman, C. West. *Challenge to Reason*. N.Y.: McGraw Hill, 1968.

———. *The Design of Inquiring Systems*. N.Y.: Basic Books, 1971.

———. *Prediction and Optimal Decision*. Englewood Cliffs: Prentice Hall, 1961.

Commoner, Barry. *The Closing Circle: Nature, Man and Technology*. N.Y.: Bantam Books, 1972.

———. *The Poverty of Power: Energy and the Economic Crisis*. N.Y.: Knopf, 1976.

Cook, Francis. *Hwa-yen Buddhism*. University Park: Pennsylvania State University Press, 1971.

Cronin, William. *Changes in the Land*. N.Y.: Hill & Wang, 1983.

Cunningham, Frank. *Democratic Theory and Socialism*. N.Y.: Cambridge University Press, 1987.

Daly, Herman E., ed. *Economics, Ecology, Ethics: Essays Toward A Steady-State Economy*. San Francisco: W. H. Freeman & Co., 1980.

Daly, Herman E., and John B. Cobb, Jr. *For the Common Good: Redirecting the Economy Toward Community, the Environment, and a Sustainable Future*. Boston: Beacon Press, 1989.

Dasmann, Raymond F. "National Parks, Native Conservation and 'Future Primitive.'" *The Ecologist* 6 (1976).

———. *Planet in Peril: Man and the Biosphere Today*. N.Y.: World Publishing, 1972.

David, Paul A., and Melvin W. Reder, eds. *Nations and Households in Economic Growth*. Stanford: Stanford University Press, 1972.

Descartes, Rene. *Discourse on Method and Meditations*, translated by Laurence J. Lafleur. N.Y.: Bobbs-Merrill, 1960.

Devall, Bill. "Deep Ecology and Its Critics." *The Trumpeter* 5 (1988): 55–60.

Devall, Bill, and George Sessions. *Deep Ecology: Living As If Nature Mattered*. Salt Lake City: Gibbs-Smith, 1985.

Devall, Bill. *Simple in Means, Rich in Ends: Practicing Deep Ecology*. Salt Lake City: Gibbs-Smith, 1988.

Dewey, John. *Experience and Nature*. N.Y.: Dover Publications, 1958.

———. *The Quest for Certainty: A Study of the Relation of Knowledge and Action*. N.Y.: G. P. Putnam, 1960.

Diamond, Stanley. *In Search of the Primitive: A Critique of Civilization*. New Brunswick: Transaction Books, 1974.

Dijksterhuis, E.J. *The Mechanization of the World Picture*. London: Oxford University Press, 1961.

Drengson, Alan. "Developing Concepts of Environmental Relationships." *Philosophical Inquiry* 8 (1986): 50–63.

Dryzek, John. "Green Reason: Communicative Ethics for the Biosphere." *Environmental Ethics* 12 (1990): 192–210.

———. *Rational Ecology: Environment and Political Economy*. N.Y.: Basil Blackwell, 1987.

Eckersley, Robyn. "Diving Evolution: The Ecological Ethics of Murray Bookchin." *Environmental Ethics* 11 (1989): 99–116.

———. *Environmentalism and Political Theory*. Albany: State University of New York Press, 1992.

Edelman, Murray. *The Symbolic Uses of Politics*. Urbana: University of Illinois Press, 1964.

Ehrenfeld, David. *The Arrogance of Humanism*. N.Y.: Oxford University Press, 1978.

Ely, John. "Lukac's Construction of Nature." *Capitalism, Nature, Socialism* 1 (1988): 107–116.

Erwin, Terry L. "An Evolutionary Basis for Conservation Strategies." *Science* 253 (1991): 750–752.

Evernden, Neil. *The Natural Alien: Humankind and the Environment*. Toronto: University of Toronto Press, 1985.

Federov, E. *Man and Nature: The Ecological Crisis and Social Progress*. N.Y.: International Publishers, 1981.

Feenberg, Andrew. "The Critical Theory of Technology." *Capitalism, Nature, Socialism* 5 (1990): 17–45.

Fox, Warwick. *Approaching Deep Ecology: A Response to Richard Sylvan's Critique of Deep Ecology*. Environmental Studies Occasional Paper 20. Hobart: University of Tasmania, 1986.

———. "The Deep Ecology-Ecofeminism Debate and Its Parallels." *Environmental Ethics* 11 (1989): 5–25.

———. *Toward a Transpersonal Ecology: Developing New Foundations for Environmentalism*. Boston: Shambala, 1990.

Fritzell, Peter A. "The Conflicts of Ecological Conscience." In *Companion to A Sand County Almanac: Interpretive and Critical Essays*, edited by J. Baird Callicott. 128–153. Madison: University of Wisconsin Press, 1987.

Galbraith, John Kenneth. *The New Industrial State.* N.Y.: New American Library, 1968.

Granit, Ragnar. "Reflections on the Evolution of Mind and Its Environment." In *Mind in Nature,* edited by Richard Q. Elvee. 96–117. San Francisco: Harper & Row, 1982.

Griffin, David Ray, ed. *Spirituality and Society: Postmodern Visions.* Albany: State University of New York Press, 1988.

Guha, Ramachandra. "Radical American Environmentalism and Wilderness Preservation: A Third World Critique." *Environmental Ethics* 11 (1989): 71–83.

Habermas, Jürgen. *Knowledge and Human Interests.* Boston: Beacon Press: 1971.

———. *Legitimation Crisis.* Boston: Beacon Press, 1975.

———. *The Philosophical Discussion of Modernity: Twelve Lectures,* translated by Frederick Lawrence. Cambridge: MIT Press, 1987.

———. "A Reply to my Critics." In *Habermas: Critical Debates,* edited by John B. Thompson and David Held. 219–283. Cambridge: MIT Press, 1982.

———. *Theory and Practice.* Boston: Beacon Press, 1973.

Hall, Charles A. S. "Sanctioning Resource Depletion: Economic Development and Neo-Classical Economics." *The Ecologist* 20 (1990): 99–104.

Hallen, Patsy. "Making Peace With Nature: Why Ecology Needs Feminism." *The Trumpeter* 4 (Summer 1987): 3–14.

Hardin, Garrett. "Carrying Capacity as an Ethical Concept." In *Lifeboat Ethics: The Moral Dilemmas of World Hunger,* edited by George R. Lucas, Jr. and Thomas W. Ogletree. 120–137. N.Y.: Harper and Row, 1976.

———. *Exploring New Ethics for Survival: The Voyage of the Spaceship Beagle.* Baltimore: Penguin Books, 1973.

———. *Filters Against Folly: How to Survive Despite Economists, Ecologists, and the Merely Eloquent.* N.Y.: Penguin Books, 1986.

Harding, Sandra. *The Science Question in Feminism.* Ithaca: Cornell University Press: 1986.

Harrington, Michael. *Socialism: Past and Future.* N.Y.: Penguin Books, 1990.

Heidegger, Martin. *The Question Concerning Technology and Other Essays.* N.Y.: Harper & Row, 1977.

Heilbroner, Robert. *An Inquiry into the Human Prospect.* N.Y.: Norton, 1980.

———. *The Nature and Logic of Capitalism.* N.Y.: Norton, 1985.

Hirsch, Fred. *Social Limits to Growth.* Cambridge: Harvard University Press, 1976.

Holbrook, Bruce. *The Stone Monkey; An Alternative Chinese-Scientific Reality*. N.Y.: William Morrow and Co., 1981.

Horkheimer, Max. *Critical Theory: Selected Essays*. N.Y.: Herder and Herder, 1972.

Horkheimer, Max, and Theodor Adorno. *The Dialectic of Enlightenment*. N.Y.: Herder and Herder, 1972.

Johns, David M. "The Relevance of Deep Ecology to the Third World." *Environmental Ethics* 12 (1990): 233–252.

Johnson, Warren. *Muddling Toward Frugality: A Blueprint for Survival in the 1980s*. Boulder: Shambala, 1978.

Jonas, Hans. *The Imperative of Responsibility: In Search of an Ethics for the Technological Age*. Chicago: University of Chicago Press, 1984.

———. *The Phenomenon of Life: Toward a Philosophical Biology*. Chicago: University of Chicago Press, 1966.

Kassiola, Joel Jay. *The Death of Industrial Civilization: The Limits to Economic Growth and the Repoliticization of Advanced Industrial Society*. Albany: State University of New York Press, 1990.

Keller, Evelyn Fox. *Reflections on Gender and Science*. New Haven: Yale University Press: 1985.

Kheel, Marti. "Ecofeminism and Deep Ecology: Reflections on Identity and Difference." *The Trumpeter* 8 (1991): 62–72.

Kilpatrick, Franklin P., ed. *Explorations in Transactional Psychology*. N.Y.: New York University Press, 1961.

Komorov, Boris. *The Destruction of Nature in the Soviet Union*. White Plains: M.E. Sharpe, 1980.

Kuhn, Thomas. *The Structure of Scientific Revolutions*. Chicago: University of Chicago Press, 1962.

Leiss, William. *The Domination of Nature*. Boston: Beacon Press, 1974.

Leopold, Aldo. *A Sand County Almanac: With Essays on Conservation from Round River*. N.Y.: Ballantine, 1970.

———. "Some Fundamentals of Conservation in the Southwest." *Environmental Ethics* 1 (1979): 131–141.

Levins, Richard, and Richard Lewontin. *The Dialectical Biologist*. Cambridge: Harvard University Press, 1985.

Locke, John. *Second Treatise of Government*, edited by C. B. Macpherson. Indianapolis: Hackett Publishing, 1980.

Lovejoy, Arthur O. *The Great Chain of Being: A Study of the History of an Idea*. Cambridge: Harvard University Press, 1936.

Lovelock, James. *The Ages of Gaia: A Biography of Life on Earth.* N.Y.: Norton, 1988.

———. *Gaia: A New Look at Life on Earth.* N.Y.: Oxford University Press, 1979.

Luntley, Michael. *The Meaning of Socialism.* La Salle: Open Court, 1989.

Machan, Tibor. "Pollution and Political Theory." In *Earthbound: New Introductory Essays in Environmental Ethics,* edited by Tom Reagan. 74–106. N.Y.: Random House, 1984.

MacIntyre, Alasdair. *After Virtue: A Study in Moral Theory,* 2nd ed. Notre Dame: University of Notre Dame Press, 1984.

Malthus, Thomas Robert. "A Summary View of the Principle of Population." In *On Population: Three Essays.* N.Y.: New American Library, 1960.

Manes, Christopher. *Green Rage: Radical Environmentalism and the Unmaking of Civilization.* Boston: Little, Brown & Co., 1990.

Marcuse, Herbert. *Eros and Civilization.* N.Y.: Vintage Press, 1962.

———. *One Dimensional Man: Studies in the Ideology of Advanced Industrial Society.* Boston: Beacon Press, 1964.

Mathiessen, Peter. *Indian Country.* N.Y.: Viking Press, 1984.

Matthews, Freya. *The Ecological Self.* Savage, MD: Barnes and Noble: 1991.

Maturana, Humberto R., and Francisco J. Varela. *Autopoiesis and Cognition: The Realization of the Living.* Dordrecht: Reidel, 1980.

Maxwell, Nicholas. *From Knowledge to Wisdom: A Revolution in the Aims and Methods of Science.* N.Y.: Basil Blackwell, 1984.

McCullough, H. B., ed. *Political Ideologies and Political Philosophies.* Toronto: Wall & Thompson, 1989.

McCully, Patrick. "A Message to the Executives and Shareholders of E. I. DuPont de Nemours and Co. and Imperial Chemical Industries, Ltd." *The Ecologist* 21 (1991): 114–116.

McDermott, John. "Technology: The Opiate of the Intellectuals." *New York Review of Books* (31 July 1969): 25–36.

McKibben, Bill. *The End of Nature.* N.Y.: Doubleday, 1989.

McLaughlin, Andrew. "Images and Ethics of Nature." *Environmental Ethics* 7 (1985): 293–319.

———. "Method and Factual Agreement in Science." In *PSA 1970: In Memory of Rudolf Carnap. Boston Studies in the Philosophy of Science* Vol. 8, edited by R. Buck and R. Cohen. 459–469. Dordrecht: Reidel, 1971.

Meadows, Donella, Dennis L. Meadows, and Jørgen Randers. *Beyond the Limits: Confronting Global Collapse, Envisioning a Sustainable Future*. Post Mills, Vt.: Chelsea Green Publishing Co., 1992.

Meadows, Donella. "Systems Paradigm." *Co-Evolution Quarterly* 34 (1982).

Merchant, Carolyn. *The Death of Nature: Women, Ecology and the Scientific Revolution*. San Francisco: Harper & Row, 1990.

Milbraith, Lester. *Environmentalists: Vanguard for a New Society*. Albany: State University of New York Press, 1984.

———. *Envisioning a Sustainable Society: Learning Our Way Out*. Albany: Sate University of New York, 1989.

Morrison, Roy. *We Build the Road We Travel*. Philadelphia: New Society Publishers, 1991.

Mumford, Lewis. *The Myth of the Machine: The Pentagon of Power*. N.Y.: Harcourt Brace Jovanovich, 1970.

———."Technics and the Nature of Man." In *Philosophy and Technology*, edited by Carl Mitcham and Robert Mackey. 77–85. N.Y.: Free Press, 1972.

Naess, Arne. "The Deep Ecological Movement: Some Philosophical Aspects." *Philosophical Inquiry* 8 (1986): 10–31.

———. *Ecology, Community and Lifestyle: Outline of an Ecosophy*. Translated and revised by David Rothenberg. N.Y.: Cambridge University Press, 1989.

———. "Identification as a Source of Deep Ecological Attitudes." In *Deep Ecology*, edited by Michael Tobias. 256–270. San Diego: Avant Books, 1984.

———. "Intrinsic Value: Will the Real Defenders of Nature Please Stand Up?" In *Conservation Biology: The Science of Scarcity and Diversity*, edited by Michael Soule. 504–515. Sunderland: Sinauer Associates, 1986.

———. "Self-Realization: An Ecological Approach to Being in the World." *The Trumpeter* 4 (Summer 1987): 35–42.

———. "The Shallow and the Deep, Long-Range Ecology Movements." *Inquiry* 16 (1973): 95–100.

Nash, Roderick Frazier. *The Rights of Nature: A History of Environmental Ethics*. Madison: University of Wisconsin Press, 1989.

———. *Wilderness and the American Mind*, 3rd ed. New Haven: Yale University Press, 1982.

Nozick, Robert. *Anarchy, State, and Utopia*. N.Y.: Basic Books, 1974.

Oelschlaeger, Max. *The Idea of Wilderness: From Prehistory to the Age of Ecology*. New Haven: Yale University Press, 1991.

Ophuls, William. *Ecology and the Politics of Scarcity*. San Francisco: W.H. Freeman & Co., 1977.

Ottman, Henning. "Cognitive Interests and Self-Reflection." In *Habermas: Critical Debates*, edited by John B. Thompson and David Held. 79–97. Cambridge: MIT Press, 1982.

Paelke, Robert C. *Environmentalism and the Future of Progressive Politics*. New Haven: Yale University Press, 1989.

Perlin, John. *A Forest Journey: The Role of Wood in the Development of Civilization*. N.Y.: W.W. Norton, 1989.

Persig, Robert. *Zen and the Art of Motorcycle Maintenance*. N.Y.: William Morrow and Co., 1974.

Plant, Judith, ed. *Healing the Wounds: The Promise of Ecofeminism*. Philadelphia: New Society Publishers, 1989.

Plumwood, Val. "Ecofeminism: An Overview and Discussion of Positions and Arguments." *Australasian Journal of Philosophy*, Supplement, 64 (1986): 120–138. See also Val Routley.

———. "Nature, Self, and Gender: Feminism, Environmental Philosophy, and the Critique of Rationalism," *Hypatia* 6 (1991): 3–27. See also Val Routley.

Polanyi, Karl. *The Great Transformation*. 1944. Reprint. Boston: Beacon Press, 1957.

Porritt, Jonathon. *Seeing Green: The Politics of Ecology Explained*. Oxford: Basil Blackwell, 1985.

Rappaport, Roy A. *Ecology, Meaning, and Religion*. Berkeley: North Atlantic Books, 1979.

Reagan, Tom. *The Case For Animal Rights*. Berkeley: University of California Press, 1983.

Robertson, James. "Toward a Multi-Level One-World Economy." *New Options* 63 (1989): 1–4.

Roelofs, Robert T., Joseph N. Crowley, and Donald L. Hardesty, eds. *Environment and Society: A Book of Readings on Environmental Policy, Attitudes, and Values*. Englewood Cliffs: Prentice Hall, 1974.

Rolston, Holmes, III. *Environmental Ethics: Duties to and Values in the World*. Philadelphia: Temple University Press, 1988.

Rorty, Richard. *Objectivity, Relativism, and Truth: Philosophical Papers*, Vol. 1. Cambridge: Cambridge University Press, 1991.

———. *Philosophy and the Mirror of Nature*. Princeton: Princeton University Press, 1979.

Roszak, Theodore. *Person/Planet: The Creative Disintegration of Industrial Society*. Garden City: Anchor Books, 1979.

Routley, R. and V. "Against the Inevitability of Human Chauvinism." In *Ethics and the Problem of the 21st Century*, edited by K. E. Goodpaster and K. M. Sayre. 36–59. Notre Dame: University of Notre Dame Press, 1979. See also Richard Sylvan and Val Plumwood.

———. "Human Chauvinism and Environmental Ethics." In *Environmental Philosophy*, edited by D. S. Mannison, M. A. McRobbie, and R. Routley. 96–189. Canberra: Australian National University, 1980. See also Richard Sylvan and Val Plumwood.

———. "Social Theories, Self Management, and Environmental Problems." In *Environmental Philosophy*, edited by D. S. Manison, M. A. McRobbie, and R. Routley. 217–332. Canberra: Australian National University, 1980. See also Richard Sylvan and Val Plumwood.

Rubin, Charles T. "Environmental Policy and Environmental Thought: Commoner and Rukelshaus." *Environmental Ethics* 11 (1989): 27–51.

Sadik, Nafis. *The State of World Population 1990*. N.Y., United Nations Population Fund, n.d.

Sagoff, Mark. *The Economy of the Earth*. N.Y.: Cambridge University Press, 1988.

Sahlins, Marshall. *Stone Age Economics*. Chicago: Aldine, 1972.

Sale, Kirkpatrick. *Dwellers in the Land: The Bioregional Vision*. San Francisco: Sierra Club Books, 1985.

Sandell, Klas, ed. *Buddhist Perspectives on the Ecocrisis*. Kandy, Sri Lanka: Buddhist Publication Society, 1987.

Sarkar, Saral. "Accommodating Industrialism: A Third World View of the West German Ecological Movement." *The Ecologist* 20 (1990): 147–152.

Schmidt, Alfred. *The Concept of Nature in Marx*. London: NLB, 1973.

Scitovsky, Tibor. *The Joyless Economy*. N.Y.: Oxford University Press, 1976.

Sessions, George. "Ecocentrism and the Greens: Deep Ecology and the Environmental Task." *The Trumpeter* 5 (1988): 65–69.

Shrybman, Steven. "Selling the Environment Short." *Earth Island Journal* (Spring 1991): 31–34.

Simon, Herbert A. *Models of Man*. N.Y.: Wiley and Sons, 1957.

Simon, Julian, and Herman Kahn, eds. *The Resourceful Earth*. Oxford: Basil Blackwell, 1984.

Singer, Peter. *Animal Liberation: A New Ethics for Our Treatment of Animals*. N.Y.: Avon Books, 1975.

———. *Practical Ethics*. N.Y.: Cambridge University Press, 1979.

Soule, Michael, ed. *Conservation Biology: The Science of Scarcity and Diversity*. Sunderland: Sinauer Associates, 1986.

———. "Conservation Tactics for a Constant Crisis." *Science* 253 (1991): 744–749.

Stretton, Hugh. *Capitalism, Socialism and the Environment*. N.Y.: Cambridge University Press, 1976.

Suppe, Frederick. "The Search for Philosophic Understanding of Scientific Theories." In *The Structure of Scientific Theories*, 2nd ed., edited by Frederick Suppe. 3–241. Urbana: University of Illinois Press, 1977.

Sylvan, Richard. *A Critique of Deep Ecology*. Discussion Papers in Environmental Philosophy, no. 12. Canberra: Australian National University, 1985. See also Richard Routley.

———. *A Critique of (Wild) Western Deep Ecology*. Unpublished manuscript. See also Richard Routley.

Szasz, Andrew. "In Praise of Policy Luddism: Strategic Lessons From the Hazardous Waste Wars." *Capitalism, Nature, Socialism* 2 (1991): 17–43.

Taylor, Paul. "In Defense of Biocentrism." *Environmental Ethics* 5 (1983): 237–243.

———. *Respect for Nature: A Theory of Environmental Ethics*. Princeton: Princeton University Press, 1986.

Thayer, H. S., ed. *Pragmatism: The Classic Writings*. Indianapolis: Hackett Publishing, 1982.

Thompson, Janna L. "Preservation of Wilderness and the Good Life." In *Environmental Philosophy: A Collection of Readings*, edited by Robert Elliot and Arran Gare. 85–105. University Park: Pennsylvania State University, 1983.

Tucker, Robert C. ed. *The Marx-Engels Reader*, 2nd ed. New York: Norton, 1978.

Turnbull, Colin. *The Forest People: A Study of the Pygmies of the Congo*. N.Y.: Simon and Schuster, 1961.

Uexküll, Jakob von. "A Stroll Through the World of Animals and Men." In *Instinctive Behavior: The Development of a Modern Concept*, Edited and translated by Claire H. Schiller. 5–80. N.Y.: International Universities Press, 1957.

Wachtel, Paul. *The Poverty of Affluence*. Philadelphia: New Society Publishers, 1989.

Warren, Karen. "Feminism and Ecology: Making Connections." *Environmental Ethics* 9 (1987): 3–20.

Warren, Karen, and Jim Cheney. "Ecological Feminism and Ecosystem Ecology." *Hypatia* 6 (1991): 179–197.

Watson, Richard A. "A Critique of Anti-Anthropocentric Biocentrism." *Environmental Ethics* 5 (1983): 245–256.

———. "A Note on Deep Ecology." *Environmental Ethics* 6 (1984): 377–379.

Weber, Max. *The Protestant Ethic and the Spirit of Capitalism*, translated by Talcott Parsons. N.Y.: Scribner's, 1958.

———. *The Theory of Social and Economic Organization*, translated by A. M. Henderson and Talcott Parsons. N.Y.: Free Press, 1964.

Weiner, Douglas R. *Models of Nature: Ecology, Conservation, and Cultural Revolution in Soviet Russia*. Bloomington: Indiana University Press, 1988.

Wenz, Peter S. *Environmental Justice*. Albany: State University of New York Press, 1988.

Weston, Anthony. "Beyond Intrinsic Value: Pragmatism in Environmental Ethics." *Environmental Ethics* 7 (1985): 321–339.

———. "Non-Anthropocentrism in a Thoroughly Anthropocentrized World." *Trumpeter* 8 (1991): 108–112.

Whitebook, Joel. "The Problem of Nature in Habermas." *Telos* 40 (1979): 41–69.

Wilcox, Bruce A. "Insular Ecology and Conservation." In *Conservation Biology: An Evolutionary-Ecological Perspective*, edited by Michael E. Soule and Bruce A. Wilcox. 95–117. Sunderland: Sinauer Associates, 1980.

Winner, Langdon. *The Whale and the Reactor: A Search for Limits in an Age of High Technology*. Chicago: University of Chicago Press, 1986.

Wooster, Donald. *Nature's Economy: The Roots of Ecology*. Garden City: Anchor Books, 1979.

World Commission on Environment and Development. *Our Common Future*. N.Y.: Oxford University Press, 1987.

Xenos, Nicholas. *Scarcity and Modernity*. N.Y.: Routledge, 1989.

Ziegler, Charles E. *Environmental Policy in the USSR*. Amherst: University of Massachusetts Press, 1987.

Zimmerman, Michael E. "Quantum Theory, Intrinsic Value, and Pantheism." *Environmental Ethics* 10 (1988): 3–30.

INDEX